A COLLECTOR'S GUIDE TO
ANTIQUES

	UK	US	AUS	NZ	SA
Price Guide 1	£10-20	$16-32	$22-44	$24-48	R74-148
Price Guide 2	£20-50	$32-80	$44-110	$48-120	R148-370
Price Guide 3	£50-100	$80-160	$110-220	$120-240	R370-740
Price Guide 4	£100-250	$160-400	$220-550	$240-600	R740-1,850
Price Guide 5	£250-500	$400-800	$550-1,100	$600-1,200	R1,850 -3,700
Price Guide 6	£500-1,000	$800-1,600	$1,100-2,200	$1,200-2,400	R3,700-7,400
Price Guide 7	£1,000-3,000	$1,600-4,800	$2,200-6,600	$2,400-7,200	R7,400-22,200
Price Guide 8	£3,000-8,000	$4,800-12,800	$6,600-17,600	$7,200-19,200	R22,200-59,200
Price Guide 9	£8,000-Plus	$12,800-Plus	$17,600-Plus	$19,200-Plus	R59,200-Plus

This edition published in 1997 by
Greenwich Editions
10 Blenheim Court
Brewery Road
London N7 9NT

Produced by Marshall Cavendish Books, London
(a division of Marshall Cavendish Partworks Ltd)

ISBN 0–86288–121–8

British Library Cataloguing Data in Publication Data:
A catalogue record for this book is available from the British Library

Printed in Malaysia

CONTENTS

FOREWORD

Today people collect antiques for a wide variety of reasons. Some like to own a piece of history, to feel that they are in touch with the past. Others see works of art as an investment, and enjoy the hunt for a bargain, others are nostalgic for their earlier years and like to collect objects which remind them of their childhood. Some look for antiques related to their trade or profession – a doctor might collect old surgical instruments, or a policeman Victorian truncheons. There are a few who will admit to buying a beautiful object just because it is beautiful, and many will tell you that they bought this chair or that set of drinking glasses simply because they needed them for their homes.

Whatever the reasons for buying antiques, it is clear that more people are collecting now than ever before. As a consequence, there is an ever-dwindling supply of the genuine article and one of the most valuable features of *A Collector's Guide to Popular Antiques* are the checklists of points to watch. Over the last few years, reproduction antiques have become big business. So huge has been the output of modern 'antiques' that they turn up everywhere and are increasingly hard to identify as the manufacturers become more sophisticated. If such reproductions can be justified as substitutes for the real thing which has become almost unobtainable, there are also reconstructed antiques and outright fakes. A period piece, particularly of furniture, can be made using antique materials or parts, but often it will contain so little that bears any relation to what it is purported to be, that it amounts to an attempt to deceive. Fortunately, outright fakes are a comparative rarity, except at the top end of the market, because to produce them demands considerable craftsmanship and is an expensive undertaking.

In *A Collector's Guide to Popular Antiques*, antique hunters can find the information they need to save themselves from most of the worst pitfalls. But the world of antiques, although it is essential to be on one's guard, need not always be treated as a minefield. There are whole new areas which have recently been opened up, in response to the growing scarcity of traditional antiques. You will find in this book plenty of information about collecting toys, golf clubs, comics, clocks and many other items that are not generally associated with the more classic antiques, such as Sèvres, and Chippendale, but which often possess as much charm and ingenuity. Many of these comparatively new fields have already been widely explored and mapped, and although it is still quite possible to blaze new trails, it is essential to realise how much has already been discovered and what outposts have been established. Even among, say, Edwardian typewriters there are Mona Lisas and rubbish, and it is useful to know whether it is more worthwhile putting grandad's old fountain pen into an auction or using it yourself until it wears out. It is as important to be able to recognise the value and collectable interest of what you already own as it is to know about what you want to buy.

Collecting antiques should not be just an exalted form of shopping. It is a fascinating pastime at which – like any other – one can always become more expert, learning by experience and finding out as much as one can. Like all forms of hunting it demands skill, tenacity and patience – even a bit of cunning. There may be long barren periods when nothing of any interest or value turns up, but every so often there will come the indescribable thrill of finding the real bargain collectable. Good luck!

Malcolm Haslam

From the finest porcelain to the simplest cottage earthenware, china has been a perenially popular collectable. Virtually everyone, the whole world over uses some kind of china every day, whether it is a bone china teacup or a stoneware rice bowl. The very appeal of ceramics lies in this immediacy – the humblest of collections can be used, as well as cherished.

Antique china is, possibly, the broadest of fields for the collector to delve into: the prospective buyer would be well advised to specialize in one particular area. By doing this it is easier to gain familiarity with the chosen subject and, by studying it in detail, make it infinitely more interesting. By concentrating on one particular kind of china, whether it be material or style, a collection, however modest, will be more valuable if it has a common theme.

Of course quality is in the eye of the beholder, and most collectors sensibly prefer to buy what pleases them rather than follow rules laid down by other people. But as an interest grows in antique china then an arbitrary purchasing of whatever takes the eye will no longer satisfy the more committed collector. Naturally, a collection's extent and subject will depend very much on pocket and space available: the shopper on a limited budget and with little display or cupboard space, will not be interested in collecting say, various *garnitures de cheminée* or several different Victorian dinner services. Most of us will acquire only one antique dinner service in a lifetime. The most practical approach here is to collect single pieces at a time and thus build up a complete set. The best advice for a prospective buyer of a dinner service is to decide on the type of china preferred – say, pottery or porcelain – and then on a favourite colour or design. It would be expensive to go straight out and buy a complete dinner service and finding an entire set

is still fairly rare. However, Victorian families were large and their mealtime crockery extensive and it was not unusual to find servings for up to 18. Most modern requirements are for eight and so it might be possible to find enough matching pieces to suffice. Similarly, with Victorian tea sets: these were generally made for 12, making it all the more easy for the modern collector to put together an attractive and interesting tea set for their own needs and a smaller setting.

Rather than concentrate on building up a complete service of tableware, the collector might be more interested in focusing on odds and ends of china. It is relatively easy and inexpensive to start a collection of small pieces – for instance, egg cups or cream jugs can be particularly attractive to the collector on a budget, and can still be used in everyday modern life. Or the antique china enthusiast might choose to look for only items made by a specific company; or only china in a particular colour or pattern. Souvenir, commemorative and novelty pieces have been made since before the 18th century and can be fun to collect.

When collecting china from a particular artist or factory there are many different factors and subjects of interest for the buyer to consider.

This brightly-coloured ewer and basin, dating from c. 1820, has a typically oriental floral design. The pattern of this octagonal-shaped jug was highly popular.

Much ornamental and domestic china was made by artists or decorated with their designs. Famous illustrators and painters, like Eric Ravillious or Mabel Lucie Attwell produced designs for children's china and specialist potters like Clarice Cliff and Susie Cooper brought a new insight and vibrancy to the ceramic art. Pieces attributable to artists such as these are hard to come by and generally too expensive for the average collector. But great finds can be made and there is nothing like the thrill of the chase. Work by famous potteries, such as Wedgwood or Minton, are extremely collectable and any prospetive purchaser must be well armed with facts and figures before contemplating an investment in such a piece. Wedgwood, for example, must be one of the most copied of manufacturers ever and the collector must study carefully available literature about the company's markings. Various, perfectly legal, variations on the name Wedgwood have been used by imitators since the 18th century and aliases such as Vedgwood, Wedgewood, Wedge Wood or Wedgwood & Co. (Josiah Wedgwood never used the words '& Co.' or 'Ltd' after the single word 'Wedgwood' impressed on the base of his company's china) can be found.

There are collectors whose taste focuses on one particular colour or design: blue and white china is so popular an area that there is even a club for enthusiasts. Ever since the invention of transfer printing, blue and white patterns have been one of the most favoured of designs for china. In its early days, it imitated the style and patterns of Chinese Export china, that mainly blue and white ware made in the Far East specifically for the connoisseurs in Europe. Then, as now, Chinese Export porcelain was expensive and the cheap and plentiful blue and white pottery being made by so many factories was an attractive substitute. Some pieces of Chinese Export occasionally come up at auction and the interested collector might well be tempted to invest.

This decorative wall plate of the 1930s features a shimmering bunch of yellow daffodils on a rich blue background.

One of the reasons why so much blue and white china was imported to Europe lies in its connections with the tea trade. As the drinking of tea grew in popularity so did the importing of the leaf from China. As a valuable cargo, it was vital to protect the tea on the long sea voyage and practicality dictated that the lowest, and wettest, levels of the ship be filled not with tea but some other non-perishable commodity. One of these was the blue and white china tea services which were needed for tea drinking. Throughout most of the 18th century, tea was supped from Chinese-style bowls and it was not until the 1770s that cups with handles began to appear. The 19th century saw further developments both in style and materials. Manufacturers constantly experimented with new methods of production, concentrating particularly on hard paste porcelain, which was a very expensive commodity. Few materials had such brilliance and translucency when fired, but cost and kiln losses were high. The results of these extensive trials was the development of bone china; it was discovered that the addition of bone ash, china clay and china stone, to the refined clay body produced a white china of good translucency at a reasonable cost. Bone china largely replaced porcelain, except for the very finest quality services.

At the same time, techniques developed in the Mason Brothers' factory resulted in 'Patent Ironstone China', made from a finely powdered felspathic rock or stone added to a stoneware or clay body. The new material, favoured for its cheapness and durability, was quickly adopted by other manufacturers, who used names like 'Stone China' or 'Opaque Porcelain'. Although manufacturers used the words 'china' and 'porcelain', the ironstone was more like a very dense and strong stoneware.

Other ware popular with antique enthusiasts is lustreware, a cheap alternative to silver and gold, developed in the 19th century. The effect of a gold lustre was achieved by adding a little powdered gold to aqua regia (a mix of hydrochloric and nitric acids that can dissolve gold), adding this to an oily amalgam of balsam of sulphur and turpentine and then brushing the compound on to the ceramic to be lustred. The medium vaporized in the firing, leaving a metallic film on the pottery. Lustreware can be extremely satisfying to collect as there is an enormous variety of styles, colours and makers to pick from on the market today.

Another kind of china popular today is Parian ware: this particular ceramic was developed to imitate marble and was used in the 19th century particularly for the manufacture of ornaments in the Classical style. The collector also has a wide range of different Parian objects from which to choose: not only are there classically-inspired busts, but ornamental vases, or figurines much more akin to Staffordshire models than Greek statues. Parian was also made by many different factories: pieces made by the Irish firm Belleek, which are technically Parian, are known by the company name. Developments in methods and techniques in the 19th century saw the industrialization of potteries throughout the Western world and work was turned out in great numbers. There is, therefore, a great wealth of collectable china available and the connoisseur might prefer to build up a collection based on other interests.

Ceramic ornaments and domestic ware can also act as a record of artistic movements and contemporary taste in the fine arts, demonstrating the filtering down of aesthetic principles to the applied arts. In the second half of the 19th century, there was a growing move away from mass-produced articles and towards the hand crafting of well-designed artifacts and this ideal found its voice in the Arts and Crafts Movement. Artists from the Pre-Raphaelite Brotherhood were influential on this artistic movement and in ceramics the term 'art pottery' was applied to those firms that rejected the methods of industrializaiton by reviving traditional techniques. Early in the 20th century, the Art Deco style was having its effect on fashions and Art Deco pottery derived its bright and colourful designs from a variety of influences: Cubism, African art and mechanization, being just a few. The potters of late,

This jug dates from about 1850 and is decorated with an idealized rural scene, complete with gnarled tree, church spire, and country picnic.

19th-century Europe were visibly influenced by the artistic principles of the Jugendstil, also known as Art Nouveau or Seccession Art. The flowing forms of Mucha's posters, the women with their swirling hair, can often be found in Jugendstil vases and ornaments. Art pottery, a term which can be used to apply to all ceramic ware produced by craftsmen rather than mass-produced, was made to be collectable. Many of the pieces are now in museums or in large private collections, just as the original potters had hoped. And when outstanding pieces come to auction, they command substantial prices. However, a large number of crafts men and women were involved, and their output was highly varied, so 'finds' can still be unearthed.

The ornamental Staffordshire figures with which the Victorian's of all classes delighted in adorning their parlours have been aptly described as 'a potted history of the period' and, as such, are of great interest to collectors today. They were a genuinely popular art form, made for the mass market and dealing, in the main, with the same type of subjects that are now the staple diet of the tabloid newspaper. Then as now, the royal family was a source of endless fascination, and sporting heroes, stage stars and public figures of all kinds also featured high on the list of favourites.

Staffordshire figures were bought not as the works of art they are now considered to be, but as everyday items that only the very poorest of homes would have been unable to afford. Until about 1910, the cheapest figures were sold to the retail trade for just a few pence. Genteel customers would have bought them in china shops, which by the mid 19th century were common sights in the high street, but, for the less well-off, they were available at fairgrounds or in the numerous street markets. The production of Staffordshire figures began

CHINA

in about 1780, but their heyday was from around 1840 to the end of the century, a period coinciding almost exactly with Queen Victoria's reign. There is no way of estimating how many figures were made at this time as they were manufactured in such large quantities and mostly produced anonymously. Marks identifying which factory they came from are rare.

Many collectors will be looking for objects with a story behind them: those artifacts that reveal either the everyday life of the past or those pieces that have some wider, historical association. For instance, in today's homes many people like to use pot-pourri (dried, scented flowers) and many collectors specialize in the ceramic jars manufactured in the 19th century purely for containing this sweet-smelling preparation. Pot-pourris and pastille burners (ceramic holders in the shape of small buildings, used for burning scented pastilles) were produced in a time before efficient plumbing, laundries, disinfectant and deodorant and when their scent was used in every room to dispel foul odours and (erroneously) to ward off disease. We may like the smell of pot-pourri today but to middle-class Victorians it made life all that more bearable.

A very direct record of history is commemorative ware, intended as it was to be a souvenir of great events or personalities. Though produced for centuries, commemoratives were in their heyday in the 19th century with the Victorian's craze for souvenirs. A patriotic and inexpensive ornament, commemorative china was also affordable by the growing working classes. In the 18th and early 19th centuries, pottery was often used for propagandist purposes, but this died down in Victoria's reign as newspapers and cartoons became the main vehicles for polemic. During the 19th century, the range of subjects for commemoratives expanded considerably to include,

The Royal family makes up one of the largest categories of Staffordshire figures. This figurine shows Queen Victoria's son, Alfred, Duke of Edinburgh.

beside the perenially popular royalty, industrial achievements, the openings of railways, political movements and military heroes and victories. Queen Victoria's coronation was the first royal crowning to be marked by commemorative ware before it happened, as well as afterwards. Momentous occasions were often not featured on china until after the event and if a subject proved popular then copies were made for some time after. An interesting area of commemoratives is those manufactured to mark personal events, such as births, christenings or retirements. Because it was produced in such large quantities, there is still a great deal of this ware to be found on the market. It is also relatively cheap, making it an ideal subject for a first collection. Prices are, however, beginning to rise as this kind of ware becomes fashionable once again, and there are now a number of dealers that specialize in them. The range of commemorative objects varies from jugs to tankards, from plaques to pin trays, and from vases to figurines. They can be made in material from soft paste porcelain to lustreware, or from Parian ware to creamware, and decorated in transfer printing or hand painting. Many factories made commemoratives, from the most famous to the unknown, but generally speaking, the factory that made the item is of less importance to the collector than the quality of the piece and the event commemorated. Many factors influence price: limited runs will add to the value, while pieces portraying unusual events, or local occasions are also sought after. For it to be truly desirable, the object should be as close as possible in date to the event commemorated. Since there is such a vast array of items for the collector to choose from, it is a good idea to concentrate on one or two particluar themes. Railways, naval, military, sporting, political, royal or coronation pieces are all good subjects. Collections on single themes are also more valuable than those apparently compiled at random. Some subjects are obviously more common than others, and it is generally the later items that are more abundant. Ceramic items can be displayed alongside commemoratives on similar subjects but in different materials. Anyone who chooses to collect objects relating to the Great Exhibition of 1851, for example, will find papier mâché boxes, tins and glasses marking the same event. There is also a growing interest in commemorative pot lids, and these could look very attractive if framed and hung on the wall in groups like miniatures.

The collector might also consider china that fits into a decorative scheme in their own home. A collection of Clarice Cliff ceramics will make the perfect display for any Deco-styled glass-fronted cabinet from the 1930s. Similarly, when buying 19th-century silver services, the collector can also look for suitable Victorian tableware to match. A collection of blue and white kitchen and breakfast ware is going to look very handsome arranged along an old-fashioned dresser. In other words, the designing and furnishing of a home can become the starting point for a collection. When renovating an older property the home-owner might find themselves drawn to a particular period and, with an eye for authenticity, begin a collection of appropriate tableware and ornaments.

Attractive and stylish ceramics have continued to be made. The angular shape and geometric pattern of this coffee pot reflects the principles of Bauhaus design.

Whatever area of antique china the collector choses to specialize in, reading around the subject and studying it in depth will soon reveal fascinating discoveries. A complete knowledge of a particular type of china will also mean that any potential purchaser will be well armed with information when considering an investment and will be able to shop more wisely. There are two main ways in which the collector can learn about ceramics: by reading and by looking at and handling pieces. A great many books have been written on all aspects of china, ranging from handy pocket guides to specialized works of research. There are also specialist journals that keep up with new discoveries and information, and the collector will also find saleroom catalogues interesting, not least for showing current prices. There are small, handy-size books available, giving details on china markings, that are an invaluable guide for any shopper to carry with them when antique-hunting at auctions or at the dealers.

The easiest way of looking at good quality china is by visiting museums. The great national collections, such as the Victoria and Albert Museum, have superb holdings, but local museums can be just as rewarding. Of course, those towns and areas around the world that were the centres of the ceramic industry will also have particularly fine collections on show, Stoke-on-Trent being a very good example. It is worth approaching museums, both large and small, for advice on antique ceramics and their information officers can be very helpful. Of course, it would be considerate, and helpful, for enquiries to be quite specific rather than general and, as a rule, museums and galleries cannot give advice on the valuation of pieces.

Visiting shops and dealers will give the collector an opportunity to handle pieces. Sympathetic and interested dealers and shop owners will probably be helpful with any queries, though the more established the business, the more reliable will be the advice. Collectors should not feel pressurized into buying and rely on their own judgement. Visiting a renowned, and more expensive, antique shop will mean that anything bought there is most likely to be authentic, but the collector looking for a bargain will be best advised to shop around. Scouring the shops, auctions and fairs can be fun, as well as rewarding. Antique markets and stalls can be a very good source of finds and the collector has the opportunity to browse widely before buying. Bric-a-brac and jumble sales can also be great hunting grounds for the enthusiast, especially in the hope that the best piece in a collection might turn up at a car boot sale. The potential collector should not be afraid of auctions, since many attractive pieces of china can come up for sale and change hands for well below shop price. It is important to go to the viewing before the auction and decide on piece to bid for. The bidder should then opt for a spending limit and stick to it during the auction. Sometimes, whole dinner services, and the like, can appear at auctions when the contents of a house are being sold and remarkable finds can be picked up.

One of the chief merits of antique china as a collectable is that, beyond normal careful handling, there is little else to guard against. Damp, woodworm, sunlight – the enemies of most types of antiques – have no damaging effect on china. It needs no constant care beyond regular dusting and washing. But this is where the danger lies for a collection, it is obviously vulnerable to damage when being handled. With ornamental figures kept in a display cabinet there is very little dust that will accumulate, but many collectors prefer to keep their pieces on mantelpieces, open shelves or on other furniture. Cleaning should then be carried out with a feather duster, taking particular care with more fragile parts. To remove nicotine film, place the piece in a detergent solution for an hour or two and allow to dry in a warm place without wiping. This is general advice only, and the cleaning of each type of china should be researched beforehand: for instance, Parian ware is porous and should not be immersed in water. Pieces repaired with

This striking 1930s, Art Deco cheese dish was made by T. Green & Co. of Derbyshire and the painted flowers are an imitation of the popular Clarice Cliff 'Crocus' design.

glue should not be soaked in water – they should just be wiped with a damp cloth andd dried immediately. China tableware that is used on a daily basis, or for special occasions, should still be treated carefully when handled. It is not a good idea to put pieces in the dishwasher and even the glaze on the most durable of blue and white china should not be harshly scrubbed. Overglaze decoration, particularly gilding, is sensitive to hot water and harsh detergents and can be more quickly worn away. Brief immersion in warm water, and gentle wiping should remove dust and dirt and any remaining patches of grease and grime can be tackled with a little white spirit on a pad of cotton wool. When washing up any china that has been used for food it is important to clean each piece separately: putting items into water with cutlery will increase the risk of damage to the china. If a favourite piece becomes broken or if something has been bought that is already damaged or with a bad repair, then the collector should consider restoration. Consulting an expert will ensure that any repairs undertaken are of the highest quality, but professionals can be expensive and may not be worth it in terms of balancing the cost against the final value of the restored piece. It might be worthwhile considering home restoration which can be an interesting and absorbing hobby. There are classes and plenty of literature on this subject and it is vital that the collector should read up on the subject, with practical advice, before tackling any repairs at home. Care and patience are needed for good results.

Thus armed with knowledge and practical information about their chosen area of specialization, the collector can enjoy their search for antique china at the same time as being able to build up and conserve an interesting and rewarding collection.

◀ A STAFFORDSHIRE TEA CUP, COFFEE CUP AND SAUCER, C.1845. THE INSIDES OF THE CUPS ARE HIGHLY DECORATED WITH A BLUE BAND AND ROSE DESIGN WITH GILT LEAVES.
PRICE GUIDE 4

▲ THE FLORAL DESIGN ON THIS MID-VICTORIAN BONE-CHINA TEA CUP AND SAUCER IS TRANSFER PRINTED. HAND-PAINTED GILDING HAS BEEN ADDED TO THE CUP RIM, BASE AND HANDLE, AND TO THE SAUCER RIM AS WELL.
PRICE GUIDE 3

◀ A RICH BLUE AND GOLD PATTERN DECORATES THIS STAFFORDSHIRE BONE-CHINA TEA CUP, COFFEE CUP AND SAUCER, C.1835. THE FLORAL DESIGN AND GILDING IS HAND-PAINTED.
PRICE GUIDE 3

▶ DERBY BONE-CHINA TEAPOT WITH MATCHING CUP AND SAUCER, C.1825. THE GILT AND BLACK PATTERN IS REPEATED ON EACH PIECE, WITH ADDITIONAL GILDING ON THE TEAPOT'S HANDLE, SPOUT AND LID.
PRICE GUIDE 5

DESIGN FEATURES

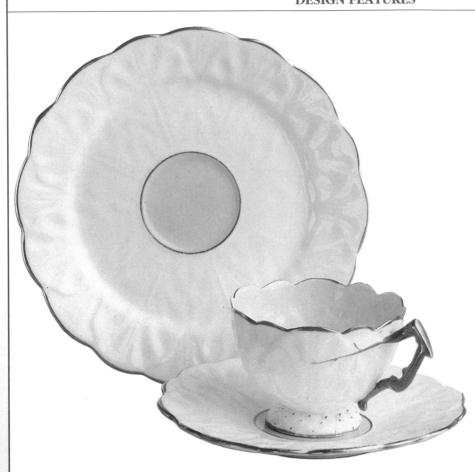

BONE CHINA TEA SETS WERE VERY POPULAR DURING THE 19TH CENTURY; NOT ONLY WERE THEY ATTRACTIVE, THEY WERE ALSO CHEAPER THAN IMPORTED PORCELAIN. THIS LATE-VICTORIAN CUP AND SAUCER IS UNMARKED, BUT THE PARTICULARLY DELICATE PINK AND WHITE LEAF-MOULD DESIGN WAS A COMMON STYLE PRODUCED IN MANY FACTORIES AT THAT TIME. THE DISTINCTIVE HANDLE IS A FORM KNOWN AS CRABSTOCK AND THIS KIND OF DAINTY WORK CAN BE SUSCEPTIBLE TO BREAKAGE. THEREFORE, COLLECTORS SHOULD CHECK TO SEE IF THERE ARE ANY REPAIRS THAT HAVE BEEN HIDDEN BY BEING GILDED OVER.

WITH POPULAR DESIGNS THERE IS A GREATER AVAILABILITY BUT COLLECTORS SHOULD LOOK CAREFULLY AT TEA SETS TO ENSURE THAT THERE HAS NOT BEEN A 'MARRIAGE' OF DIFFERENT ITEMS FROM DIFFERENT SETS TO MAKE A NEW SET.

▼ COFFEE CUP AND SAUCER, C.1880, FROM STAFFORDSHIRE. THE GRASSES PAINTED ON A WHITE BACKGROUND SHOW AN ORIENTAL INFLUENCE IN THEIR STYLE, AS DOES THE CUP HANDLE AND RIM OF THE SAUCER, PAINTED TO LOOK LIKE BAMBOO.
PRICE GUIDE 2

◀ A LATE VICTORIAN, JAPAN-PATTERNED TEAPOT. THE PAINTED GILDING, FUNDAMENTAL TO THIS PARTICULAR DESIGN, HAS BEEN USED TO GREAT EFFECT ON THE SPOUT, HANDLE, RIM AND BODY OF THE TEAPOT.
PRICE GUIDE 3

▼ DERBY JAPAN-PATTERNED TEA CUP AND COFFEE CUP WITH MATCHING SAUCERS. THE TEA CUP (LEFT) IS C.1830 AND THE COFFEE CUP C. 1900. THIS ENDURINGLY POPULAR DESIGN BECAME MORE WIDELY AVAILABLE FROM THE LATE EIGHTEENTH CENTURY.
PRICE GUIDE 4

▼ PART OF A PARAGON TEA SET. THE FULL SET IS FOR SIX AND INCLUDES TWO CAKE PLATES. TRIANGULAR DESIGNS DATE FROM THE EARLY 1930S.
PRICE GUIDE 5

▲ ROYAL DOULTON'S 'TANGO' TEA SET COMBINES CLASSICAL TOUCHES WITH TYPICAL GEOMETRIC DECO MOTIFS.
PRICE GUIDE 6

▼ PART OF A 'BUTTERFLY WING' PATTERNED SHELLEY MODE TEA SERVICE. INCORPORATING CLASSIC DECO DETAILS, SUCH AS THE SOLID TRIANGULAR HANDLE, THIS IS ONE OF THE MORE VALUABLE SETS.
PRICE GUIDE 4

▼ NOVELTY TEA POTS, SUCH AS THIS ONE, WERE VERY MUCH A FEATURE OF THE THIRTIES. THIS IS ONE OF JAMES SADLER AND SONS' DESIGNS, 'YE DAINTY LADYEE' OR THE 'CRINOLINE LADY'.
PRICE GUIDE 3

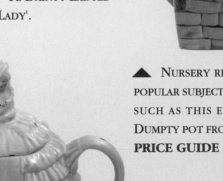

▲ NURSERY RHYME CHARACTERS MADE POPULAR SUBJECTS FOR NOVELTY TEAPOTS, SUCH AS THIS EXAMPLE OF A HUMPTY DUMPTY POT FROM THE 1930S.
PRICE GUIDE 4

▼ THIS 'CROWN DEVON' COFFEE SET, WITH TYPICAL GREEN, CREAM AND GOLD DECORATION, HAS A PEARL LUSTRE GLAZE ON THE INSIDE OF THE CUPS.
PRICE GUIDE 5

▼ PART OF THE BURLEIGH WARE RANGE, THE PATTERN OF THIS TEAPOT-FOR-ONE IS KNOWN AS BALMORAL.
PRICE GUIDE 1

▲ TEA WARE IN SHELLEY'S 'REGENT' SHAPE WITH A GEOMETRIC PATTERN DATING FROM 1933.
PRICE GUIDE 3

▶ UNUSUAL AS PART OF COMPLETE COFFEE SET, THIS IS A 'CARLTON' WARE BISCUIT BARREL MADE IN 1932.
PRICE GUIDE 5

▲ THE STYLE OF THIS SHELLEY MILK JUG AND BOWL WAS KNOWN AS 'BUTTERFLY', NAMED BECAUSE OF THE SHAPE OF THE HANDLE RATHER THAN THE PAINTED FLORAL DESIGN.
PRICE GUIDE 4

▲ A CLARICE CLIFF MILK JUG. PART OF A TEA SET, THE DESIGN OF SUNFLOWERS WAS KNOWN AS 'SUNRISE'.
PRICE GUIDE 6

▲ A MILK JUG AND SUGAR BOWL IN CLARICE CLIFF'S 'BONJOUR' RANGE. AMONGST THE COMPLETE COFFEE SET WAS INCLUDED A TOAST-RACK.
PRICE GUIDE 5

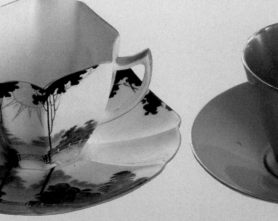

▲ PART OF THE SHELLEY 'ANEMONE BUNCH'- PATTERN TEA SET FOR TWO, A DEPARTURE FROM THE MORE USUAL GEOMETRIC DECO DESIGN.
PRICE GUIDE 5

▲ A CLASSIC SHELLEY DESIGN, THIS EIGHT-SIDED CUP, WITH ITS MATCHING SAUCER, IS PART OF A LATE 1920s SET.
PRICE GUIDE 5

▲ A 1930s SHELLEY COFFEE CUP AND SAUCER WITH TRIANGULAR HANDLE. IT IS PART OF A SET.
PRICE GUIDE 5

▲ A COMPORT, USED FOR CAKES OR FRUIT, DECORATED WITH A CHINTZ PATTERN AND SHOWING TRACES OF A GOLD-PAINTED RIM.
PRICE GUIDE 4

▼ AN EARLY VICTORIAN TEA-CUP AND SAUCER, WITH A TYPICAL RUSTIC SCENE OF FISHERMEN IN FRONT OF A COTTAGE ON BOTH CUP AND SAUCER.
PRICE GUIDE 3

▲ SOMETIMES CONFUSED WITH SUGAR BOWLS, SLOP BOWLS, SUCH AS THIS ONE, WERE, IN FACT, RECEPTACLES FOR THE DREGS OF THE FIRST CUP OF TEA.
PRICE GUIDE 3

▲ THIS CREAMER, IN POPULAR BLUE AND WHITE, IS DECORATED WITH A PATTERN OF FLOWERS, LEAVES AND SCROLLS BOTH INSIDE AND OUT.
PRICE GUIDE 4

▲ A SUGAR BOWL WITH A DEEP BLUE FLORAL DECORATION AND A SCALLOPED EDGE, DATING FROM THE MID-1820S.
PRICE GUIDE 5

▶ A 'BREADALBANE' TEA PLATE WITH A PLAID BORDER, SHOWING A CASTLE SET IN A SCOTTISH LANDSCAPE WITH MOUNTAIN PEAKS AND A LOCH.
PRICE GUIDE 3

◀ A LOW COMPORT WITH TWO HANDLES FOR TEATIME DAINTIES. THE LARGE, VINE-LIKE LEAVES IN THE DECORATION ARE A PARTICULARLY UNUSUAL FEATURE.
PRICE GUIDE 4

▼ THIS TEAPOT FROM THE 1820S HAS A DESIGN SHOWING CHILDREN IN CONTEMPORARY COSTUME PLAYING. REPAIRS TO THE LID ARE JUST VISIBLE.
PRICE GUIDE 5

▼ THE UNUSUAL SHAPE OF THIS C.1800 TEAPOT MAKES IT A RARE PIECE. IT IS DECORATED ON BOTH BASE AND LID WITH A CHINESE-INSPIRED PATTERN.
PRICE GUIDE 5

▼ THIS TEA PLATE FROM 1830 IS DECORATED IN A DARK BLUE DESIGN SHOWING AN IDYLLIC COUNTRY SCENE WITH BOATS AND FISHERMEN.
PRICE GUIDE 3

▲ A PLATE FROM THE DON POTTERY IN YORKSHIRE, FROM C.1820, SHOWS COWS GRAZING IN ENGLISH PASTURES.
PRICE GUIDE 5

▲ FROM THE 'BRITISH HISTORY' SERIES BY JONES AND SONS, THIS 1827 DINNER PLATE FEATURES A PICTURE OF THE SIGNING OF THE MAGNA CARTA.
PRICE GUIDE 4

▲ A SPODE SOUP PLATE MADE OF AN IRONSTONE CALLED 'NEW STONE', THAT WAS INTRODUCED BY SPODE EARLY IN THE 19TH CENTURY.
PRICE GUIDE 3

◀ MADE BY A STAFFORDSHIRE POTTERY IN ABOUT 1830, THIS VEGETABLE DISH, DECORATED WITH COUNTRYSIDE SCENES. ALSO INCORPORATED IS THE FIGURE OF A LION AS THE HANDLE.
PRICE GUIDE 5

▲ A SMALL TUREEN FROM AROUND 1820, WITH A LATTICE PATTERN AND SPECKLED HANDLES. ITS SIZE SUGGESTS THAT IT WAS USED FOR SERVING SAUCES.
PRICE GUIDE 5

▲ THIS CREAMER, USED FOR POURING MILK OR CREAM AT THE DINNER TABLE, IS DECORATED WITH AN UNIDENTIFIED FLORAL PATTERN AND LANDSCAPE SCENES, IN TWO TONES OF BLUE.
PRICE GUIDE 4

◀ THE LADLE ON THE LEFT HERE HAS A FLORAL DESIGN AND A SILVER BAND ON THE HANDLE; WHILE THE ONE ON THE RIGHT IS DECORATED WITH ORIENTAL SCENES. BOTH ARE MID-VICTORIAN.
PRICE GUIDE 3

▲ THIS MEAT PLATTER IN SPODE 'STONE CHINA' DATES FROM ABOUT 1820 AND IS DECORATED WITH THE GRASSHOPPER PATTERN. A CHANNEL RUNS ALONG THE CENTRE OF THE PLATTER TO COLLECT THE MEAT JUICES IN THE WELL AT THE END.
PRICE GUIDE 5

▼ A MINTON SOUP PLATE DATING FROM AROUND 1820. THE DIMINUTIVE CHINESE FIGURES IN THE CENTRE ARE TYPICAL OF THE PATTERN 'MANDARIN'.
PRICE GUIDE 5

▲ A LARGE SALAD BOWL MADE BY AN UNIDENTIFIED STAFFORDSHIRE POTTER IN THE MID 1820S. THE PATTERN SHOWS A RUINED TEMPLE AND PYRAMID SET IN AN IDEALIZED, ARCADIAN LANDSCAPE.
PRICE GUIDE 5

◀ VICTORIAN HONEY POTS IN THE SHAPE OF BEEHIVES WERE A POPULAR FEATURE. THE WHITE POT IS EARLY TO MID-19TH CENTURY AND MADE IN THE CLASSIC SHAPE OF AN OLD-FASHIONED BEEHIVE. THE QUAINTNESS AND NOVELTY VALUE OF THE OTHER POT IS INCREASED BY ITS THATCHED LID AND LEGGED STAND.
PRICE GUIDE 3

▶ THIS SPODE ITALIAN BLUE-AND-WHITE DESIGN WAS A VICTORIAN FAVOURITE AND THE PATTERN IS STILL PRODUCED TODAY IN BOTH DINNER AND BREAKFAST CHINA.
PRICE GUIDE 4

▶ THIS FINE MAJOLICA JAM POT, IN A POPULAR ORIENTAL DESIGN, IS ELABORATELY MOULDED IN THE ORNAMENTAL STYLE TYPICAL OF THIS ENGLISH ITALIANATE WARE.
PRICE GUIDE 4

▶ THE DAVENPORT POTTERY WAS RENOWNED FOR ITS FINE QUALITY EARTHENWARE AND STONEWARE. THIS RIDGED MEAT PLATE WITH HOLLY DESIGN ON THE BORDER IS DATED c.1850.
PRICE GUIDE 5

▲ THE COW ON THE LID OF THE LEFT-HAND BUTTER DISH OFFERS A CLUE TO ITS CONTENTS; WHILE THE HAT DISH ON THE RIGHT IS A MORE FANCIFUL EXAMPLE OF VICTORIAN BREAKFAST CHINA.
PRICE GUIDE A

▼ TWO LATE VICTORIAN MUFFIN DISHES: ON THE LEFT IS A SIMPLE DISH WITH A FLORAL PATTERN ON THE RIM AND PLATE; THE DISH ON THE RIGHT IS DECORATED IN A LEAF DESIGN IN THE MAJOLICA WARE POPULAR IN 19TH-CENTURY BRITAIN.
PRICE GUIDE 2 & 5

▶ SHAPED LIKE A COFFEE POT, THIS STONEWARE JUG IS ACTUALLY A TEAPOT. THE STRAINER IN THE SPARROW-BEAK LIP GIVES IT'S USE AWAY.
PRICE GUIDE 4

▼ THIS SIMPLE, BUT ELEGANT, CHINA TOAST RACK WAS A POPULAR VICTORIAN DESIGN. SIMILAR, SMALLER RACKS INTENDED FOR ONE PERSON ARE ALSO SOMETIMES FOUND.
PRICE GUIDE 3

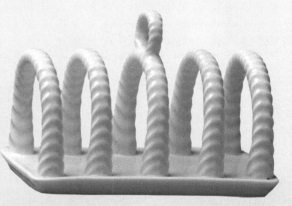

◀ A WHITE CHINA TOAST RACK IN A TWISTED, TWIG-LIKE DESIGN. TOAST RACKS, LIKE THIS ONE, WERE DESIGNED TO CATCH THE DRIPS FROM BUTTERED TOAST.
PRICE GUIDE 2

▶ THIS BLUE-AND-WHITE TOAST RACK IS THE IMITATION DELFTWARE THAT WAS POPULAR IN THE SECOND HALF OF THE 19TH CENTURY. TRUE ENGLISH DELFT IS DATED 1550 – 1800.
PRICE GUIDE 4

▲ THE SAUCE TUREEN, LIKE BOTH OF THESE EXAMPLES WITH THEIR OWN MATCHING PLATES, HAS DISAPPEARED FROM TODAY'S DINNER SERVICES.
PRICE GUIDE 4

▼ STILL POPULAR TODAY, 'NEST-EGGS' LIKE THIS STAFFORDSHIRE EXAMPLE ORIGINATED IN THE MID-19TH CENTURY AND WERE DESIGNED TO STORE EGGS.
PRICE GUIDE 4

▼ THIS BASKET-SHAPED MAJOLICA EGG-CUP STAND WITH FRUIT, FLOWER AND LEAF DESIGN IS AN UNUSUAL EXAMPLE OF THIS KIND OF SERVING CHINA.
PRICE GUIDE 4

▼ THIS EGG-CUP BASKET DATES FROM THE LATE 19TH CENTURY AND IS NOTABLE BECAUSE IT IS MADE OF PORCELAIN RATHER THAN EARTHENWARE.
PRICE GUIDE 5

▲ THESE MAJOLICA SERVING PLATTERS SHOW THE WIDE RANGE OF MOULDED SHAPES AND DESIGNS THAT COULD BE PRODUCED IN THIS STONEWARE. THE BRILLIANT, OFTEN STRIDENT, COLOURS ARE TYPICAL OF THIS STYLE.
PRICE GUIDE 5

▶ THESE MAJOLICA SARDINE BOXES CONTAINED THE SALTED SARDINES COMMON TO VICTORIAN BREAKFASTS. BOTH BOXES HAVE THE CHARACTERISTIC MODELLED FISH ON THEIR LIDS.
PRICE GUIDE 4

▲ A GREEN-GLAZED EARTHENWARE LEAF DISH BY WEDGEWOOD. DEVELOPED IN THE 18TH CENTURY, THIS WAS NAMED AFTER THE LUSTROUS, GREEN LIQUID GLAZE USED THAT VARIED IN SHADE FROM YELLOW-GREEN TO DEEP-GREEN.
PRICE GUIDE 3

▲ THIS SHELL-SHAPED SALAD PLATE BY HAMILTON, HAS A LATER ADDITION OF ENAMEL GLAZE, KNOWN AS 'CLOBBERED'.
PRICE GUIDE 5

◄ A LOBED PEARLWARE DISH, C.1812. A REFINEMENT OF CREAMWARE, PEARLWARE WAS IDEAL FOR TRANSFER PRINTING.
PRICE GUIDE 4

▼ A GROUP OF MASON'S IRONSTONE SAUCE TUREENS AND SERVING PLATES. THE STRIKING DESIGN OF IRONSTONE CHINA MAKES IT POPULAR WITH COLLECTORS EITHER AS PART OF A SET OR AS INDIVIDUAL PIECES.
PRICE GUIDE 3 – 5

DESIGN FEATURES

WHEN TRYING TO DISTINGUISH BETWEEN EARTHENWARE OR PORCELAIN IN WILLOW PATTERN CHINA, THE COLOURS ON EARTHENWARE (LEFT) ARE MUCH STRONGER THAN THOSE ON PORCELAIN (RIGHT), WHICH APPEAR MORE TRANSLUCENT.

▶ A C.1830 PURPLE AND BLUE PIE DISH DECORATED WITH A DESIGN INSPIRED BY THE DECORATIVE ARTS OF THE FAR EAST.
PRICE GUIDE 4

▼ A SELECTION OF BLUE, WHITE AND GILT SOUP TUREENS COMPLETE WITH THEIR LIDS AND UNDERPLATES.
PRICE GUIDE 4 – 7

DESIGN FEATURES

COLLECTABLE COW CREAMERS DATE FROM 1750 TO 1850. THEY ARE HARDLY EVER MARKED AND CAN RARELY BE ATTRIBUTED TO A PARTICULAR POTTER. THE BASIC DESIGN HAS BARELY CHANGED, EXCEPT FOR SOME VARIATIONS IN THE BASES AND GLAZES.

MOST COW CREAMERS ORIGINATE EITHER IN STAFFORDSHIRE OR WALES; STAFFORDSHIRE CREAMERS WERE MADE IN SALT-GLAZED STONEWARE, JET-BLACK JACKFIELD WARE, BONE CHINA, AGATE WARE OR PEARLWARE. THE COMMONEST FINISH WAS A TAN GLAZE DAPPLED WITH BLUE, GREEN, BLACK, ORANGE OR YELLOW, THOUGH LUSTRE GLAZES WERE ALSO USED. THE COW'S TAIL CURVES ON TO ITS BACK, USUALLY TO MAKE THE HANDLE. IN THE EXAMPLE HERE, THE CROOKED ARM OF A FIGURE SERVES AS A HANDLE IN PLACE OF THE TAIL. CREAMERS LIKE THIS ONE BEAR CLOSE RESEMBLANCE TO THE STAFFORDSHIRE FLAT-BACK FIGURES, WITH DETAILS AND DECORATION CONFINED TO THE FRONT AND SIDES OF THESE FIGURES.

EARLY WELSH EXAMPLES ARE IN SPLASHED LUSTRE WARE, BUT LATER EXAMPLES HAVE TRANSFER-PRINTED RURAL SCENES ON BOTH SIDES AND SOMETIMES THE BASE AS WELL. COW CREAMERS WERE ALSO MADE IN YORKSHIRE AND THESE HAVE WAISTED OBLONG BASES WITH CHAMFERED CORNERS, AND MANY HAVE THEIR EYES OUTLINED IN BLUE. THE SUNDERLAND FACTORY MADE COLOURFUL LUSTRE CREAMERS UNTIL IT CLOSED DOWN IN 1878. OTHER POTTERIES IN SCOTLAND AND THE WEST OF ENGLAND TURNED OUT YET MORE NAIVE WORK, STILL APPEALING TO TODAY'S COLLECTORS.

▲ A BLACK COW CREAMER WITH GOLD LUSTRE SPOTS. THE STRAIGHT HORNS SET ON TO THE SIDES OF THE HEAD GIVE IT AN UNUSUAL APPEARANCE WHILE THE LOW TAIL POSITION MAKES IT AWKWARD TO PICK UP AND POUR OUT THE MILK.
PRICE GUIDE 4

▼ THE ONLY NATURALISTICALLY COLOURED COW CREAMERS WERE THOSE THAT TRIED TO MIMIC THE COAT OF HEREFORDSHIRE CATTLE. THIS 1877 EXAMPLE IS ALSO VERY REALISTIC IN THE MODELLING OF THE COW'S STOUT BUILD.
PRICE GUIDE 5

◀ THIS MID-VICTORIAN, SUNDERLAND COW CREAMER DISPLAYS TYPICAL RUST AND LILAC COLOURING, AND HAS AN UNUSUALLY REALISTIC FACE AND SMILING EXPRESSION. THE LID SET INTO THE BACK WAS A PRACTICAL FEATURE, PRESERVING THE MILK OR CREAM FROM DIRT AND FLIES.
PRICE GUIDE 6

▲ THE RANDOM DAUBS OF LILAC AND RUST LUSTRE MARK THIS C.1800 CREAMER AS ANOTHER SUNDERLAND MODEL. OTHER VARIATIONS COMBINED PINK OR LILAC WITH BLUE OR GREEN.
PRICE GUIDE 5

◀ CREAMERS LIKE THIS 19TH-CENTURY, BLACK STAFFORDSHIRE COW ARE SOMETIMES, ERRONEOUSLY, CALLED 'JACKFIELD'. ORIGINAL JACKFIELD COWS WERE PRODUCED IN SHROPSHIRE BETWEEN 1750 AND 1775 BUT THE TYPE HAS BEEN MUCH REPRODUCED SINCE.
PRICE GUIDE 5

▼ THE LOW, BOAT SHAPE OF THIS JUG, REMINISCENT OF A MODERN GRAVY BOAT, WAS A TYPICAL FEATURE OF MANY EARLY 19TH-CENTURY JUGS. THIS WEDGWOOD JUG DATES FROM AROUND 1810 AND IS A VERY GOOD EXAMPLE OF THE 'FISH ROE' PATTERN.
PRICE GUIDE 3

◀ METALLIC LUSTRE GLAZES WERE USED ON EARTHENWARE AND BONE CHINA FROM THE EARLY 19TH CENTURY ONWARDS. THIS MID-VICTORIAN STAFFORDSHIRE JUG HAS A COPPER LUSTRE BAND ABOVE A HAND-PAINTED ENAMEL DESIGN ON SKY-BLUE GROUND.
PRICE GUIDE 3

▼ AN UNUSUAL, MAJOLICA CREAM JUG MOULDED TO RESEMBLE A CAULIFLOWER. MINTON PRODUCED A HUGE RANGE OF QUALITY MAJOLICA WARE BETWEEN 1851 AND 1862. THESE WERE SOON IMITATED BY A HOST OF LESSER POTTERS.
PRICE GUIDE 5

▶ THE VICTORIANS OFTEN DREW ON EARLIER STYLES. THIS WHITE PORCELAIN JUG WITH SPREADING FOOT (C.1880) IS INFLUENCED BY THE BALUSTER SHAPE.
PRICE GUIDE 2

DESIGN FEATURES

CREAM JUG SHAPES WENT IN AND OUT OF FASHION IN THE 18TH AND 19TH CENTURIES, BUT THE UNDERLYING TREND WAS AWAY FROM TALL, SLENDER JUGS TOWARDS WIDER, SHORTER FORMS. THE UNUSUAL DESIGN OF THE REGENCY CHINA CREAM JUG, SHOWN HERE, HAS A SPOUT INSTEAD OF A LIP, GIVING THE JUG A TEAPOT-LIKE APPEARANCE.

▶ THOUGH UNMARKED, THIS JUG IS PROBABLY MID-VICTORIAN. A MAUVE, TRANSFER-PRINTED DESIGN, HIGHLIGHTED WITH TRAILING LINES OF LUSTRE, MAKES FOR AN UNUSUAL, ABSTRACT PATTERN.
PRICE GUIDE 3

▶ A HIGH-HANDLED, BROAD-SPOUTED PORCELAIN CREAM JUG, C.1840. THE SMALL FEET ON THIS CHARACTERISTIC VICTORIAN JUG WERE DERIVED FROM EARLIER 18TH-CENTURY EXAMPLES. THIS ONE IS DECORATED WITH ELABORATE GILDED PATTERNING.

PRICE GUIDE 2

◀ A MINIATURE VERSION OF THE POPULAR OCTAGONAL MASON'S IRONSTONE JUG – THESE WERE MADE IN A GRADUATED RANGE OF SIZES. THIS EXAMPLE SHOWS THE JAPANESE-INFLUENCED IMARI PATTERN, PAINTED IN TYPICALLY RICH COLOURS.

PRICE GUIDE 4

▶ AN EARLY VICTORIAN PORCELAIN CREAM JUG WHICH FOLLOWS THE CONTEMPORARY SAUCE-BOAT SHAPE. ORIENTAL PATTERNS, LIKE THE ONE SHOWN HERE, VARIED IN POPULARITY THROUGHOUT THE 19TH CENTURY.

PRICE GUIDE 3

▲ COMPORT AND PLATES FROM A
WORCESTER DESSERT SERVICE, WITH
VARIOUS PAINTED LANDSCAPES IN THE
CENTRE AND A GILDED BORDER. THESE
PIECES BELONG TO A SET OF FOUR
COMPORTS AND 16 DESSERT PLATES.
PRICE GUIDE 8

DESIGN FEATURES

JOHN DAVENPORT FOUNDED HIS
STAFFORDSHIRE FACTORY IN 1793 AND
BEGAN BY PRODUCING CREAMWARE AND
EARTHENWARE. PORCELAIN STARTED TO
BE PRODUCED EARLY IN THE 19TH
CENTURY AND THE FACTORY EXPANDED.

DAVENPORT EMPLOYED PAINTERS FROM
THE DERBY WORKS AND PRODUCED A
BETTER QUALITY PORCELAIN, IMITATING
DERBY DESIGNS. THESE INCLUDED FRUIT
AND FLORAL MOTIFS, STILL-LIFES AND
LANDSCAPES IN BRILLIANT COLOURS AND
GILDING. HERE, A COLOURFUL FLORAL
DECORATION HAS BEEN PAINTED ON A
PLAIN WHITE CENTRE AND GILDING HAS
REINFORCED THE CURVILINEAR LINES OF
THE SCALLOPED EDGE.

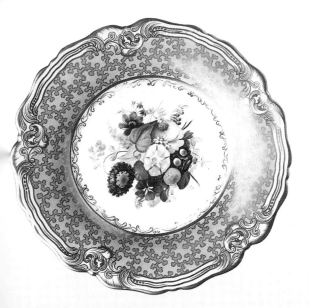

◀ THIS FLORAL PINK PLATE WITH GILDING IS BY CHAMBERLAIN OF WORCESTER. THESE TWO NAMES WERE ASSOCIATED FROM 1783 TO 1840.
PRICE GUIDE 4

▶ WORCESTER PLATE SHOWING CAREW CASTLE, SIGNED BY J.STINTON. SETS DECORATED WITH LANDSCAPES WERE PRODUCED BY WORCESTER FROM 1813.
PRICE GUIDE 5

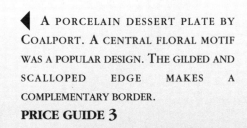

◀ A PORCELAIN DESSERT PLATE BY COALPORT. A CENTRAL FLORAL MOTIF WAS A POPULAR DESIGN. THE GILDED AND SCALLOPED EDGE MAKES A COMPLEMENTARY BORDER.
PRICE GUIDE 3

▼ TWO DERBY PLATES: THE OVAL PLATE ON THE LEFT IS IN EXCELLENT CONDITION AND DATES FROM BETWEEN 1878 TO 1890; THE ROUND PLATE IS SLIGHTLY RUBBED AND IS FROM AROUND 1840.
PRICE GUIDE 5 & 3

POINTS TO WATCH

● JAPANNED GILDING AND HONEY GILDING WERE USED ON BEST PORCELAIN UNTIL THE 1850S.

● SOLID GILDING WAS INTRODUCED IN 1810 FOR BONE CHINA, GIVING A GLITTERING EFFECT.

● MERCURY GILDING, NOT IN COMMON USE UNTIL THE 1830S, IS RESILIENT AND PERMANENT AND IT APPEARS BRASSIER THAN OTHER FORMS OF GILDING.

● TRANSFER-GILDING AND LIQUID GOLD BOTH HAVE AN EXCEEDINGLY BRILLIANT FINISH.

POINTS TO WATCH

● See if a piece is porcelain by holding it up to a strongish light to see if it is translucent. Tap with a fingernail: hard-paste porcelain gives a clear ring; repaired or soft-paste porcelain has a duller sound.

● Look out for makers' marks, but treat them as guides rather than guarantees.

● In soft-paste porcelain, colours tend to fuse with the glaze; in hard-paste porcelain, the colours will generally be crisper.

▶ This Coalport plate, dating from about 1820, has been prettily decorated with pink flowers between blue and gold bands.
PRICE GUIDE 3

▼ A Ridgway teapot in deep peach with gold trim. The brothers Job and George Ridgway established a firm at Hanley, Staffordshire, in 1794, producing mainly tableware.
PRICE GUIDE 4

▲ A Coalport vase of c.1830 with a floral design on a blue background. The simple trumpet shape was very popular for small vases during the Regency period.
PRICE GUIDE 4

▼ A COALPORT BREAKFAST CUP AND SAUCER OF C.1825, WITH EXTREMELY LAVISH ORNAMENTATION. BREAKFAST CUPS ARE GENERALLY LARGER IN SIZE THAN STANDARD TEA OR COFFEE CUPS.
PRICE GUIDE 5

DESIGN FEATURES

THESE CUP AND SAUCER SETS, DATING FROM ABOUT 1770, SHOW THE RANGE OF POSSIBILITIES IN DECORATING PORCELAIN. THE SET ON THE LEFT IS ORNATE IN SHAPE AND FORM, WITH ITS RIBBING AND ELABORATE HANDLE, BUT WITH SPARSE PAINTED DECORATION. THE RIGHT-HAND CUP AND SAUCER ARE SIMPLE IN FORM, BUT THE DESIGN IS EXTREMELY RICH IN COLOUR AND PATTERN.

▶ A SOUP PLATE DATING FROM ABOUT 1825, POSSIBLY MADE BY COALPORT. IT IS PRINTED WITH A BOLD AND LUSH FLORAL DESIGN IN ENAMEL COLOURS.
PRICE GUIDE 6

▲ A PAIR OF EGG CUPS OF C.1825 WITH PREDOMINANTLY BLUE AND GOLD DECORATION. EGG CUPS SOMETIMES COME IN SETS ON A STAND.
PRICE GUIDE 3

◀ A WORCESTER COFFEE POT, C.1806. SIMPLE IN PROPORTION, IT FEATURES A PATTERN OF GOLD LEAVES ARRANGED BETWEEN A SERIES OF GOLD BANDS ON A WHITE BACKGROUND.
PRICE GUIDE 6

▼ A WORCESTER CREAMER AND CUP AND SAUCER, C.1810. THE VERY DELICATE DECORATION TAKES THE FORM OF GREY PRINT FLOWERS AND GOLD TRIMMING ON A WHITE BACKGROUND.
PRICE GUIDE 4 & 3

◀ A WORCESTER CUP AND SAUCER DATING FROM ABOUT 1820, IN A DELICATE PEACH AND GOLD DESIGN.
PRICE GUIDE 3

▲ A WORCESTER COMPORT WITH
GOLD HANDLES AND A BLUE AND GOLD
TRIM THAT FOLLOWS THE ELEGANT
OUTLINES OF THE PIECE.
PRICE GUIDE 5

▲ A HANDSOME WORCESTER PLATE IN
A TYPICAL BLUE AND GOLD COLOURS,
DECORATED IN THE CENTRE WITH WHAT IS
KNOWN AS A HO-HO BIRD, A DECORATIVE
MOTIF TAKEN FROM CHINESE ART.
PRICE GUIDE 6

▶ A WORCESTER DESSERT PLATE,
DATING FROM ABOUT 1815. WITH
ORNATE SCALLOPED EDGES AND
DECORATION IN THE FORM OF ROSES AND
PANSIES, THIS PLATE IS IN VERY GOOD
CONDITION FOR ITS AGE.
PRICE GUIDE 4

POINTS TO WATCH

- MAKE SURE THAT A CUP AND SAUCER OR THE PIECES IN A SET REALLY MATCH.
- GOOD BUYS ARE OFTEN PIECES MADE BY LESSER-KNOWN FACTORIES, OR SINGLE PIECES FROM AN INCOMPLETE SET.
- GILDING SHOULD BE BRIGHT AND CRISP AND PAINTING CLEAR AND CLEAN.
- HANDLE PIECES WITH CARE, KEEPING FINGERS OFF THE GILDED AREAS.
- SIGNATURES OF A RENOWNED ARTIST CAN ADD TO THE VALUE OF THE PIECE BUT ITEMS SHOULD BE JUDGED ON THEIR OWN MERITS.

▼ A VIENNA PORCELAIN CUP AND SAUCER, C.1825, WITH A FLARED CUP AND SCROLLING HANDLE. THE RICH GILT BACKGROUND ON BOTH CUP AND SAUCER IS DECORATED WITH A BAND OF DELICATE, HAND-PAINTED FLOWERS.

PRICE GUIDE 6

▲ THIS VIENNA PORCELAIN TEACUP AND SAUCER WAS MADE C.1820. THE CYLINDRICAL CUP AND DEEP SAUCER ARE DECORATED WITH SPRAYS OF ROSES IN OVAL GILT FRAMES.

PRICE GUIDE 6

◀ THE RUBIES, EMERALDS AND SAPPHIRES PAINTED ON TO THIS VIENNA CUP, C.1825, AND SAUCER HAVE A THREE-DIMENSIONAL, *TROMPE-L'ŒIL* EFFECT.
PRICE GUIDE A

▶ THIS LARGE VIENNA CUP, MADE IN C.1825, HAS A DELICATE FLORAL BOUQUET WITHIN A BORDER, PAINTED ON ONE SIDE, ON A GILT BACKGROUND.
PRICE GUIDE 5

◀ TWO KPM TEACUPS, BOTH GILDED INSIDE AND OUT. THE INITIALS KPM STAND FOR THE KÖNIGLICHE PORZELLAN MANUFAKTUR, OR ROYAL PORCELAIN FACTORY, IN BERLIN, ONE OF THE CHIEF MAKERS OF BIEDERMEIER PORCELAIN.
PRICE GUIDE 6

▼ ANOTHER KPM PIECE, THIS IS A CABINET CUP AND SAUCER, C.1840, INTENDED FOR DISPLAY RATHER THAN USE. THE GILT DECORATION IS PAINTED ON TO A NATURAL WHITE PORCELAIN.
PRICE GUIDE 4

DESIGN FEATURES

ONE OF THE FEATURES OF LUSTREWARE IS RESIST LUSTRE. THIS IS PRODUCED BY BLOCKING OUT THE PATTERN WITH GLYCERINE AND COATING THE BACKGROUND WITH METAL.

A NUMBER OF PINK LUSTREWARE DESIGNS ARE DECORATED WITH HAND PAINTING, WHICH CAN BE IDENTIFIED BY ITS IRREGULAR, BOLD STROKES.

EARLY LUSTRE WAS INTENDED TO IMITATE METALS SUCH AS GOLD AND SILVER, ALTHOUGH LATER EXAMPLES ARE OFTEN MORE SUBTLE AND HAVE A LESS OBVIOUS METALLIC SHEEN. THE BEST CLUES TO THE AGE OF LUSTREWARE ARE ONLY REVEALED BY WEAR OR CHIPPING. FOR EXAMPLE, A PURPLISH GLAZE SHOWING UNDER A GOLD LUSTRE INDICATES THE USE OF PURPLE OF CASSIUS, A MIXTURE OF GOLD AND TIN OXIDES USED ONLY IN EARLY WARES.

▲ SOME OF THE MOST VALUED LUSTREWARE IS PURPLE OR PINK SPLASHED, WHICH WAS CHIEFLY MADE IN SUNDERLAND. THE EFFECT WAS ACHIEVED BY APPLYING THE LUSTRE AND THEN SPLASHING IT WITH OIL WHICH PRODUCED THE MOTTLED EFFECT DURING FIRING.
PRICE GUIDE 5

▶ THIS SMALL DISH, PRODUCED IN C.1880, HAS A PINK LUSTRE BORDER. THE PRINT ON THE BOTTOM IS AN AMUSING ILLUSTRATION OF A LADY PLAYING WITH A MONKEY ON A SOFA.
PRICE GUIDE 3

▶ A PINK RESIST LUSTRE JUG WITH A PATTERN POPULAR IN THE 19TH CENTURY. THE SHADE OF PINK ACHIEVED DEPENDS ON THE RATIO OF GOLD TO TIN; ONE PART TO FOUR PRODUCED A LIGHT PURPLE, ONE TO FIVE, A PALER ROSE SHADE.
PRICE GUIDE 4

▼ DATING FROM C.1820, THIS DELICATE TEACUP HAS A PINK LUSTRE BORDER AROUND THE TOP AND A HAND-PAINTED SCENE OF A COTTAGE IN THE COUNTRYSIDE ON THE BOWL.
PRICE GUIDE 3

▼ A STAFFORDSHIRE JUG WITH PINK LUSTRE DECORATION PRODUCED IN 1815. THE BORDER AT THE TOP HAS A MOTTLED EFFECT, AS DOES THE HANDLE.
PRICE GUIDE 3

▲ A PARTICULARLY DELICATE PINK, LUSTRE LINE HIGHLIGHTS THE DECORATION OF THIS SMALL MILK JUG, C.1810, BY A STAFFORDSHIRE POTTERY.
PRICE GUIDE 4

▼ PLATES INSCRIBED WITH MOTTOES, SUCH AS THIS ONE, ARE ALSO POPULAR WITH MANY LUSTREWARE COLLECTORS. DECORATED WITH A MOTTLED LUSTRE BORDER, PLATES LIKE THIS WOULD HAVE BEEN HUNG ON THE WALL.
PRICE GUIDE 4

▼ A LARGE PINK LUSTRE MUG FROM THE STAFFORDSHIRE POTTERIES, HAND-PAINTED WITH A SCENE OF HOUSES,
PRICE GUIDE 4

◀ A SMALL CUP AND SAUCER DECORATED WITH A SMALL SILVER LUSTRE BORDER AND HAND-PAINTED, ORIENTAL-STYLE DESIGN.
PRICE GUIDE 3

DESIGN FEATURES

RELIEF PATTERNS WERE SOMETIMES USED TO DECORATE MUGS AND VASES. THE EXAMPLE SHOWN HERE IS RATHER CRUDELY HAND PAINTED.

IN A REVERSE PROCESS OF RESIST, THE SILVER LUSTRE SEEN HERE WAS STENCILLED ON OVER THE SURFACE AND THEN DECORATED WITH PAINT.

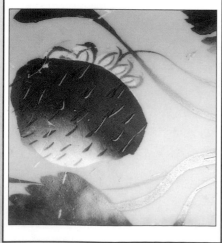

▶ THIS SILVER LUSTRE COFFEE POT WAS MADE IN STAFFORDSHIRE IN AROUND 1860. ALL-OVER SILVER LUSTRE WAS FIRST USED TO MIMIC THE METAL ITSELF AND WAS KNOWN AS POOR MAN'S SILVER.
PRICE GUIDE 5

▲ A DELICATELY CRAFTED COPPER LUSTRE JUG BANDED IN ORANGE WITH A RESIST PATTERN OF LEAVES, MADE IN STAFFORDSHIRE IN ABOUT 1850.
PRICE GUIDE 5

◀ THIS LARGE MUG, FROM 1860, IS DECORATED WITH A GOLD LUSTRE THAT IS ALMOST YELLOW IN COLOUR. PRODUCED FROM GOLD OXIDES, GOLD LUSTRE HAS WIDELY VARYING HUES BECAUSE OF THE DIFFERENT CARATS OF GOLD USED.
PRICE GUIDE 3

▼ A SILVER LUSTRE TEAPOT WITH A DELICATE PATTERN IN RESIST WHICH HAD BEEN USED SINCE 1810. WHITE OR CREAM GLAZE WAS MOST COMMONLY USED UNTIL THE 1830s.
PRICE GUIDE 5

▲ A SMALL STAFFORDSHIRE COPPER LUSTRE BOWL WITH MUSTARD-COLOUR AND BLUE BANDS. THE LUSTRE HAS A SMOOTH, ALMOST MIRROR-LIKE SURFACE WHICH WAS OFTEN USED TO GIVE COPPER LUSTRE A CONSISTENT DEPTH AND RICHNESS OF TONE NORMALLY ASSOCIATED WITH GOLD LUSTRE.
PRICE GUIDE 2

▲ THE HAND-PAINTED FLOWERS SET ON A DEEP-BLUE BAND ARE, IN FACT, MOULDED IN RELIEF ON THIS COPPER LUSTRE MUG. THE BRONZE COLOUR WAS ACHIEVED BY THE USE OF MORE COPPER IN THE GOLD ALLOY.
PRICE GUIDE 3

◀ A STAFFORDSHIRE GOBLET FROM THE 1820s IS DECORATED WITH COPPER LUSTRE. THIS KIND OF LUSTRE WAS SCARCE UNTIL AROUND 1823.
PRICE GUIDE 5

POINTS TO WATCH

● JUDGE THE ITEM FIRST AS A PIECE OF POTTERY BEFORE CONSIDERING THE QUALITY OF THE LUSTRE.

● A GOOD, PLAIN JUG WITH A LITTLE LUSTRE BANDING MAY SOMETIMES BE A BETTER BUY THAN A FLASHIER PIECE WITH ALL-OVER DECORATION.

● FALSE MARKS ARE RARE ON LUSTRE, BUT LOOK CAREFULLY TO MAKE SURE NO MARKS HAVE BEEN REMOVED TO MAKE THE PIECE SEEM OLDER.

● BE WARY OF VERY EARLY DATES ASCRIBED TO SILVER LUSTRE. EARLY PIECES SHOULD HAVE BECOME GREY AND DULL IN APPEARANCE, BUT THIS IS NOT AN INFALLIBLE TEST.

▲ A PATÉ JAR, C.1820, IN THE POPULAR JAPAN IMARI PATTERN. THE DECORATION WAS UNDERGLAZE, COLOURED WITH ADDED OVERGLAZE COLOUR.

PRICE GUIDE 5

▲ A PEARLWARE COFFEE POT, C.1780, DECORATED WITH DELICATE LEAFY SPRIGS PICKED OUT IN BROWN, BLUE, GREEN AND ORANGE. THE WHITE BODY OF PEARLWARE WAS PRODUCED BY USING A HIGH PROPORTION OF WHITE CLAY AND FIRING IT AT A HIGH TEMPERATURE.

PRICE GUIDE 6

▲ PEARLWARE'S CHARACTERISTIC IRIDESCENT APPEARANCE IS CLEARLY SEEN IN THIS BOTANICAL PLATE OF ABOUT 1810. THE PAINTED DECORATION INSIDE IS OF A TANGIER PEA.

PRICE GUIDE 6

◀ A QUINTAL STAFFORDSHIRE VASE, C.1810, WITH UNDERGLAZE COLOURS IN BLUE, ORANGE, GREEN AND BROWN. DESPITE DAMAGE, THIS UNUSUAL PIECE IS STILL VALUABLE TODAY.

PRICE GUIDE 7

▼ A LATE 18TH-CENTURY HAND-PAINTED PEARLWARE POT POURRI, PROBABLY MADE BY THE LEEDS POTTERY. THE HOLES IN THE LID OF THIS PIECE WERE SO THAT THE AROMA OF THE DRIED FLOWERS OR LIQUID CONTAINED WITHIN COULD ESCAPE AND SCENT THE ROOM. **PRICE GUIDE 5**

▲ A PEARLWARE CUP AND COVER DATED C.1815, WITH PUCE TRANSFER-PRINTED DECORATION AND FEATURING HANDLES IN THE SHAPE OF RAMS' HEADS. **PRICE GUIDE 5**

▲ THIS LATE 18TH-CENTURY DINNER PLATE WITH SHELL EDGE IS DECORATED WITH A NAIVE AND VIGOUROUS PAINTING OF A CHINESE PAGODA. **PRICE GUIDE 4**

▲ AN EARLY 19TH-CENTURY PEARLWARE GOBLET WITH BOLD FLORAL DECORATION, INSPIRED BY IMARI, IN UNDERGLAZE BLUE, GREEN AND DEEP ORANGE. IT WAS PROBABLY MADE BY SPODE. **PRICE GUIDE 4**

DESIGN FEATURES

IT IS FAIRLY EASY TO TELL CREAMWARE AND PEARLWARE APART. THE BLUISH TINGE OF THE SLOP BOWL, C. 1810, ON THE LEFT DISTINGUISHES IT AS PEARLWARE; THE BOWL ON THE RIGHT IS A CREAMWARE PIECE OF ABOUT 1790.

▲ DATING FROM ABOUT 1820, THIS SAUCE TUREEN IS DECORATED WITH A BLUE AND WHITE TRANSFER-PRINTED CHINOISERIE PATTERN. THE BODY OF PEARLWARE WAS PARTICULARLY SUITABLE FOR TRANSFER PRINTING AND MUCH WAS MADE IN BLUE AND WHITE. **PRICE GUIDE 5**

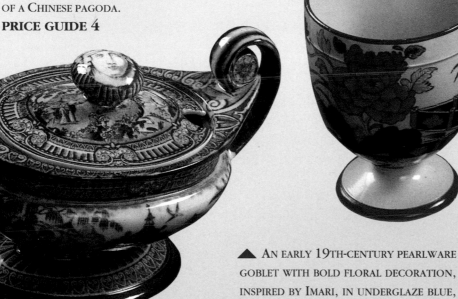

▶ A WEDGWOOD CREAMWARE DIAMOND-SHAPED COMPORT WITH BLACK AND YELLOW BORDER DECORATION, FROM ABOUT 1810. THE PIECE HAS BEEN REPAIRED IN ONE CORNER.
PRICE GUIDE 3

▲ A JUG FROM ABOUT 1810, DECORATED WITH A BAND OF FLOWERS AROUND THE RIM AND A SCENE OF A MAN HUNTING GAME.
PRICE GUIDE 5

▲ THIS ELONGATED CREAMWARE DISH WITH A PIERCED EDGE DECORATION IS UNMARKED, BUT IT IS LIKELY TO BE 18TH-CENTURY. IT WAS PROBABLY USED FOR SERVING SWEETMEATS.
PRICE GUIDE 5

◀ THIS CREAMWARE URN FOR FRUIT OR NUTS IS DECORATED WITH A FRET PATTERN AND SWAGS. THE SLIGHTLY BUFF COLOUR OF THE PIECE SUGGESTS AN EARLY DATE.
PRICE GUIDE 3

▲ A LATE 18TH-CENTURY CREAMWARE JUG WITH PIERCED AND FLUTED DECORATION AND AN UNUSUAL HANDLE IN THE FORM OF A KNOT.
PRICE GUIDE 3

◀ THIS SMALL CREAMWARE POT WITH A PIERCED LID AND BASKET-WEAVE BASE WAS MADE IN THE LATE 18TH CENTURY.
PRICE GUIDE 3

POINTS TO WATCH

- EARLY PIECES OF CREAMWARE ARE VERY LIGHT IN THE HAND AND WITH A DEEP-YELLOW GLAZE, APPLIED UNEVENLY.
- ANY 'WEDGWOOD' PIECE WITH A NETWORK OF FINE LINES (CRAZING) IN ITS GLAZE IS EITHER PRE-1764 OR, MORE LIKELY, A FAKE.
- ONLY THE SINGLE IMPRESSED WORD 'WEDGWOOD' IS USED ON WARES ACTUALLY MADE BY THE FAMOUS FIRM.
- WARES WITH AMERICAN SCENES MAY WELL HAVE ORIGINATED AT LIVERPOOL POTTERY.

▲ A CREAMWARE PLATE FROM C.1790, SHOWING A PICTURE OF A SHIP IN FULL SAIL. BY 1764, WEDGWOOD HAD DEVELOPED CREAMWARE AS A DURABLE, BUT PLEASING, LIGHT-COLOURED AND MODESTLY PRICED CHINA. HIS INNOVATION ENJOYED AN IMMEDIATE AND LASTING POPULARITY AND POTTERS CATERED FOR A VARIETY OF TASTES AND MARKETS. THEREFORE, COLLECTORS OF CREAMWARE CAN EXPECT TO FIND WARES VARYING FROM PLAIN AND UNADORNED TO PAINTED AND DECORATED.
PRICE GUIDE 5

▲ A 'VEILLEUSE', OR FOOD WARMER, IN CREAMWARE, C.1800, USED FOR MAKING INFUSIONS. THE SIMPLE WHITE SHAPE IS UNADORNED, EXCEPT FOR THE UNUSUAL, TWISTED HANDLES.
PRICE GUIDE 3

▶ A WEDGWOOD CREAMWARE DISH MADE IN ABOUT 1810. THE RAISED SIDES OF THIS DISH ARE ADORNED WITH A PATTERN OF GRAPES AND LEAVES.
PRICE GUIDE 5

◀ THE SIMPLE SHIP DESIGN IN THE CENTRE OF THIS LARGE, SUSIE COOPER SERVING PLATTER OF THE 1930S, IS SET AGAINST A MORE ABSTRACT BORDER PATTERN REPRESENTING WAVES AND FISH.
PRICE GUIDE 5

▼ SUSIE COOPER BEGAN TO USE LITHOGRAPHIC TRANSFER TO DECORATE HER PIECES IN THE LATE 1930S. THIS SMALL TEAPOT'S LITHOGRAPHED TULIP DESIGN IS IN THE THEN FASHIONABLE SHADES OF PINK AND GREEN.
PRICE GUIDE 4

▼ THIS HORS-D'ŒUVRES DISH IS DECORATED WITH A SUBTLE PATTERN OF STYLIZED LEAVES IN GREEN AND BEIGE. MOTIFS INSPIRED BY PLANTS FEATURED STRONGLY IN SUSIE COOPER'S WORK.
PRICE GUIDE 4

▼ IN THE EARLY 1930S, SUSIE COOPER CONTRACTED WOOD & SONS' CROWN WORKS IN BURSLEM TO PRODUCE HER DESIGNS. THIS COFFEE SET, WHICH ALSO HAS A MATCHING DINNER SERVICE, WAS MADE THERE.
PRICE GUIDE 6

SUSIE COOPER LEFT A.E.GRAY'S BURSLEM POTTERY FIRM IN 1930, AFTER WORKING THERE EIGHT YEARS, SO ANYTHING PRODUCED BY HER OWN BUSINESS, AT THE CROWN WORKS, DATES AFTER THEN.

MOST OF HER MOTIFS AND PATTERNS HAVE BEEN INSPIRED BY NATURAL FORMS AND FINE HAND PAINTING OF HER DESIGNS IS AN UNMISTAKABLE SIGN OF AN ORIGINAL SUSIE COOPER.

▲ A PARTICULARLY LIGHT AND DELICATE DESIGN IN MUTED COLOURS, THIS SUSIE COOPER PLATE SHOWS HER USE OF *SGRAFFITO*, WHERE THE DESIGN WAS CUT INTO THE COLOURED GLAZE.
PRICE GUIDE 2

▲ THIS HAND-PAINTED FLOWER VASE HAS AN UNUSUAL ABSTRACT DESIGN BASED ON LEAVES AND FLOWERS.
PRICE GUIDE 5

▼ AS WELL AS CREATING PATTERNS FOR CHINA, SUSIE COOPER ALSO DEVELOPED NEW SHAPES. THE 'KESTRAL' SHAPE WAS DESIGNED IN THE 1930S AND REMAINED POPLULAR FOR MANY YEARS. THIS TEAPOT DATES FROM THE 1950S.
PRICE GUIDE 3

▼ THE CROCUS PATTERN WAS ONE OF CLARICE CLIFF'S BEST-SELLING DESIGNS AND IT CAME IN SEVERAL COLOURWAYS. THIS TOAST-RACK WAS MADE IN 1936.
PRICE GUIDE 4

▲ THE VIBRANT PATTERN ON THIS CLARICE CLIFF BISCUIT PLATE IS KNOWN AS 'MELON'. THIS PIECE IS PART OF THE 'FANTASQUE' RANGE.
PRICE GUIDE 6

▼ THIS CYLINDRICALLY-SHAPED CONTAINER IS A SUGAR BOWL PRODUCED IN 1935 AND IS AN EXAMPLE OF CLARICE CLIFF'S 'BONJOUR' SHAPE.
PRICE GUIDE 5

▼ MADE IN 1933, THIS CIGARETTE AND MATCH HOLDER IS PART OF CLARICE CLIFF'S 'BIZARRE' RANGE.
PRICE GUIDE 5

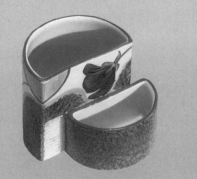

DESIGN FEATURES

THIS PARTICULARLY STRIKING CONICAL BOWL IS A GOOD EXAMPLE OF THOSE FEATURES THAT MAKE CLARICE CLIFF'S DESIGNS COLLECTABLE. THE OVERALL SHAPE OF THE BOWL IS BASED ON GEOMETRIC PRINCIPLES AND IN 1931 THIS CONICAL FORM WAS THE FIRST OF HER INNOVATIVE SHAPES PATENTED.

THE DESIGN IS CALLED 'UMBRELLAS AND RAIN' AND THE COLOURS AND PATTERNS USED INCOPORATE FEATURES OF MANY CONTEMPORARY ARTISTIC MOVEMENTS. HER FAVOURITE COLOURS WERE THE BRIGHTEST ORANGES, YELLOWS, GREENS AND BLUES. THE CLEAR, BOLD STROKES ARE A FEATURE OF CLARICE CLIFF'S DESIGNS, AND ARE OFTEN LACKING IN FAKES AND REPRODUCTIONS.

◀ THIS TEAPOT AND CUP AND SAUCER ARE PART OF A SMALL TEA SERVICE IN THE 'BONJOUR' SHAPE THAT COMPRISES OF POT, TWO CUPS AND SAUCERS, MILK AND SUGAR BOWL.

PRICE GUIDE 5

▼ THIS VASE WAS INTENDED AS A RECEPTACLE FOR SPILLS (THIN STRIPS OF WOOD USED FOR LIGHTING CANDLES, FIRES AND CIGARETTES), IT IS DECORATED WITH THE 'UMBRELLAS AND RAIN' DESIGN AND DATES FROM 1929.

PRICE GUIDE 5

▲ THIS STRIKING DINNER PLATE WAS PRODUCED IN 1930 AND IS PART OF CLARICE CLIFF'S 'FANTASQUE' RANGE.

PRICE GUIDE 6

▶ THIS CONICAL-SHAPED PIECE OF CHINA IS, IN FACT, A SUGAR SHAKER, DATING FROM 1930, AND DECORATED WITH THE POPULAR 'CROCUS' PATTERN.

PRICE GUIDE 5

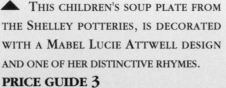

▼ A MUG AND PLATE, PART OF A PLACE SETTING FOR ONE, ILLUSTRATED WITH A SCENE CAPTIONED 'YOUR LICENCE PLEASE!' AS FAMILIES BECAME SMALLER IN THE 1930S MORE PEOPLE WERE PREPARED TO PROVIDE THEIR CHILDREN WITH PERSONAL CROCKERY AND CUTLERY, AND INDIVIDUAL PLACE SETTING BECAME MORE AND MORE POPULAR.
PRICE GUIDE 2

▲ THIS CHILDREN'S SOUP PLATE FROM THE SHELLEY POTTERIES, IS DECORATED WITH A MABEL LUCIE ATTWELL DESIGN AND ONE OF HER DISTINCTIVE RHYMES.
PRICE GUIDE 3

◀ THIS PORCELAIN CHLDREN'S BEAKER FROM THE SIMPLE SIMON NURSERY TEA SERVICE, WAS FIRST PRODUCED BY ROYAL DOULTON IN 1920.
PRICE GUIDE 2

DESIGN FEATURES

THIS PLATE DESIGNED BY MABEL LUCIE ATTWELL IS TYPICAL OF CROCKERY INTENDED FOR CHILDREN. TOO HEAVY TO SLIDE AROUND THE TABLE, OR TO BE EASILY THROWN, THE CERAMIC IS STRONG TO MAKE BREAKAGE LESS LIKELY. THE LIP ON THE INSIDE OF THE RIM IS DESIGNED TO PUSH FOOD ON TO THE SPOON RATHER THAN SHOVELLING IT OVER THE EDGE OF THE BOWL.

MABEL LUCIE ATTWELL DESIGNED HER NURSERY TEA SERVICE IN 1926. MANUFACTURED BY THE SHELLEY POTTERY, IT FEATURED HER DISTINCTIVE DRAWINGS OF SMALL CHILDREN AND LITTLE ELVES, KNOWN AS 'THE BOO-BOOS'. EACH PIECE HAS A SHORT RHYME PRINTED ON IT AND ALL ITEMS FEATURE THE DESIGNER'S SIGNATURE.

▼ ANOTHER ROYAL DOULTON SERIES WAS 'ALICE IN WONDERLAND' AND THIS IS A CUP AND PLATE FROM A TEA SET. THE DESIGN WAS BASED ON TENNIEL'S DRAWINGS FOR LEWIS CARROLL'S BOOK.
PRICE GUIDE 3

▼ THE NURSERY RHYME ON THIS CHILD-SIZE MUG IS 'OLD MOTHER HUBBARD'. THIS PARTICULAR RANGE WAS PRODUCED FROM 1903 TO 1939.
PRICE GUIDE 3

▲ DECORATED WITH BLACK AND WHITE LINE DRAWINGS AND A NURSERY RHYME THIS JUG WAS MANUFACTURED FROM 1907 UNTIL 1934.
PRICE GUIDE 3

▶ THIS DISH, EGG CUP AND SMALL PLATE WERE PART OF A SERIES DESIGNED BY HEATH ROBINSON.
PRICE GUIDE 5

▼ THIS PARAGON BOWL FEATURES MICKEY AND MINNIE MOUSE AT THE PIANO. THEY ARE PAINTED IN DISNEY'S EARLY STYLE FOR HIS CARTOON CHARACTERS.
PRICE GUIDE 3

▼ THIS DIMINUTIVE CHINA ORNAMENT OF AN ALERT FOX TERRIER WOULD HAVE BEEN A POPULAR CHOICE FOR CHILDREN IN THE 1930S. THIS PIECE WAS MADE BY SHAW AND COPESTAKE.
PRICE GUIDE 2

▲ THESE ARE TWO SYLVAC TERRIERS IN GREEN AND BUFF, WITH THEIR HEADS CHARACTERISTICALLY COCKED TO ONE SIDE. THOUGH NOT INTENDED AS SPECIFICALLY CHILDREN'S CHINA, SYLVAC WARE FEATURED ENDEARING LITTLE DOGS, RABBITS AND CATS THAT WERE PERENIALLY POPULAR WITH GIRLS AND BOYS.
PRICE GUIDE 3

◄ THESE TWO LONG-NECKED, CARTOON DOGS, IN DIFFERENT SIZES, ARE ALSO PART OF THE SYLVAC AND COPESTAKE RANGE.
PRICE GUIDE 2

◄ THIS SOULFUL-LOOKING, CERAMIC SETTER'S HEAD IN A RING, FORMS A RELIEF PLAQUE THAT, TYPICALLY, WOULD HAVE HUNG ON THE WALL OF A CHILD'S ROOM.
PRICE GUIDE 2

▼ THESE TWO CERAMIC BOOKENDS WERE MADE IN GERMANY. THEY SHOW A BOY ON ONE BOOKEND WITH A POSY AND A GIRL ON THE OTHER, HOLDING A BOOK. BOTH CHILDREN ARE DRESSED IN 18TH-CENTURY COSTUME.
PRICE GUIDE 3

◀ SYLVAC CHINA WAS AN EARTHENWARE MADE BY SHAW AND COPESTAKE AND WHICH CAME IN PALE GREEN, BUFF, BLUE AND, OCCASIONALLY, YELLOW. THIS BUTTON TIDY, WITH ITS SCOTTIE DOG, IS IN BUFF AND PALE GREEN.
PRICE GUIDE 2

▶ THIS ENDEARING WHITE AND TORTOISESHELL KITTEN WITH GREEN EYES IS ALSO IN THE SYLVAC RANGE AND DATES FROM THE 1930S.
PRICE GUIDE 3

◀ THIS CERAMIC MONEY BOX IS IN THE SHAPE OF A RABBIT. THE DETAILS OF THE NOSE, EYES AND CLAWS HAVE BEEN HAND-PAINTED LATER ADDITONS.
PRICE GUIDE 2

▼ THESE TWO TINY SYLVAC RABBITS ARE IN SUBTLY DIFFERENT STYLES. THE GREEN RABBIT HAS A HERRINGBONE PATTERN ON HIS EARS.
PRICE GUIDE 1

▲ THESE BOOKENDS ARE ALABASTER BUT THE FIGURES OF GIRLS THAT ADORN THEM ARE CERAMIC. ONE GIRL HOLDS A CAMERA AND THE OTHER A ROSE.
PRICE GUIDE 2

▶ THE ALLIES WERE NOT FORGOTTEN IN MEMORABLILIA AND THIS CERAMIC FIGURE OF THE FRENCH LEADER MARSHAL FOCH SHOWS HIM DRINKING FROM A BOTTLE SAYING 'TO THE DEVIL WITH THE KAISER.
PRICE GUIDE 6

▼ SOME POTTERIES PRODUCED SMALL CERAMIC MODELS OF THE TOOLS OF WAR — SHIPS, TANKS, SHELLS AND GUNS WERE ALL INCLUDED. THIS WORLD WAR I AMBULANCE WAS MADE BY CARLTON AND BEARS A CREST AND THE RED CROSS SYMBOL. THE TANK WAS BY SWAN AND IS DECORATED WITH A REGIMENTAL CREST AND GOLD PAINT HIGHLIGHTS.
PRICE GUIDE 3 & 5

DESIGN FEATURES

ONE OF THE MOST POPULAR AND RESPECTED OF BRITISH COMMANDERS DURING WORLD WAR I, GENERAL HAIG WAS A FITTING SUBJECT FOR A CARRUTHERS GOULD TOBY JUG. THIS DIGNIFIED PORTRAIT OF HIM PAYS CLOSE ATTENTION TO DETAIL WITH HIS UNIFORM — RIGHT DOWN TO THE DETAILS OF THE DOUBLE ROW OF GENERAL'S BRAID ON HIS CAP'S PEAK.

▲ IN 1918, THIS CERAMIC BEAKER WAS MADE TO CELEBRATE THE CONCLUSION OF HOSTILITIES. THE FLAGS OF THE ALLIES — AMERICA, GREAT BRITAIN, FRANCE AND ITALY — SURROUND A GLOBE EMBLAZONED WITH THE WORD 'PEACE'.
PRICE GUIDE 3

▼ BAIRNSFATHER'S 'OLD BILL' CHARACTER BECAME THE MODEL FOR THIS PATRIOTIC TOBY JUG.
PRICE GUIDE 4

▼ PIECES THAT POKED FUN AT THE ENEMY WERE VERY POPULAR. PIECES LIKE THIS ORNAMENT THAT SHOWS THE TWO-FACED KAISER AND THAT CHALLENGES THE OWNER TO DECIDE THE GERMAN RULER'S FATE. WILL HE BE ALLOWED TO 'BOSS THE LOT' OR WILL THE OLD DEVIL BE DEFEATED?
PRICE GUIDE 4

▲ THIS BOWL AND SMALL TEAPOT ARE DECORATED WITH CARTOONS BY BRUCE BAIRNSFATHER, WHOSE POPULAR 'OLD BILL' CHARACTER BECAME THE EPITOME OF THE BRITISH TOMMY.
PRICE GUIDE 4

▶ ANOTHER CARRUTHERS GOULD TOBY JUG HAS AN UNIDENTIFIED GENERAL DRINKING FROM A JUG PROCLAIMING 'FRANCE FOR THE FRENCH'.
PRICE GUIDE 6

◀ BRITISH POTTERIES RESPONDED TO THE CHALLENGE OF WORLD WAR I WITH AN ASTONISHING OUTPUT OF CHINA MEMORABLILIA. TOBY JUGS, ALWAYS POPULAR ITEMS, WERE ADAPTED TO REPRESENT WARTIME LEADERS AND HEROES. THIS EXAMPLE WAS MADE BY CARRUTHERS GOULD AND SHOWS ADMIRAL BEATTIE HOLDING A SHELL.
PRICE GUIDE 6

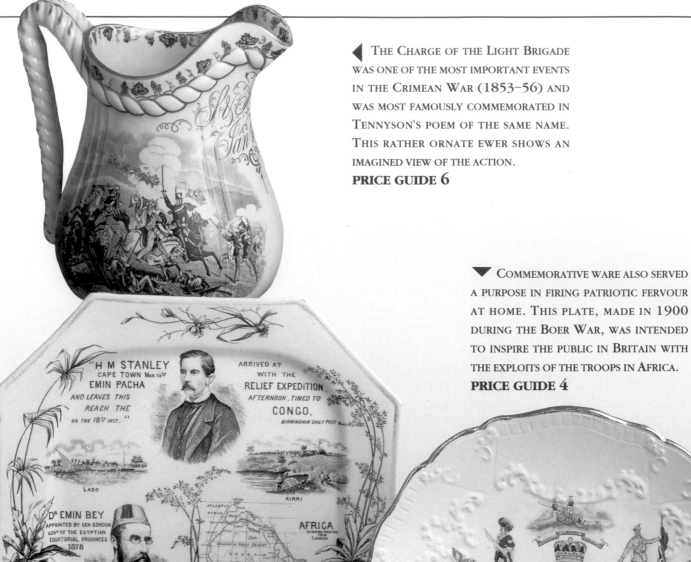

◀ THE CHARGE OF THE LIGHT BRIGADE WAS ONE OF THE MOST IMPORTANT EVENTS IN THE CRIMEAN WAR (1853–56) AND WAS MOST FAMOUSLY COMMEMORATED IN TENNYSON'S POEM OF THE SAME NAME. THIS RATHER ORNATE EWER SHOWS AN IMAGINED VIEW OF THE ACTION.
PRICE GUIDE 6

▼ COMMEMORATIVE WARE ALSO SERVED A PURPOSE IN FIRING PATRIOTIC FERVOUR AT HOME. THIS PLATE, MADE IN 1900 DURING THE BOER WAR, WAS INTENDED TO INSPIRE THE PUBLIC IN BRITAIN WITH THE EXPLOITS OF THE TROOPS IN AFRICA.
PRICE GUIDE 4

▲ BRITAIN'S COLONIAL PAST IS EVOKED IN THIS PLATE OF 1871, WHICH COMMEMORATES STANLEY'S DISCOVERY OF DR. LIVINGSTONE, AS WELL AS OTHER BRITISH EXPLOITS IN AFRICA.
PRICE GUIDE 5

▶ THE CHARMING AND RATHER CARTOON-LIKE PICTURE ON THIS PLATE ILLUSTRATES AN INCIDENT IN THE CRIMEAN WAR (1853–56). THE ORDINARY SOLDIERS ARE SHOWN RECEIVING THEIR MAIL BEFORE THE SIEGE OF SEBASTOPOOL IN 1854.
PRICE GUIDE 5

▶ As a national hero, Lord Nelson, remained a popular feature for commemorative ware throughout the 19th century. This jug, however, is of particular value as it was actually made as a souvenir at the time of his death in 1805.
PRICE GUIDE 7

▼ This plate had a dual purpose: not only did it commemorate the striking of 7,500 men in support of a nine-hour day, it also served to advertise J.Greaves' tea – 'Many imitate, none excell'. Dating from 1871, the rather naive illustration running around this plate enhance the charm of the piece.
PRICE GUIDE 6

▶ The politician Sir Robert Peel was most famous for creating the first British police force. But other notable events in his career are also commemorated on this plate, produced at his death in 1850.
PRICE GUIDE 5

▲ This octagonal plate shows the British statesman Benjamin Disraeli. Made by Walter Gimson in 1887, the primrose, known to be Disraeli's favourite flower, was chosen to decorate the plate's background.
PRICE GUIDE 4

POINTS TO WATCH

● LOOK TO SEE IF THERE IS THE NAME OF A FACTORY ON THE BASE OF THE PIECE. MODERN REPRODUCTIONS, ESPECIALLY OF LIVERPOOL AND SUNDERLAND WARE, ARE COMMON BUT THESE ARE ALWAYS MARKED AS SUCH.

● MAKE SURE THAT THE EVENT COMMEMORATED IS A REAL ONE, BACKED UP BY HISTORICAL EVIDENCE.

● LOOK AT THE QUALITY OF THE PRINTING. POOR OR SMUDGED EXAMPLES ARE LESS VALUABLE.

● AS WITH ALL CERAMIC WARES, CRACKS, CRAZING AND OBVIOUS REPAIRS WILL ALL MAKE THE OBJECT LESS DESIRABLE.

▼ THIS GILDED STAFFORDSHIRE FIGURE OF KING EDWARD VII WAS MADE TO MARK HIS CORONATION IN 1902.
PRICE GUIDE 5

▼ QUEEN VICTORIA'S CORONATION WAS A YEAR AFTER HER ACCESSION AND THIS PLATE COMMEMORATES THAT EVENT. THE ILLUSTRATION IN THE CENTRE IS REMARKABLY SIMILAR TO THE 1837 PLATE BUT IN THIS ONE THE DATE OF THE CORONATION IS INCLUDED AND THE DESIGN IS COLOURED.
PRICE GUIDE 6

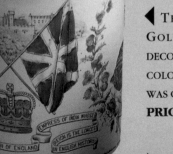

▲ THIS PLATE IS UNUSUAL, AND, THEREFORE, MORE VALUABLE, BECAUSE IT COMMEMORATES THE PROCLAIMATION OF VICTORIA AS QUEEN ON 20TH JUNE 1837. ANY EARLY ROYAL COMMEMORATIVES WILL ALSO BE OF GREATER VALUE.
PRICE GUIDE 6

◄ THIS MUG MADE FOR VICTORIA'S GOLDEN JUBILEE HAS A 'CLOBBERED' DECORATION, THAT IS, IT HAS ENAMELLED COLOURS ADDED TO IT. THIS TECHNIQUE WAS OFTEN USED IN THE 19TH CENTURY.
PRICE GUIDE 3

▶ A VISIT BY THE PRINCE OF WALES TO THE DOULTON FACTORY IN 1885 RESULTED IN THIS UNUSUAL SALTGLAZE VASE.
PRICE GUIDE 6

▼ THE MAYOR OF WORCESTER GAVE A DINNER TO CELEBRATE QUEEN VICTORIA'S GOLDEN JUBILEE IN 1887. THIS SPECIAL PLATE TO COMMEMORATE THE JUBILEE IS MARKED WITH THE MAYOR'S NAME AND WAS A GIFT FOR THE LADIES PRESENT AT THE DINNER.
PRICE GUIDE 4

▶ A SIMPLE BLACK AND WHITE TRANSFER PRINT OF THE PRINCE AND PRINCESS OF WALES DECORATES THIS PLATE OF 1888.
PRICE GUIDE 4

▼ DOULTON PRODUCED THIS SCALLOP-EDGED BONE CHINA PLATE TO MARK EDWARD VII'S CORONATION. IT SHOWS PORTAITS OF THE KING AND QUEEN.
PRICE GUIDE 4

▲ A YOUTHFUL-LOOKING PRINCE OF WALES, THE FUTURE EDWARD VII, FEATURES ON THE SIDE OF THIS LARGE JUG.
PRICE GUIDE 5

◀ A PORTRAIT OF QUEEN VICTORIA AND HER CONSORT, PRINCE ALBERT, ADORNS THIS TRANSFER-PRINTED AND LUSTREWARE MILK JUG.
PRICE GUIDE 6

▲ THIS IS A STAFFORDSHIRE DOG OF A PARTICULARLY FINE QUALITY. THESE DOGS WERE MODELLED ON THE KING CHARLES SPANIEL AND THE 'COMFORTER' DOG WHICH WAS A KIND OF LAP-DOG, NOW NO LONGER BRED. NO VICTORIAN PARLOUR WOULD HAVE BEEN COMPLETE WITHOUT ONE OF THESE DOGS ON THE MANTELPIECE.
PRICE GUIDE 6

▲ FIGURES IN RURAL SETTINGS WERE ALWAYS A POPULAR THEME, ESPECIALLY WITH THE MANY NEW TOWN DWELLERS. ORNAMENTS SUCH AS THIS SPILL HOLDER WITH A PAIR OF LOVERS SEATED BESIDE A FLOWING STREAM WERE TYPICAL.
PRICE GUIDE 5

▶ ORNAMENTS IN THE FORM OF EXOTIC ANIMALS WERE A POPULAR KIND OF STAFFORDSHIRE FIGURE. SO GREAT WAS DEMAND FOR ZEBRAS THAT MOULDS ORIGINALLY MEANT FOR HORSES WERE OFTEN USED AND THEN PAINTED MORE APPROPRIATELY WITH STRIPES.
PRICE GUIDE 6

▶ THESE STAFFORDSHIRE SHEEP SPILL HOLDERS ARE MADE IN WHAT WAS KNOWN AS THE 'BOCAGE' STYLE. THE REALISTIC WOOL TEXTURE WAS CREATED USING GRANULATED CLAY.
PRICE GUIDE 5

▲ FLORENCE NIGHTINGALE (1820–1910) ACHIEVED FAME IN HER OWN TIME AS A PIONEERING NURSE IN THE CRIMEA. STILL A POPULAR HISTORICAL CHARACTER, FIGURES LIKE THIS ARE OF GREAT INTEREST TO MODERN COLLECTORS.
PRICE GUIDE 5

▶ UNNAMED, UNKNOWN FIGURES ARE GENERALLY PRICED LOWER THAN SPECIFICALLY NAMED OR IDENTIFIED EXAMPLES. THE QUALITY OF MOULDING AND HAND-PAINTING, HOWEVER, WILL ALWAYS ADD VALUE. THIS WELL-MOULDED DOUBLE FIGURE OF LOVERS HAS A FRAGILE LOOK WITH ITS THIN CLAY UMBRELLA, THE HANDLE HELD IN THE MAN'S HAND.
PRICE GUIDE 5

▶ THE EXOTICISM OF TRAVEL AND EXPLORATION WAS SUMMED UP FOR THE VICTORIANS IN THE VAST RANGE OF NAVAL FIGURES AND SAILORS MADE IN STAFFORDSHIRE. THE BROAD-BRIMMED HAT AND THE BAGGY SHIRT INDICATE THAT THE MALE FIGURE IN THIS PAIR IS A SAILOR.
PRICE GUIDE 5

POINTS TO WATCH

● INSPECT THE GLAZE CAREFULLY, FORGERIES TEND TO HAVE MORE UNIFORM CRAZING THAN ORIGINALS
● STUDY THE UNDERSIDE – ORIGINALS ARE OFTEN PARTIALLY GLAZED AND SHOWING RESIDUES OF KILN GRIT, RATHER THAN UNGLAZED AND CLEAN.

DESIGN FEATURES

THIS PORCELAIN PASTILLE BURNER IN THE SHAPE OF A SMALL CHURCH IS UNMARKED. THE WINDOWS AND THE TOWER ARE LEFT OPEN FOR THE FRAGRANCE OF THE PASTILLE TO ESCAPE AND SCENT THE ROOM. THE PASTILLES WERE INSERTED AT THE BACK. OTHER MODELS HAVE LIFT-OFF WALLS AND ROOF, OR SOMETIMES JUST THE ROOF LIFTS OFF. AN UNUSUAL FEATURE HERE IS A DRAWER AT THE BACK FOR STORING EXTRA PASTILLES. THE ROOF IS ADORNED WITH TYPICAL *COTTAGE ORNÉE* FLOWERS.

▲ A LARGE TREE, OR POSSIBLY A HILLOCK, LOOMS BEHIND THE GABLED ROOF OF THIS LATE VICTORIAN COTTAGE.
PRICE GUIDE 5

▲ THIS MUSHROOM-SHAPED PORCELAIN COTTAGE IS A FINE EXAMPLE OF RUSTIC FANTASY DESIGN. THE CIRCULAR ROOF AND BASE OF THE COTTAGE ARE DOTTED WITH OUT-SIZED FLOWERS.
PRICE GUIDE 3

◀ A WATER MILL, SUCH AS THIS STAFFORDSHIRE EXAMPLE, WAS A POPULAR SUJECT FOR THE *COTTAGE ORNÉE*. THE WINDOWS OF THE MILL ARE LEFT UNFILLED TO LET THE INCENSE ESCAPE.
PRICE GUIDE 5

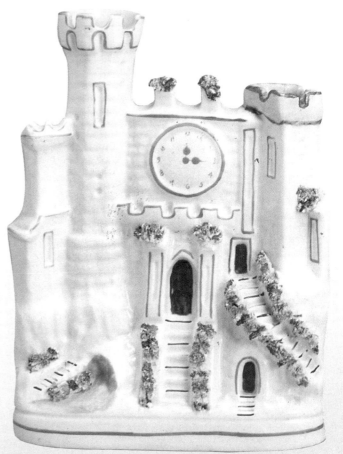

▲ THIS STAFFORDSHIRE COTTAGE IS IN
A SLIGHTLY GRANDER STYLE. A THREE-
TIERED MODEL, THIS IS DECORATED WITH
FLOWERS AND IS RATHER A CURIOUS
FANTASY OF THE RUSTIC STYLE.
PRICE GUIDE 5

▲ THIS PASTILLE BURNER IN THE SHAPE
OF A CASTLE DATES FROM 1870. SPECIAL
CONTAINERS FOR BURNING PASTILLES OF
SWEET-SMELLING GUM HAVE BEEN USED
SINCE THE 18TH CENTURY.
PRICE GUIDE 5

▲ THIS *COTTAGE ORNÉE* IS DESIGNED IN
A GOTHIC STYLE, WITH SLENDER WINDOWS
AND TOWERS FLANKING EITHER SIDE.
PRICE GUIDE 5 .

▲ THATCHED COTTAGES LIKE THIS ONE,
FROM 1860, WERE AMONGST THE MOST
POPULAR OF *COTTAGE ORNÉE* SUBJECTS.
PRICE GUIDE 5

▲ A STAFFORDSHIRE CASTLE WITH
TURRETS, DATING FROM 1870. EACH
DOOR HAS A CRUCIFIX ABOVE IT.
PRICE GUIDE 5

POINTS TO WATCH

- CHECK CONDITION; SMALL REPAIRS DO NOT NECESSARILY DECREASE VALUE.
- MAKE SURE THAT THE STYLE, THE NUMBER AND MARK, IF ANY, AND THE SUBJECT ALL POINT TO THE SAME DATE AND FACTORY.
- CHECK THAT ANY CRAZING IS NATURAL. UNIFORM CRAZING MAY INDICATE A REPRODUCTION PIECE WITH A MODERN GLAZE THAT CRACKLES DURING FIRING.
- THE CAPTION SHOULD BE LEGIBLE.

▶ FAIRINGS WERE CHINA ORNAMENTS AND TRINKETS MAINLY SOLD AS MOMENTOES AT FAIRS IN THE 19TH CENTURY. THIS MATCH STRIKER, C. 1880, SHOWS A YOUNG BOY CRYING OVER A SPILT BASKET OF EGGS. THE ROUGH TEXTURE OF THE WALL WAS FOR STRIKING PHOSPHORUS MATCHES AGAINST.
PRICE GUIDE 3

▶ ALSO SOMETIMES KNOWN AS COTTAGE MANTELSHELF CHINA, FAIRINGS WERE AT THE HEIGHT OF THEIR POPULARITY BETWEEN 1860 AND 1900. THIS UNUSUAL PIECE, SHOWING THREE WELSH LADIES AT A TEA PARTY, IS, IN FACT, A SPILL HOLDER ENTITLED 'WELSH COSTUME' AND DATES FROM THE 1890s.
PRICE GUIDE 3

▶ THIS REASONABLY COMMON MATCH HOLDER, DATING FROM 1862–1870, SHOWS A GIRL AT AN OYSTER STAND AND IS ENTITLED 'OYSTERS, SIR.'
PRICE GUIDE 3

▲ THIS RARE MATCH HOLDER IS CALLED COME AT ONCE' AND SHOWS A MAN TALKING TO HIS SWEETHEART THROUGH A WINDOW WHILE HER FATHER APPROACHES WITH A STICK. THE MATCHES WERE KEPT IN THE RECEPTACLE BEHIND THE FIGURE OF THE GIRL.
PRICE GUIDE 4

◀ AN EDWARDIAN MATCH STRIKER AND HOLDER WITH 'SCRATCH MY BACK' PRINTED ON THE BIG PIG AND 'ME TOO' ON THE SMALLER ONE. BEFORE THE INVENTION OF THE SAFETY MATCH, JUST SCRATCHING A MATCH ACROSS A ROUGH SURFACE, LIKE THE BACK OF THESE ENDEARING PIGS, WOULD LIGHT IT.
PRICE GUIDE 3

▼ THIS EDWARDIAN FAIRING IS ALSO A MATCH HOLDER AND SHOWS TWO SMILING PIGS SITTING BESIDE A WOODEN TUB.
PRICE GUIDE 2

▲ THIS EDWARDIAN SPILL HOLDER IS MADE OF THREE CROSSED HOLLOW BRANCHES. THE PIGLET AND TINY BANJO PLAYER AT THE BOTTOM ARE RATHER CRUDELY PAINTED.
PRICE GUIDE 3

▼ INTENDED TO BE USED AS A PIN HOLDER, THIS FAIRING IS MODELLED IN THE FORM OF A FIREPLACE.
PRICE GUIDE 3

▼ THIS NOVELTY, PIG FAIRING DATES FROM THE EDWARDIAN PERIOD. THE PIG HAS ITS FRONT TROTTERS IN A HOLLOWED-OUT TRAY THAT WAS PROBABLY INTENDED FOR PINS OR BUTTONS.
PRICE GUIDE 2

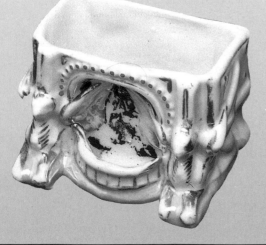

DESIGN FEATURES

CAPTURING THE HUMOUROUS SENTIMENT OF THE MAJORITY OF 19TH-CENTURY FAIRINGS, THIS DRAMATIC EXAMPLE SHOWS A MAN HAVING HIS TOOTH PULLED OUT. AS AN ASSISTANT HOLDS THE PATIENT'S HEAD THE DENTIST PULLS HIS TOOTH OUT WITH A STRONG TUG. CAPTIONED 'A LONG PULL AND A STRONG PULL', IT IS A RARE DESIGN. THERE WAS A COMPANION PIECE TO THIS; ENTITLED 'OUT! BY JINGO!!!', IT SHOWED ALL THREE FIGURES ON THE FLOOR WITH THE PATIENT WITH HIS LEGS IN THE AIR.

THIS MODEL IS NUMBERED 3335, WHICH HELPS TO DATE IT AT C.1880. THE CLOTHES WORN BY FIGURES CAN HELP DATE FAIRINGS WHEN UNMARKED AND BRIGHT-COLOURED PAINTS WERE NOT USED UNTIL THE 1850S.

▼ FAIRINGS WITH THE POPULAR MOTTO 'THE LAST IN BED TO PUT OUT THE LIGHT', WERE ORIGINALLY MADE IN 1860. THE CAPTIONS FOR FAIRINGS WERE USUALLY HUMOUROUS IN INTENT AND PUNS WERE COMMON. THE MOST CHARACTERISTIC STYLE WAS SLIGHTLY RISQUÉ.
PRICE GUIDE 3

▶ FAIRINGS WERE NOT ALL FUNCTIONAL, ORNAMENTAL FIGURES MADE UP A LARGE PROPORTION OF THIS KIND OF COTTAGE MANTELSHELF CHINA. THIS VERY RARE FAIRING SHOWS THE FIGURE OF A WIDOW IN MOURNING AND IS, RATHER POIGNANTLY, CAPTIONED 'TO LET'. IT DATES FROM BETWEEN 1860 AND 1870.
PRICE GUIDE 5

▶ THIS IS A VERY RARE FAIRING, PROBABLY MADE IN C.1880, SHOWING A YOUNG GIRL EMBRACING HER LOVED ONE AND WHICH IS ENTITLED 'JUST AS IT SHOULD BE'.
PRICE GUIDE 5

▲ FAIRINGS WERE USUALLY ENGLISH BUT SOME EXAMPLES OF FRENCH AND GERMAN WARE ARE FOUND. THIS DESIGN WAS FIRST MADE BY CONTA & BOEHME, AND IT WAS COPIED BY MANY OTHER GERMAN FACTORIES. THE ORIGINAL MODEL IS NOW VERY RARE.
PRICE GUIDE 3

▼ DATING FROM BETWEEN 1863 AND 1875, THIS FAIRING WHICH SHOWS A MONK KISSING A YOUNG GIRL, IS WITTILY ENTITLED 'ANIMATED SPIRITS'.
PRICE GUIDE 5

▼ ENTITLED 'THE POWER OF LOVE', THIS HUMOUROUS FAIRING SHOWS A WIFE PEEPING BEHIND A SCREEN AS HER HUSBAND KISSES THE MAID.
PRICE GUIDE 4

▲ THIS VERY RARE FAIRING IS ENTITLED 'IF YOU PLEASE SIR', AND SHOWS A BUXOM MAID POINTING OUT A CORK IN HER CLEAVAGE TO A SEATED GENTLEMAN.
PRICE GUIDE 5

▼ ENTITLED 'GOING TO THE BALL', THIS FAIRING FROM C.1870 SHOWS A YOUNG GIRL BEING DRESSED BY HER MOTHER TO GO TO A PARTY. FAIRING FIGURE GROUPS WERE ALWAYS SMALL WITH BASES NO MORE THAN 5 INCHES (13CMS) LONG.
PRICE GUIDE 4

▲ THE CAPTION TO THIS TYPICALLY COARSE FAIRING OF A COUPLE IN FRONT OF A ROSE BUSH SAYS 'COME ALONG, THESE FLOWERS DON'T SMELL TOO GOOD'. TURNING THE PIECE AROUND REVEALS THE FIGURE OF A YOUNG BOY RELIEVING HIMSELF BEHIND THE BUSH.
PRICE GUIDE 5

CHINA *Parian Ware*

DESIGN FEATURES

PARIAN WAS THE NAME GIVEN TO A KIND OF UNGLAZED PORCELAIN PERFECTED IN THE 1840s. IT WAS SO CALLED BECAUSE ITS SLIGHT TRANSLUCENCE AND DELICATE, CREAMY OFF-WHITE SURFACE RESEMBLED THE CELEBRATED MARBLE FROM THE ISLAND OF PAROS, USED BY PRAXITELES AND OTHER GREAT GREEK SCULPTORS. THIS ILLUSTRIOUS ASSOCIATION AND ITS SIMILARITY WITH MARBLE MEANT THAT PARIAN BECAME THE ESTABLISHED CERAMIC MEDIUM FOR PORTRAIT BUSTS AND FIGURINES OF CLASSICAL CHARACTERS OR SUBJECTS.

THIS PIECE WAS KNOWN AS 'CLYTIE', AND WAS ONE OF THE MOST POPULAR OF THE PARIAN CLASSICAL BUSTS. IN GREEK MYTHOLOGY, CLYTIE WAS THE MISTRESS OF THE SUN GOD HELIOS. HER JEALOUSY OF HER SISTER LUCOTHEA, WHO SHARED HIS AFFECTION, CAUSED HER TO PLOT HER SISTER'S DEATH. WHEN SHE REALISED THAT HER ACTIONS HAD LOST HER HELIOS' LOVE, SHE DIED OF DISPAIR HERSELF. REFUSING TO EAT OR DRINK HER BODY BEGAN TO TAKE ROOT IN THE SOIL AND, EVENTUALLY, SHE WAS TRANSFORMED INTO THE APTLY-NAMED HELIOTROPE, THE FLOWER THAT ALWAYS TURNS ITS HEAD TOWARDS THE SUN.

LIKE MANY OTHER PARIAN BUSTS, 'CLYTIE' WAS BASED ON AN ORIGINAL SCULPTURE – IN THIS CASE A GRECO-ROMAN FIGURE IN THE BRITISH MUSEUM. THE DESIGN WAS INTRODUCED BY COPELAND IN 1855, BUT A STAMP ON THE BASE OF THIS PIECE REVEALS THAT THIS PARTICULAR EXAMPLE WAS PRODUCED IN 1876. THE ART UNION OF LONDON DISTRIBUTED COPIES TO ITS MEMBERS AS PRIZES FOR COMPETITIONS.

▶ THIS PARIAN GROUP IS A NEW TESTAMENT SUBJECT TAKEN FROM ACTS 10 AND SHOWS THE CONVERTED ROMAN CENTURION, CORNELIUS, GREETING THE APOSTLE, SIMON PETER. THE PIECE DATES FROM ABOUT 1855.
PRICE GUIDE 5

▶ A MINTON GROUP FROM 1857 DEPICTING THE OLD TESTAMENT FIGURES OF NAOMI AND HER DAUGHTERS-IN-LAW, RUTH AND ORPAH. ALL THREE WOMEN WERE WIDOWED AND EXILES, HENCE THEIR TRAGIC EXPRESSIONS.
PRICE GUIDE 6

▼ A TERRACOTTA-COLOURED, GLAZED PARIAN FIGURE OF THE WATER NYMPH, UNDINE, THE HEROINE OF A FRIEDRICH DE LA MOTTE FOUQUÉ STORY. THE MODEL, WHICH IS BASED ON A BRONZE STATUETTE BY THE SCULPTOR J.B.KLAGMANN, WAS INTRODUCED BY MINTON POTTERIES IN 1859, BUT THIS PARTICULAR EXAMPLE DATES FROM AROUND 1898.
PRICE GUIDE 6

◀ THIS WORCESTER GROUP FROM 1855 IS BASED ON A SCULPTURE BY W.B.KIRK. IT DEPICTS THE HERO OF GOETHE'S *FAUST*, WITH HIS SWEETHEART, MARGUERITE.
PRICE GUIDE 6

▲ THIS PARIAN FIGURE IS MADE BY COPELAND, IN AROUND 1880, AND IT REPRESENTS THE CHARACTER MIGNON, TAKEN FROM GOETHE'S NOVEL *WILLHELM MEISTER'S APPRENTICESHIP*. SHE IS ALSO THE SUBJECT OF A WELL-KNOWN VICTORIAN PAINTING AND AN OPERA.
PRICE GUIDE 6

POINTS TO WATCH

● SEEK EXPERT ADVICE BEFORE ATTEMPTING TO CLEAN UNGLAZED PARIAN; IT IS SLIGHTLY POROUS AND SHOULD NOT BE IMMERSED IN WATER. CERTAIN CHEMICALS CAN ALSO DAMAGE THE SURFACE.

● DO NOT PAY FOR THE NAME OF A FAMOUS POTTERY IF YOU THINK THE MODELLING IS NOT UP TO SCRATCH.

● IF A PIECE IS GLAZED, MAKE SURE THE GLAZE HAS BEEN APPLIED SKILFULLY AND HAS NOT OBSCURED THE FINE DETAIL OF THE PIECE.

● NEARLY ALL PARIAN FIGURES AND BUSTS ARE COPIES OF SOMETHING, EITHER A CONTEMPORARY WORK OR A CLASSICAL MASTERPIECE. THE ORIGINAL MAY NOT ALWAYS BE A STATUE; IT COULD BE A DETAIL OF A WELL-KNOWN PAINTING.

● A SCULPTOR'S NAME IMPRESSED ON A PARIAN COPY IS NOT NECESSARILY A GUARANTEE OF QUALITY.

▼ SAMUEL ALCOCK MANUFACTURED THIS PARIAN FIGURE OF THE DUKE OF WELLINGTON, SEATED ON A CURIOUSLY DRAPED CHAIR, AS A MOMENTO AFTER THE DUKE'S DEATH IN 1852.
PRICE GUIDE 6

▶ THIS PARIAN FIGURINE SHOWS ALBERT EDWARD, PRINCE OF WALES AND FUTURE EDWARD VII, AS A BOY, DRESSED IN A SAILOR SUIT. THE PIECE WAS MADE BY MINTON IN ABOUT 1849.
PRICE GUIDE 6

▼ THIS BUST OF QUEEN VICTORIA'S GRANDSON, PRINCE ALBERT VICTOR, DUKE OF CLARENCE, WAS PRODUCED FOLLOWING THE PRINCE'S DEATH FROM PNEUMONIA IN 1892.
PRICE GUIDE 6

▲ THIS GERMAN PARIAN BUST OF QUEEN VICTORIA WAS MANUFACTURED IN 1897. THE BASE IS ACTUALLY CERAMIC AND ONLY PAINTED TO RESEMBLE MARBLE.
PRICE GUIDE 4

▶ THIS DIGNIFIED PARIAN PORTRAIT OF PRINCE ALBERT, QUEEN VICTORIA'S CONSORT, WAS PRODUCED BY COPELAND IN 1862. IT WAS PROBABLY INTENDED AS A COMMEMORATIVE PIECE, AS THE PRINCE HAD DIED THE PREVIOUS YEAR.
PRICE GUIDE 7

▲ THIS UNUSUAL AND BEAUTIFULLY OBSERVED PARIAN GROUP WAS MADE BY COPELAND. THE SCENE IS FLORENCE NIGHTINGALE MINISTERING TO A WOUNDED MAN.
PRICE GUIDE 7

◀ THE MARRIAGE OF ONE OF QUEEN VICTORIA'S DAUGHTERS, PRINCESS LOUISE, TO THE MARQUESS OF LORNE IN 1871 IS CELEBRATED IN THIS CHARMING PORTRAIT OF THE BRIDAL COUPLE, WHICH IS UNUSUAL IN BEING GLAZED.
PRICE GUIDE 5

▼ WITH A COSTUME BASED ON THAT OF AN 18TH-CENTURY SHEPHERDESS, THIS DOULTON FIGURE WAS NAMED 'DELIGHT'. THE DESIGN WAS MANUFACTURED BETWEEN 1936 AND 1967; THIS EXAMPLE DATES FROM THE 1930s.
PRICE GUIDE 7

▼ COYLY HIDING BEHIND HER PARASOL, THIS FIGURE IS KNOWN AS 'MISS DEMURE'. ALTHOUGH DRESSED IN A COSTUME THAT LOOKS MID-VICTORIAN, THIS PIECE WAS ACTUALLY IN PRODUCTION BETWEEN 1930 AND 1975.
PRICE GUIDE 5

▲ THE 'BUTTERFLY GIRL' WAS ONE OF THE MOST ENDURINGLY POPULAR OF ROYAL DOULTON'S ART DECO FIGURES. SHE FIRST APPEARED IN 1925 AND WAS STILL BEING MADE FIFTY YEARS LATER. THIS VERSION DATES FROM THE 1930s. WHEN SHOPPING FOR DOULTON FIGURES, IT IS WORTH TAKING ALONG A RELIABLE GUIDE TO FACTORY REFERENCE NUMBERS AND PRICES.
PRICE GUIDE 7

▼ LESLIE HARRADINE FIRST MODELLED THIS FIGURE, 'LADY CLARE', IN 1931. HARRADINE'S WORK IN THE 1930'S RARELY INCLUDED CONTEMPORARY FIGURES, HE PREFERRED TO MODEL FIGURES LIKE THIS VICTORIAN LADY.
PRICE GUIDE 6

▼ THIS DOULTON PIECE IS CALLED 'PHYLLIS' AND IS INTENDED TO REPRESENT AN 18TH-CENTURY FLOWER-SELLER. THE RICH EFFECT OF THE DRAPERY IS ACHIEVED BY THE APPLICATION OF SEVERAL COLOURS, EACH FIRED SEPARATELY.
PRICE GUIDE 7

▲ THIS IS ONLY ONE OF MANY DIFFERENT VERSIONS OF THE FIGURINE PIERETTE. OTHERS SHOW HER WEARING A HARLQUIN SKIRT, OR WITH PLAYING CARDS CASCADING DOWN HER DRESS.
PRICE GUIDE 7

◀ FACTORIES IN EUROPE WERE MADE A VARIETY OF ART DECO FIGURES IN THE 1920S AND 1930S. THIS GROUP OF TWO YOUNG LOVERS WERE MADE BY THE LENCI FACTORY IN TURIN.
PRICE GUIDE 8

▶ A CONTEMPORARY FASCINATION WITH THE MYSTERIES OF THE ORIENT IS EVIDENT IN THIS COLOURFUL AND EXOTIC DANCING FIGURE, MADE BY THE GERMAN FIRM OF ROSENTHAL IN THE 1930S.
PRICE GUIDE 7

▶ THIS 1930S FIGURINE SHOWS A GRACEFUL, BUT RATHER DARING, TOPLESS LADY CARRYING A TRAY. THE MANUFACTURER WAS THE CZECH FIRM ROYAL DUX (THE TRADEMARK FOR THE NAME OF DUXER PORZELLAN-MANUFAKTUR), WHO PRODUCED MANY DANCERS, SINGLE LADIES AND COUPLES , AS WELL AS SAUCY BATHERS.
PRICE GUIDE 6

▶ THE SIMPLIFIED GEOMETRIC FORMS OF MODERN ART ARE REFLECTED IN THIS FIGURINE BY THE FRENCH DESIGNER, SIBYLLE MAY.
PRICE GUIDE 6

◀ A CHEEKY-LOOKING PIERROT IN 18TH-CENTURY COSTUME, WITH A MONKEY ON HIS SHOULDER. HE WAS MADE BY AMPHORA, AN AUSTRIAN MANUFACTURER.
PRICE GUIDE 6

▼ THIS ALLURING DANCING GIRL IN HER UNUSUAL POSE AND SEDUCTIVE COSTUME WAS MADE IN THE GOLDSCHEIDER FACTORY OF VIENNA.
PRICE GUIDE 8

▲ THIS ACROBATIC PIERROT, BENDING LOW TO DOFF HIS HAT, WAS MADE BY SITZENDORF IN THE 1930S. IT WAS APPARENTLY MODELLED ON THE FAMOUS DANCER ROBERT HELPMANN.
PRICE GUIDE 7

▲ THIS ELEGANT LADY STEPPING FORWARD FROM HER PLINTH IS MADE BY THE KATZHUTTE FIRM. PIECES BY THIS FIRM ARE MARKED BY THE COMPANY'S PICTOGRAM – A CAT IN A HOUSE. THIS FIGURE'S POSE IS HIGHTLY REMINISCENT OF THOSE SEEN IN DECO BRONZES.
PRICE GUIDE 6

▲ THESE TWO SPODE POT-POURRI VASES ARE BOTH ABOUT 1830. THE PERFORATED LIDS LET THE FRAGRANCE OUT BUT THE INNER LIDS WERE INTENDED TO PRESERVE THE SMELL OF THE POT POURRI WHEN NOT IN USE. THE RICH COLOURED DECORATION OF BOTH VASES IS ON A CRACKED ICE BACKGROUND.

PRICE GUIDE 6

DESIGN FEATURES

POT POURRI LIDS ARE DIFFERENTLY PIERCED DEPENDING ON THE DESIGN OF THE POT-POURRI CONTAINER. LARGE, SYMMETRICAL APERTURES MAY APPEAR ON THE LARGER POTS, WHEREAS A SERIES OF TINY HOLES OR COMBINATION OF LARGE AND SMALL ARE SUITED TO THE SMALLER DESIGNS OF CONTAINER.

▲ AN OVAL, TUREEN-SHAPED POT-POURRI CONTAINER WITH PIERCED LID. THIS PIECE IS MADE FROM CREAMWARE WITH BROWN DECORATION AND HAS TWO HANDLES. THIS IS A RARE EXAMPLE, REMINISCENT OF CANEWARE.

PRICE GUIDE 7

◀ THIS MID-VICTORIAN POT-POURRI URN IS IN WHITE PORCELAIN. THE CONTAINER IS DECORATED WITH BLUE AND PINK FLORAL DESIGNS AND GILT EDGING.
PRICE GUIDE 6

▶ THIS PALE MAUVE, GINGER-JAR SHAPED POT, C.1830 WITH GOLD DECORATION IS SPODE. EMBELLISHED WITH MOULDED CHERUBS AROUND THE BASE, THE JAR IS SLIGHTLY CHIPPED.
PRICE GUIDE 5

▲ A STAFFORDSHIRE POT-POURRI CONTAINER IN AN UPRIGHT, VASE SHAPE. IN THIS EARLY 19TH-CENTURY EXAMPLE, THE GREY CHINA IS DECORATED WITH BLUE MOULDING AND HAS BEEN ATTRACTIVELY FINISHED WITH A GILT EDGE.
PRICE GUIDE 5

◀ THIS SMALL BASKET-SHAPED POT-POURRI WITH GILT DECORATION WAS MADE AROUND 1820 BY MINTON.
PRICE GUIDE 5

POINTS TO WATCH

- COCKERELS, USED IN THE DESIGNS OF ALLER VALE POTTERIES, OFTEN HAVE THE WORDS 'GOOD MORNING' ISSUING FROM THE BEAK.
- COTTAGES PAINTED ON WATCOMBE WARE ALWAYS HAD TWO STOREYS. AND BIRDS ALWAYS DIVED FROM LEFT TO RIGHT, EXCEPT ON PAIRS OF VASES THAT MIRRORED EACH OTHER.
- SINGLE-MASTED FISHING BOATS WERE A FAVOURITE MOTIF OF LONGPARK, AS WAS THE THATCHED COTTAGE SET BETWEEN TWO TREES.
- EARLY HONITON JACOBEAN PATTERNS ARE PAINTED IN BROWNS, RUSTS AND GOLDS. LATER PATTERNS USE DARK BLUES AND TURQUOISE.

▶ EVEN THE TINIEST OF OBJECTS MADE BY THE WEST COUNTRY POTTERIES, LIKE THIS PINCH-POT, HAD HAND-PAINTED DESIGNS BASED ON COUNTRY MOTIFS.
PRICE GUIDE 1

▼ A POPULAR NOVELTY WITH TOURISTS, THE IDEA WITH PUZZLE JUGS, SUCH AS THIS ONE, WAS TO GUESS WHICH WAY THE WATER POURED. THE WATER TRAVELLED UP THE HOLLOW HANDLE BUT CAME OUT THROUGH ONLY ONE OF THE HOLES IN THE RIM. MOST EXAMPLES WERE DECORATED WITH COTTAGES AND MOTTOES.
PRICE GUIDE 2

▲ ALLER VALE WAS THE FIRST OF THE ART POTTERIES AND PRODUCED THIS BLUE AND WHITE SCROLL PATTERN, CALLED 'SANDRINGHAM WARE'. THE PRINCESS ALEXANDRA, LATER QUEEN, SO LIKED THE DESIGN ON A VISIT TO THE POTTERY THAT IT WAS NAMED AT HER REQUEST.
PRICE GUIDE 4

▶ IN THE LATE 19TH AND EARLY 20TH CENTURY, THE WEST COUNTRY OF BRITAIN BECAME A CENTRE FOR HAND-CRAFTED CERAMICS, KNOWN AS 'ART' POTTERY. THE CROWN DORSET POTTERY WAS SET UP IN 1905 BY CHARLES COLLARD, PRODUCING WARE SUCH AS THIS VASE, PAINTED BY COLLARD HIMSELF.
PRICE GUIDE 4

▼ CHARLES COLLARD ONCE WORKED AT ALLER VALE WHERE HE WAS INFLUENCED BY THE ARTS AND CRAFTS MOVEMENT. COLOURED SLIPS WERE A VERSATILE MEDIUM FOR DESIGN AND THIS STORK VASE WAS THOUGHT TO BE PAINTED BY COLLARD HIMSELF.
PRICE GUIDE 5

▶ THE CROWN DORSET POTTERY, BASED IN POOLE, OFTEN ADOPTED PATTERNS FROM THE TORQUAY FACTORIES, SUCH AS THE MOTIF OF A BLACK COCKEREL, SHOWN ON THIS C. 1905 BEAKER.
PRICE GUIDE 2

▼ BEACH SCENES DEPICTING A LONE CHILD LOOKING OUT TO SEA WERE OFTEN ACCOMPANIED BY THE NAME OF THE SEASIDE TOWN WHERE THEY WERE SOLD. THE CHILDREN'S STYLE OF DRESS WAS TYPICAL OF THE PERIOD WITH SMOCKS, SAILOR SUITS AND LARGE STRAW HATS.
PRICE GUIDE 3

POINTS TO WATCH

● CERAMICS CAN BE RESTORED – LOOK FOR CAREFULLY DISGUISED SIGNS OF GLUEING OR FILLING.

● QUITE A FEW WALL VASES AND MASKS WERE FINISHED IN A SLIGHTLY CRACKLED GLAZE. FAULTS SUCH AS CRACKS ARE HARD TO SPOT.

● A SOUND PIECE SHOULD RING SWEETLY WHEN TAPPED. IT WILL SOUND DULL IF IT IS FAULTY.

● BEWARE OF FAKES – IF IN DOUBT TAKE EXPERT ADVICE.

▶ THIS CLASSIC-SHAPED VASE WITH A GOLD BORDER DATES FROM THE 1930s AND WAS MANUFACTURED BY CARLTON AS A MATCHING PAIR, IDEAL FOR DISPLAYING ON EITHER SIDE OF THE FIREPLACE.
PRICE GUIDE 4

▼ THIS HAT-SHAPED WALL VASE WAS PRODUCED BY BESWICK. THE BESWICK FACTORY WAS ESTABLISHED IN 1896, BUT THE COMPANY REALLY TOOK OFF IN THE THIRTIES, PRODUCING DECO WARE.
PRICE GUIDE 4

▲ THIS WALL VASE, SHAPED LIKE A STRAW HAT, IS MADE IN GLAZED CREAM AND GREEN POTTERY. A HOLLOWED OUT SPACE IN THE CROWN OF THE HAT ALLOWED THIS PIECE TO BE USED AS A VASE. THE FLOWERS WERE PLACED IN A HOLE IN THE HAT BAND, PRODUCING A RATHER SURREAL EFFECT.
PRICE GUIDE 3

▲ THIS WALL POCKET IS ALMOST A CROSS BETWEEN A WALL MASK AND A WALL VASE. IT WAS PRODUCED BY THE CZECH FIRM, ROYAL DUX, AND IS THOUGHT TO BE MODELLED ON THE FAMOUS FILM STAR, GRETA GARBO.
PRICE GUIDE 5

▶ THE BESWICK FACTORY'S MOST FAMOUS DESIGN IS THEIR WIDELY IMITATED FLYING DUCKS. THE SET SHOWN HERE WAS PROBABLY PRODUCED BY THE KEELE STREET POTTERY. BESWICK ACTUALLY PRODUCED A WHOLE FLOCK OF FLYING BIRDS, INCLUDING SEAGULLS, PHEASANTS, KINGFISHERS AND HUMMING BIRDS.
PRICE GUIDE 3

◀ THIS UNUSUAL 1930s PLAQUE SHOWS A FLIGHT OF THREE DUCKS TOGETHER IN A LANDSCAPE. THIS MODEL WAS PRODUCED BY ROYAL DUX IN CZECHOSLOVAKIA.
PRICE GUIDE 3

◀ THIS SOLIAN WARE WALL VASE IS BASED ON A FAN-TAILED DOVE. CUT FLOWERS WERE DISPLAYED IN A HOLE AT THE TOP OF THE BIRD'S BODY.
PRICE GUIDE 4

▼ THIS CRINOLINED LADY IN A FOREST IS ACTUALLY BY CLARICE CLIFF. IT IS VASTLY DIFFERENT IN BOTH STYLE AND COLOURS TO THE MAJORITY OF HER OTHER CERAMICS AND WOULD, THEREFORE, BE OF INTEREST TO COLLECTORS OF HER WORK.
PRICE GUIDE 4

◀ PRODUCED BY CARLTON IN THE 1930s, THIS GLADIOLI WALL VASE IS UNUSUAL IN THAT THERE ARE THREE SEPARATE POCKETS FOR DISPLAYING THREE DIFFERENT SPRAYS OF FLOWERS.
PRICE GUIDE 5

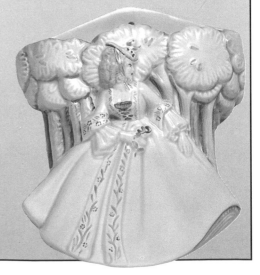

DESIGN FEATURES

THIS SET OF FIVE PORCELAIN GARNITURES IS IN ABSOLUTELY PERFECT CONDITION. MADE BY SPODE IN 1810, THEY ARE PAINTED IN THE ORIGINAL STYLE. THE BACKGROUND IS WHITE AND THEY ARE TRIMMED IN GILT AND FINISHED WITH WHITE BEADED RIMS. BLUE WAS OFTEN A FAVOURITE BACKGROUND COLOUR FOR THIS TYPE OF DECORATION. THREE OF THESE GARNITURES HAVE LITTLE GILT FEET AND THE CENTRAL VASE HAS A LID WITH HOLES IN IT, USED TO SUPPORT FLOWER ARRANGEMENTS.

DECORATION OF GARNITURES VARIES TREMENDOUSLY FROM ORIENTAL PATTERNS AND CLASSICAL LANDSCAPES TO FLORA AND FAUNA.

▼ DATING FROM AROUND 1800, THESE ELEGANT FRENCH WHITE URNS ARE TYPICAL OF EMPIRE STYLING, DRAWING HEAVILY ON THE INFLUENCE OF CLASSICAL GREECE AND ROME. THEY RELY ON THEIR LEAFY GILT HANDLES AND SIMPLE GILT TRIM FOR ORNAMENTATION.

PRICE GUIDE 6

▲ THIS PAIR OF TRUMPET-SHAPED PORCELAIN SPILL JARS WERE MADE IN 1810. WITH FLORAL SPRAYS ON A DELICATE, LIGHT BLUE BACKGROUND, THEY ARE EDGED IN GOLD WITH BEADED RIMS AND GILT HANDLES.

PRICE GUIDE 8

THESE TWO PIECES ARE FROM A MEISSEN-STYLE *GARNITURE DE CHEMINÉE* SET OF PORCELAIN. EARLY REGENCY, THEY ARE DECORATED WITH CLASSICAL RURAL SCENES. THE FRENCH TERM *GARNITURE DE CHEMINÉE* IS USED TO DESCRIBE A SET OF VASES OR ORNAMENTS MADE TO DECORATE A CHIMNEYPIECE.

PRICE GUIDE 4

A GARNITURE SET OF THREE PORCELAIN VASES. TRUMPET-SHAPED, THE GILT HANDLES ARE IN THE FORM OF SMALL LIONS' HEADS. THE BODIES OF THE VASES ARE DECORATED WITH OVALS SHOWING A WIDE RANGE OF FLOWERS, RANGING FROM ROSES TO TULIPS; NO TWO DESIGNS ARE THE SAME. THEY DATE FROM 1820. A COMPLETE SET OF *GARNITURES DE CHEMINÉE* IS OBVIOUSLY WORTH MORE TO THE COLLECTOR THAN AN INCOMPLETE SET, ALTHOUGH SUCH A SET MAY ALSO BE ATTRACTIVE AND WORTH COLLECTING.

PRICE GUIDE 6

ONE OF A PAIR OF LARGE PORCELAIN CAMPANA VASES WITH GILT HANDLES, DATING FROM 1820. PANELS OF FLOWERS ARE PAINTED ON TO A DARK BLUE BACKGROUND WITH TOUCHES OF GILT.

PRICE GUIDE 8

POINTS TO WATCH

● A *GARNITURES DE CHEMINÉE* SET ALWAYS CONSISTS OF AN ODD NUMBER OF PIECES. AN EVEN-NUMBERED GROUP OF ITEMS IS INCOMPLETE.

● THE LETTERS 'Rd' WITHIN A DIAMOND-SHAPED MARK SHOW THAT THE DESIGN WAS REGISTERED BETWEEN 1842 AND 1883.

● CHECK THE HANDLES AND OTHER POINTS FOR SIGNS OF WEAR. IF THEY ARE ABSENT, THE PIECE MAY HAVE BEEN SKILFULLY REPAIRED.

● THE PRESENCE OF AN INNER FLANGE IN THE NECK OF A LIDLESS VASE INDICATES THAT IT DID ONCE HAVE A LID, WHICH HAS NOW BEEN LOST.

▼ A SET OF PORCELAIN SPILL JARS DATING FROM AROUND 1830. RURAL SCENES OF ARCADIAN IDYLLS BECAME POPULAR IN THE REGENCY PERIOD AND HERE THEY HAVE BEEN APPLIED BY TRANSFER PRINTING IN A PUCE COLOUR ON TO A WHITE BACKGROUND.
PRICE GUIDE 7

▲ BEFORE THE INCREASED AVAILABILITY OF MATCHES, SPILL JARS WERE A POPULAR PART OF *GARNITURES DE CHEMINÉE*; SPILLS BEING NEEDED EITHER TO LIGHT THE FIRE OR TO TAKE A LIGHT FROM IT FOR CANDLES AND LAMPS. THESE 1810 SPILL JARS ARE TRANSFER-PRINTED IN BLACK ON TO WHITE AND DECORATED WITH COUNTRY SCENES OF RUINS AND RURAL BUILDINGS.
PRICE GUIDE 8

◀ THIS POTTERY GARNITURE WAS MADE SOMEWHERE BETWEEN 1820 AND 1830 AND SHOWS A MALE AND FEMALE MUSICIAN ARRANGED ON EITHER SIDE OF A TRUMPET-SHAPED SPILL JAR.
PRICE GUIDE 8

▼ GARNITURES RANGED FROM CLASSICAL DESIGNS IN PORCELAIN, TO POTTERY FIGURES. SEEN HERE ARE TWO 1780s POTTERY SPILL JARS WITH ANIMALS.
PRICE GUIDE 8

▲ POTTERY, AS OPPOSED TO PORCELAIN, GARNITURES BECAME MORE AND MORE COMMON IN THE 19TH CENTURY AS THE MARKET FOR DECORATIVE CHINA EXPANDED WITH THE GROWING MIDDLE CLASSES. THIS SET OF YELLOW POTTERY GARNITURES WITH LION HANDLES AND A CLASSICAL PRINT IN SILVER LUSTRE, DATES FROM AROUND 1820.
PRICE GUIDE 7

POINTS TO WATCH

● THE PRINCIPAL ARTISTS OF THE ROYAL COPENHAGEN FACTORY ALWAYS SIGNED THEIR PIECES.

● SINCE MANY OF THE COPENHAGEN FACTORY'S PIECES HAVE BEEN IN PRODUCTION FOR MANY YEARS, REPRODUCTIONS FROM OTHER SOURCES ARE NOT A PROBLEM.

▼ THIS PORCELAIN VASE FROM THE ROYAL COPENHAGEN FACTORY DATES FROM 1900 AND IS DECORATED WITH AN UNDERGLAZE DESIGN OF DANDELION FLOWERS AGAINST A PALE BLUE GROUND.
PRICE GUIDE 4

▲ A POLAR BEAR MADE IN PORCELAIN, AND DATING FROM AROUND 1900, ILLUSTRATES THE COPENHAGEN FACTORY ARTISTS' SKILLS IN RENDERING ANIMALS.
PRICE GUIDE 6

▼ THIS BOWL WAS DESIGNED BY ANNA PEDERSEN AND IS DECORATED WITH TWO SWALLOWS AT THE EDGES OF THE DISH.
PRICE GUIDE 7

▲ THIS TINY PORCELAIN VASE IS VERY SIMPLY DECORATED WITH STYLIZED SNOWDROP FLOWERS AND LEAVES.
PRICE GUIDE 4

▶ THIS KIND OF DISH IS KNOWN AS A *VIDE POCHE* AND IT WAS USED TO HOLD THE CONTENTS OF A GENTLEMAN'S POCKET WHEN HE HAD UNDRESSED. THIS EXAMPLE FEATURES A MOULDED FISH SURROUND AND A PAINTED CRAB ON THE BOTTOM.
PRICE GUIDE 4

◀ THIS LARGE VASE WAS DECORATED BY
BERTA NATHANIELSON. THE DESIGN IS A
FINELY-PAINTED, INTERWOVEN PATTERN
OF LEAVES, VINES AND BUTTERFLIES.
PRICE GUIDE 8

▲ PRODUCED AT THE COPENHAGAN
FACTORY IN THE EARLY 1900s, THIS
PORCELAIN VASE IS DECORATED WITH A
SUBTLE, ELEGANT PINK ROSE AGAINST A
WHITE BACKGROUND.
PRICE GUIDE 5

▲ THIS SHALLOW DISH IS ANOTHER
EXAMPLE OF A *VIDE POCHE* AND SHOWS A
MERMAID IN THE WATER SURROUNDED
WITH SWIRLING HAIR AND FISH.
PRICE GUIDE 8

▲ THIS PORCELAIN VASE WAS HAND-
PAINTED AND SIGNED BY JENNY MEYER,
AN ARTIST WORKING FOR THE FACTORY IN
1909. AFTER 1886, AN ORIENTAL
INFLUENCE BEGAN TO MAKE ITSELF FELT
AND MANY ROYAL COPENHAGEN PIECES
HAD A JAPANESE STYLE.
PRICE GUIDE 7

DESIGN FEATURES

THIS TRICOLOUR JASPER WARE MEDALLION IS DECORATED WITH PUTTI (SMALL, WINGED BOYS) PLAYING MUSICAL INSTRUMENTS. A SMALL PIECE, THIS WOULD PROBABLY HAVE BEEN MADE INTO A BROOCH OR INTO A SIMILAR PIECE OF JEWELLERY.

THE BAS-RELIEF FIGURES IN JASPER ARE MODELLED WITH INTAGLIO MOULDS. THEY WERE THEN CAREFULLY APPLIED TO THE MEDALLION. JASPER WARE WAS CAPABLE OF BEING 'UNDERCUT', THAT IS, OF HAVING THE RELIEF WORK CUT AND PICKED OUT WITH A SPECIAL TOOL BEFORE FIRING. THIS GIVES DEPTH AND DETAIL SO THAT THE FINISHED WORK RESEMBLES SHELL CAMEOS.

▼ THIS JASPER URN, DECORATED WITH THE DANCING HOURS, REVEALS THE CLASSICAL INFLUENCES THAT INSPIRED MANY WEDGEWOOD DESIGNS.
PRICE GUIDE 5

▲ WEDGWOOD'S DISTINCTIVE JASPER WARE WAS NOT ONLY PRODUCED IN BLUE. THIS PLATE HAS A LIGHT GREEN BACKGROUUND WITH DECORATION IN AN OFF-WHITE AND YELLOW.
PRICE GUIDE 7

▼ THIS BLUE AND WHITE JASPER WARE PLAQUE WAS MADE AROUND 1800. IT MIGHT HAVE BEEN HUNG ON A WALL OR INSERTED INTO SOME ARCHITECTURAL DETAIL AROUND THE HOME.
PRICE GUIDE 6

▲ THIS DISH IS IN SOLID BLUE JASPER. MADE AROUND 1789, IT IS DECORATED WITH A CLASSICALLY-INSPIRED SCENE KNOWN AS THE INFANT ACADEMY.
PRICE GUIDE 7

▼ JASPER WARE WAS A DENSE WHITE STONEWARE THAT COULD BE MADE TO RESEMBLE PORCELAIN AND IT CAME IN VARIOUS COLOURS — BLUE, DARK BLUE, LILAC, GREEN, YELLOW AND BLACK.
PRICE GUIDE 6

▲ THIS FLOWERPOT HOLDER AND MATCHING STAND ARE IN DARK BLUE JASPER. THEY WERE MADE IN ABOUT 1780 BY WEDGWOOD.
PRICE GUIDE 6

▲ THIS TRICOLOUR JASPER COFFEE CUP AND SAUCER WERE MADE IN 1790.
PRICE GUIDE 6

▲ THIS SOLID JASPER PLATE IS DECORATED WITH SWAGS AROUND THE EDGE AND CUPID WITH A SWAN IN THE CENTRE. THE RELIEF DESIGNS ARE OF WHITE JASPER WHICH WERE SEPARATELY MOULDED BEFORE BEING APPLIED TO THE LIGHT BLUE PLATE.
PRICE GUIDE 6

▲ THIS JASPER SUGAR BOWL, C.1820, HAS GREEN MOULDING THAT FORMS FOLIAGE MOTIFS AROUND THE BOWL.
PRICE GUIDE 6

POINTS TO WATCH

● CHECK THAT THE ITEM BEARS THE IMPRESSED MARK FOR WEDGWOOD.
● ENSURE THAT THE RELEIF MOULDING IS CRISP AND CLEARLY DEFINED.
● THE SURFACE SHOULD BE SMOOTH AND FREE OF SCOURING MARKS.
● ENSURES THAT THE BLUE COLOUR IS NOT TOO LIGHT.

◀ A TYPICAL CLASSICALLY INSPIRED JUG DECORATED WITH SWAGS. WEDGWOOD WERE NOT THE ONLY MANUFACTURERS OF BLACK STONEWARE; STAFFORDSHIRE POTTERS HAD ALREADY BEEN PRODUCING SOMETHING CALLED EGYPTIAN BLACK WARE. THE MAKER OF THIS JUG, C.1805, IS NOT KNOWN.
PRICE GUIDE 4

▼ THIS KANTHAROS CUP, OF 1780, IS DECORATED WITH ENCAUSTIC PAINTING WHERE ENAMEL COLOURS WERE BURNT INTO THE BODY OF THE CERAMIC.
PRICE GUIDE 8

▲ BY ADDING MANGANESE DIOXIDE AND COBALT TO BLACK STONEWARE, WEDGWOOD PRODUCED A RICHER AND FINER VERSION OF EGYPTIAN BLACK WARE THAT WAS CHRISTENED BLACK BASALTES. THIS SQUAT TEAPOT IN THE MATERIAL WAS MADE BY WEDGWOOD IN 1820.
PRICE GUIDE 5

▼ THIS POT-POURRI WITH TWIN HANDLES, C.1800, HAS BEEN DESIGNED IN A SHAPE REMINISCENT OF A CLASSICAL GREEK VASE. THE TERRACOTTA RELIEF DECORATION WAS APPLIED TO THE PIECE.
PRICE GUIDE 6

▼ THIS CANDLE HOLDER IS IN THE SHAPE OF A SPHINX. IT WAS PRODUCED IN AROUND 1800 BUT THERE IS NO MARK BY WHICH TO ATTRIBUTE THE PIECE.
PRICE GUIDE 6

▼ THESE THREE ITEMS ARE FROM A
MATCHING TEA AND COFFEE SET MADE BY
AN UNKOWN FACTORY IN ABOUT 1795.
THE FIGURE OF A WOMAN APPEARS AS A
FINIAL ON THE LID OF EACH PIECE. SHE IS
MEANT TO REPRESENT THE CLASSICAL
FIGURE OF A SYBIL, REPUTED IN ANCIENT
TIMES TO BE THE MOUTHPIECE OF THE
GODS. THE DESIGNS PAINTED AROUND THE
POTS ARE IN SILVER; FINE VERTICAL BANDS
ARE DELICATELY CUT INTO THE CERAMIC.
PRICE GUIDE 7

▲ THIS LARGE PEDASTAL BOWL WAS
MADE BY WEDGWOOD IN C.1830. THE
APPLIED RELIEF DECORATION ON THIS
BLACK BOWL IS ALSO IN BLACK.
PRICE GUIDE 6

▼ THIS LIDDED BUTTER DISH COMES
WITH AN ATTACHED SAUCER. IT HAS
APPLIED TERRACOTTA DECORATION ON
LID, DISH AND SAUCER, AND WAS MADE BY
WEDGWOOD IN ABOUT 1800.
PRICE GUIDE 6

POINTS TO WATCH

● THE WORK OF STUDIO POTTERS AND PIECES BY FAMOUS ARTISTS TEND TO BE TOO EXPENSIVE. TABLEWARE DECORATED WITH JUGENDSTIL INSPIRED PATTERNS, BUT NOT ATTRIBUTED TO MAJOR DESIGNERS, ARE MORE AFFORDABLE.

● BUYING VERY OBVIOUSLY DAMAGED JUGENDSTIL PIECES IS NOT A WISE OR WORTHWHILE INVESTMENT.

● SOME TOP QUALITY PORCELAIN PIECES HAVE BEEN RESTORED SO EXPERTLY THAT YOU ARE UNABLE TO DETECT ANY REPAIR AND PRICES ARE STILL HIGH.

● A SPECIALITY OF THE HUNGARIAN FIRM, ZSOLNAY, WAS AN IRIDESCENT GLAZE CALLLED 'EOSIN'.

● GET EXPERT ADVICE BEFORE INVESTING IN 'EOSIN' WARE; MODERN ORIGINAL MOULDS HAVE BEEN USED WHICH PRODUCE VERY SIMILAR WARE TO CONTEMPORARY PIECES.

▲ THE COMPANY RIESSNER, STELLMACHER AND KESSEL OF TURN-TEPLITZ IN CZECHOSLOVAKIA BECAME KNOWN AS AMPHORA AFTER 1903. THEY MADE THIS GILDED VASE, PART OF A PAIR, SET WITH CERAMIC STONES AND A WITH A FEMALE FIGURE AS A HANDLE.
PRICE GUIDE 9

▶ THE ANGULAR SHAPE OF THIS DEEP BLUE ZSOLNAY VASE COMPLEMENTS THE INCISED GEOMETRIC GOLD PATTERN.
PRICE GUIDE 7

◀ THE SLIP-TRAILED DESIGN OF THIS FLAME-COLOURED STYLIZED IRIS IS SET AGAINST A DARK BACKGROUND ON THIS VASE, c.1900, MADE BY AN UNKNOWN AUSTRIAN POTTERY.
PRICE GUIDE 4

▼ THIS PAIR OF PORCELAIN VASES WERE MADE BY AMPHORA. THE DESIGN IS KNOWN AS 'MELTING'; THE SOLID CERAMIC MEDIUM IS MANIPULATED TO APPEAR ALMOST A LIQUID FORM.
PRICE GUIDE 6

▼ THIS EARTHENWARE VASE WAS MADE AROUND 1904 BY EICHWALD, A CZECH FIRM. IT FEATURES A GILDED, SWAYING MOTIF OF WHITE FLOWERS ON A DEEP SALMON-PINK BACKGROUND.
PRICE GUIDE 5

◀ A WOMAN'S HEAD WITH FLOWING HAIR AND FLOWERS WAS A TYPICAL JUGENDSTIL MOTIF, AS ON THIS EARTHENWARE VASE MADE BY AMPHORA IN AROUND 1900
PRICE GUIDE 6

POINTS TO WATCH

- BLUE AND WHITE PIECES SHOULD BE IN REASONABLE CONDITION.
- SLIGHT DETERIORATION IN THE DECORATION OF MULTICOLOURED PIECES IS ACCEPTABLE.
- BE WARY – SOME 19TH-CENTURY CHINESE-STYLE JARS AND VASES MAY BEAR A REIGN MARK AS EARLY AS THE 15TH CENTURY.
- GOOD RESTORATION TECHNIQUES ARE AVAILABLE, BUT WORTHWHILE ONLY WITH RARE OR VALUABLE PIECES.

▲ IN THE 18TH AND 19TH CENTURIES SPECIALLY DECORATED CANTONESE PORCELAIN WAS EXPORTED TO EUROPE IN VAST AMOUNTS. PIECES SUCH AS THIS TEA CADDY, OF AROUND 1780, WERE MADE IN SHAPES AND PATTERNS THAT REFLECTED A MORE EUROPEAN TASTE.

PRICE GUIDE 5

▲ THIS PLATE DATES FROM 1790 AND HAS AN UNUSUAL SCALLOPED EDGE AND ELABORATE BORDER. THE CENTRE PICTURE IS RATHER WORN WITH AGE AND SHOWS A CHINESE DOMESTIC SCENE. THIS IS PAINTED IN AN ORIENTAL STYLE THAT CONTRASTS WITH THE MORE EUROPEAN TASTE OF THE BORDER.

PRICE GUIDE 5

▼ THIS LARGE BOWL, DATING FROM ABOUT 1780, WAS PROBABLY USED FOR PUNCH. THE DESIGN IS IN WHAT IS KNOWN AS *FAMILLE ROSE*, A COMBINATION OF COLOURS IN WHICH LUMINOUS PINK PREDOMINATES. SCENES OF CHINESE LIFE ARE SHOWN ON THE OUTSIDE WITH AN ELEABORATE FLORAL BORDER WITH CARTOUCHES, ON THE INSIDE.

PRICE GUIDE 6

▶ THIS SMALL LOBED BOWL, PERHAPS ONCE USED FOR SUGAR, DATES FROM AROUND 1780. THE EXTERIOR IS PAINTED WITH MANDARIN FIGURES IN A TYPICALLY CHINESE LANDSCAPE.

PRICE GUIDE 4

▶ THIS DINNER PLATE DATES FROM 1790, AND IS PAINTED WITH A CHINESE RIVERSCAPE SHOWING MOUNTAINS, TREES, FLYING DUCKS AND A SMALL BOAT.

PRICE GUIDE 5

▼ THIS VERY SIMPLE BOWL IS DATED FROM 1790 AND IS DECORATED WITH CHINESE FLOWERS AND BLOSSOMS. BEING BADLY CRACKED AND REPAIRED IT WOULD FETCH A LOWER PRICE THAN USUAL.

PRICE GUIDE 3

▶ THE EARLIEST CHINESE EXPORT WARE WAS IN BLUE AND WHITE PORCELAIN, AND THIS CONTINUED TO BE MADE, RIGHT UP TO THE 18TH CENTURY. THIS BALUSTER SHAPED VASE DATES FROM 1770.

PRICE GUIDE 6

▼ THIS VASE IN THE TRADITIONAL CHINESE DOUBLE GOURD SHAPE, WITH LOOP HANDLES, BEARS THE QIANLONG REIGN MARK (1736–1795). IT IS COVERED WITH A RICH AND EVEN TEA-DUST GLAZE. IN THE 18TH CENTURY SOME WESTERN COLLECTORS BEGAN TO BUY AUTHENTIC CHINESE WARE AS WELL AS EUROPEAN-STYLE EXPORT CHINA BUT FEW PIECES OF THE QUALITY OF THIS VASE FOUND THEIR WAY TO EUROPE AND THEY ARE COMPARATIVELY EXPENSIVE.

PRICE GUIDE 9

▲ THIS JAR AND COVER CARRIES THE JINQING REIGN MARK (1796–1820), AND IS DECORATED WITH FIVE-CLAWED DRAGONS CHASING THROUGH STYLIZED SCROLLS OF CLOUDS. TRADITIONALLY ASSOCIATED WITH VIGILANCE AND GUARDIANSHIP, THE DRAGON, AND PARTICULARLY ONE SHOWN WITH FIVE-CLAWS, WAS A REVERED SYMBOL OF THE IMPERIAL FAMILY OF CHINA.

PRICE GUIDE 9

◄ THIS LAVANDER-GLAZED BOTTLE IS IN 'IMPERIAL STYLE' AND DATES FROM THE 18TH CENTURY. IT IS A LATER CHINESE IMITATION OF A MEDIEVAL SUNG PIECE; THIS HAS A MARK DATING IT TO THE QIANLONG REIGN (1736–1795).

PRICE GUIDE 9

FURNITURE

Most collectors of antiques take great pleasure in using their treasured pieces, whether it is on a day-to-day basis or for special occasions only, and antique furniture probably has more daily use than any other kind of collectable. Functional rather than ornamental by nature, antique chairs, tables, desks, cabinets, and the like, are usually bought to furnish the home. Very few of us have the financial wherewithal or storage space necessary to house an extensive collection of, for instance, wardrobes. Anyone buying furniture will be looking for the most pleasing and suitable items, or will be aiming to replace their existing furniture with pieces of better quality and greater value. Many people decorate and furnish their homes in period style and will, therefore, be hunting for appropriate furniture in age and style. Good pieces of furniture can be a very sound investment; a Georgian cabinet or a Chippendale chair, if cherished, can fetch a good price at the right auction house. However, serious care and consideration should go into buying antique furniture; its very size, by comparison to china, glass and other small collectables, makes it a much more expensive option and really top quality pieces can easily fetch very high prices. The prospective purchaser would be well advised to take expert advice and to read around the subject before buying.

Furniture has been around from earliest times; since man first thought to sit or sleep off the ground, or realised the wisdom of keeping food out of the way of the household animals and the dirt of the floor, chairs, cupboards and tables have become part of daily life. Wood has nearly always been used, with or without the addition of other materials, as it is one of the most readily available, easily adapted and durable of medium. From the first chests made out of hollowed-out trunks to the most delicate of lady's writing tables, wood has been fashioned by man to his own ends and devices. As time went on, other materials have been combined with wood – glass, metal, ivory, and, more latterly, plastic. But it was not until the onset of the machine age that whole pieces of furniture in metal began to appear. Other, more natural, mediums have also been used; such as in cane, rattan and wicker furniture, Different fabrics and coverings have been added and even paper has been adapted to make chairs, tables, and even settees. But despite all this, wood remains the most enduring of materials for furniture.

Wood has a great aesthetic appeal and, for centuries, connoisseurs have appreciated the different grains and patinas that can be found in either solid or veneered pieces. Most of us will have some kind of wood furniture in our homes, even if it is only a few rough kitchen chairs, and only the most modern and hi-tech of offices have totally abandoned the wooden desk. Over the years, many different kinds of wood have been endowed with magical properties; rowan was thought to guard against witches and many of us still look to 'touch wood' to ward off threatened evils. In furnishing the home with wooden furniture, one collector might prefer the light colour of oak or pine over the dark richness of mahogany or rosewood, but as in anything, this is a matter of taste. Older furniture is usually made in rarer, and, therefore, now more expensive hard woods like mahogany and teak and some collectors will clearly be drawn to the investment potential of such pieces. By buying older items, the antique collector is going a little way towards helping conservation. In a sense, as furniture passes between one owner and the next, the wood is being recycled. This is, of course, particularly important today as regards the hard woods, since demand for these kinds

This late, 19th-century dressing chest features two central jewellery drawers beneath the triple mirror that is supported by Arts and Crafts style gallery uprights.

of woods is a partial cause of the environmentally harmful deforestation of the tropical rain forests.

Keen collectors can familiarize themselves with the different kinds of woods and will soon be able to spot varieties and to recognise veneers. To ensure a good buy it is vital to be able to assess the wear and tear that the wood has taken in its lifetime. Since most pieces of antique furniture have been subjected to years of use, and abuse, many pieces will be showing their age. The well-informed collector will be able to spot the signs and recognise where dealers may have tried to disguise the effects of ageing. For instance, kitchen table legs, after many years of being pushed around on hard and damp floors, will sometimes splinter and fray. An unscrupulous dealer might slice the end off legs like these, or even splice on a new piece of wood to cover up the wear. Alternatively, some dealers might artificially 'age' objects to pass them off as older and, therefore, more expensive antiques. When buying any furniture it is a good idea to be familiar with the methods of construction in the past as it will help in spotting fakes, 'marriages' of different, unrelated parts, and dubious restoration work.

Not all furniture is wood; Victorian craftsmen produced a great deal of papier mâché furniture. Sturdy pieces of papier mâché are still around and it is hard to imagine they began life as paper pulp. Literally meaning 'chewed paper', papier mâché was introduced into France from the Far East in the early 18th century. Originally it was made from waste paper, pulped and bound with glue. The mixture was then dried in moulds and used to make objects as varied as chairs and snuff boxes. Later in the 18th century, methods were developed for glueing whole sheets of paper together, shaping them over a mould, then compressing and baking them. This produced heat resistant panels that

Dating from the 1880s, this bentwood rocking chair with a dark finish has a seat and back support in woven cane.

retained their shape remarkably well. Because the dried paper had such a smooth surface it was often varnished and painted to look like oriental lacquer, a process that became known as 'japanning'.

In the 1930s, Lloyd Loom developed their now famous technique of weaving paper fibre into maleable sheets of a wicker-like material that could be bent into new forms. This process put a new kind of affordable furniture on the market and, despite being made of paper fibre, Lloyd Loom furniture is remarkably tough, solid and resistant to wear. Many pieces survive today and Lloyd Loom remains very popular with collectors. Who knows, the 1960s op-art chairs made of folded cardboard might be the collectables of the future. Cane and wicker have been in use since ancient times – initially in the craft of basket weaving, and later in the making of some furniture. Lightweight, yet strong, wicker proved ideal and it was enthusiastically taken up in the 19th century. Particularly popular in the colonies, the lighter frame was suitable in hotter climates. With industrialization, working in metal became more feasible and materials such as cast iron became fashionable for all sorts of pieces. Christopher Dresser, one of the great designers of the Arts and Crafts Movement, created a complete set of hall furniture in iron, the metal wire being bent into delicate plant-like forms. In the early years of the 20th century, European furniture makers, like Breuer or Thonet, developed a method of using tubular steel to make mainly chairs and tables. Practical, as well as modernistic in appearance, tubular steel easily lent itself to mass-production techniques and is still often used by modern furniture makers.

What was once cheap mass-produced furniture is now highly sought after. For example, bentwood furniture, developed at the end of the last century, and the tubular metal pieces of Art Deco are all found at auction and in antique shops today. Bentwood chairs are fairly common, as they were often made for seating in public places, such as in cafés and restaurants, and they are easily afforded by most collectors. More unusual pieces, such as magazine racks and nests of tables, can fetch higher prices. Part of the popularity of more modern furniture stems from its suitability for our own homes. In the early part of the 20th century, more and more people began to live in flats and smaller homes in general. Out of necessity, demand grew for smaller and less ornate pieces of furniture and for new styles that could be folded away or stacked for easy storage.

Mass-production put the comfort of upholstered furniture within the reach of most people and the 1920s saw the advent of the sofa and armchair as we know them today. Prior to that, upholstery was the preserve of the wealthy, and padded and fabric-covered furniture was limited. The buyer of antique upholstered furniture should try and familiarize themselves with the different kinds of fabric that were used in furnishings. Obviously, any fabric used to cover a seat is going to have taken a lot of punishment, and any covering that has survived is likely to be showing the signs of wear and tear. Needlework and tapestry fabrics have stood up well over the years because their characteristic, densely-worked stitches have made for a hard-wearing surface. Velvet and plush will not have lasted so well and will very often have been replaced. The discerning and knowledgeable collector will be able to judge if modern replacements have effected value, and will know when renovation is necessary. Leather is one fabric that will have survived well and sometimes replacing worn leather will not necessarily be beneficial. Not only chairs are covered, some particular kinds of tables and desks can be found

Originating in China, this eight-leaved lacquer screen is inlaid with gold and silver and was made specifically for the European market.

with baize or leather tops. A practised eye will soon be able to tell the imitation fabrics.

More expensive and rare pieces of antique furniture are not generally within the range of the majority of collectors though, occasionally, the cost of buying that one extraordinary piece will be offset by the value of the investment. Most collectors will be hoping to find a bargain that proves to be the one purchase of a lifetime. Either way, buying a collector's item takes some consideration. Nobody wants to buy a set of Chippendale chairs only to find they are 'Chippendale-style' or just good reproductions. It is important to read up on the subject, whether it is occasional tables or Art Deco cocktail cabinets, especially if a piece is bought with its future value in mind. During the 19th century, many reproduction versions of earlier pieces were produced. Some were faithful copies and others were adaptations of styles. Furniture like this is collectable in its own right, but no one wants to spend a lot of money on a Georgian bureau only to find it is a Victorian imitation. By keeping abreast of current prices and market developments through the relevant antique trade journals and auction catalogues, the prospective buyer can, hopefully, ensure a sound and secure investment in their purchases and collection.

Unlike china, glass and other smaller objects, furniture is a less frequent purchase for the collector, who will not want to learn by mistakes that could prove costly. The wise collector will read around and seek advice. It is also a good idea to shop around; this will provide an opportunity to look at and judge the different merits of various pieces as well as to learn more about antique furniture. Auctions are a good place to buy and there is always an opportunity to view before bidding. Shops and antique markets outside of city centres are often very good places to buy and genuine bargains can be found. Larger pieces are sometimes advertised in the classified sections of local and trade papers though it is imperative to view before making an offer. Impulse buys should generally be avoided – there are all sorts of considerations that should be taken into account. A bargain buy will not turn out to be such an investment if it costs the earth to have it transported home. Nor will there be much value or pleasure derived from a piece if it is too large to get into the house! It is a good idea to measure the space available at home before going on a shopping expedition – it is not always easy to judge the size of an object at the dealers and a piece might turn out to dominate a room rather than complement the rest of the furnishings. If collecting chairs, then care should be taken to ensure that they are not too flimsy for daily use. Bearing in mind that people today are generally taller than in the past, it is advisable to check that tables are tall enough and beds long enough so that they will be a comfortable fit.

As with any antiques, it is vital to care for pieces and furniture can be particularly vulnerable to the elements and to daily wear and tear. Over the years, exposure to sunlight can lighten the colour of wood items and it is well worth positioning valuable or treasured objects away from direct sunlight; if just a corner is in direct light then just that portion will be bleached by the sun, considerably affecting the price. Central heating is the enemy of wood – it dries out furniture which can then crack and warp beyond repair. The internal parts of wooden cabinets, drawers and chests were often made of cheaper and untreated woods and these can dry out at a quicker rate than the rest of the piece. As a result, the internal compartments and drawers can often collapse before the main body. It might be advisable to limit the amount of central heating in rooms containing antique furniture – it is worth turning off radiators and storage heaters when rooms are unoccupied. One measure that can go some way towards combating the effects of heating and to increase humidity is to place a bowl of water under the radiator, or alternatively, to invest in a humidifier.

The restoration of furniture can, beyond the most basic of repairs, be a complex and costly business. Certain renovations will be beyond most amateurs and should be left to professionals. The more valuable the antique, the more expert the restorer needs to be. Some pieces might need sanding down or re-varnishing, which is easily enough done, but it is a good idea to seek advice first – over-hasty or unnecessary treatment can detract from a piece's value. There are specialist polishes on the market that can be helpful in preserving and protecting pieces. There are courses available in the restoration of furniture, and upholstery is a very popular hobby among many. The interested collector should also improve their knowledge of the other material furniture is made in – papier mâché, cane, iron and brass, for instance, will all need different treatment and care. There is a lot of literature and expert advice available to guide the collector to the correct preparation, polishes, and the like, that can enhance and protect an item.

The Davenport was a particular type of lady's writing desk that featured many small drawers in its sides. It was produced in large numbers in the 19th century.

Many people will consider buying antique furniture and this is one of the most interesting of areas for the antiques enthusiast. Since pieces will be on permanent display around the home, the collector can make daily use of their treasures and can pick out those pieces that can be incorporated into their personal scheme of interior design. Being a major purchase, antique furniture can prove to be a valuable investment and, if cherished and protected, can give the collector years of pleasure and reward.

◄ THIS RICHLY CARVED VICTORIAN FENDERSTOOL WAS, AS THE NAME SUGGESTS, INTENDED FOR IN FRONT OF THE FIRE. THE VELVET AND BEADWORK COVERING OF THIS STOOL IS ORIGINAL; IN BEADWORK, DIFFERENT COLOURED GLASS BEADS WERE SEWN ON TO THE CHOSEN FABRIC TO MAKE THE DESIGN.
PRICE GUIDE 6

▶ THIS MAHOGANY FENDERSTOOL IS ALSO VICTORIAN. THE EMBOIDERY COVERING THE STOOL'S PAD IS WORKED IN A STITCH KNOWN AS FLORENTINE, POPULAR IN THE 19TH CENTURY. THIS EXAMPLE IS, HOWEVER, A LATER ADDITION.
PRICE GUIDE 4

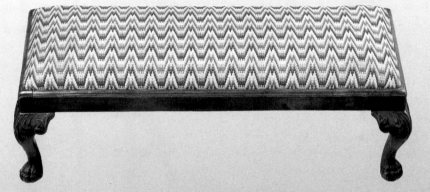

▲ A LOW FOOTSTOOL WAS A VALUABLE ASSET TO THE VICTORIAN HOME – WHEN SEATED IN FRONT OF THE FIRE THE FEET COULD BE RAISED ABOVE THE DRAUGHTS ON THE FLOOR AND NEARER THE WARMTH OF THE FLAMES. THIS VICTORIAN MAHOGANY FOOTSTOOL HAS RETAINED ITS ORIGINAL DEEP RED VELVET PAD.
PRICE GUIDE 4

▶ THIS 19TH-CENTURY FRENCH WALNUT FOOTSTOOL HAS A NEEDLEWORK COVER OF SKY BLUE WITH A POSY OF BRIGHT FLOWERS. MANY FOOTSTOOLS FROM THE 19TH CENTURY FEATURE THIS KIND OF COVERING BECAUSE NEEDLEWORK WAS A VERY POPULAR PASTIME FOR GENTLEWOMEN AT THE TIME. AS WELL AS BEING DECORATIVE, THE DENSE ARRANGEMENT OF TINY TENT STITCHES ON CANVAS MADE FOR AN EXTREMELY DURABLE COVER. THIS IS WHY SO MANY WOOLWORK STOOLS SURVIVED.
PRICE GUIDE 4

▼ ALL THREE OF THESE VICTORIAN FOOTSTOOLS HAVE NEEDLEWORK COVERS. THE TWO LARGER STOOLS ARE VICTORIAN AND MAHOGANY, THE SMALLER IS ALSO 19TH-CENTURY AND IS OF WALNUT.
PRICE GUIDE 4

▼ THIS LOW-BACKED, 19TH-CENTURY WINDSOR CHAIR HAS THE STANDARD PIERCED SPLAT IN THE CENTRE OF THE BACK. THE SUCCESS OF THE WINDSOR CHAIR IS LARGELY DUE TO THE FACT THAT THE CHAIRS WERE USUALLY PRODUCED BY A GROUP OF CRAFTSMEN, WITH SPECIALIZED SKILLS IN MAKING THE VARIOUS COMPONENT PARTS.

PRICE GUIDE 5

▲ THIS STURDY ROCKER HAS A CARVED CENTRAL SPLAT RATHER LIKE A WINDSOR CHAIR, AND HEAVILY TURNED SUPPORTS TO THE ARM RESTS.

PRICE GUIDE 6

▲ THIS LATE 19TH-CENTURY YEW AND FRUIT WOOD LADDER BACK CHAIR HAS WHAT IS KNOWN AS CUPID BOW RAILS. THE SEAT IS MADE OF RUSH.

PRICE GUIDE 5

▼ THIS KIND OF CHAIR IS KNOWN AS A SMOKER'S BOW. THIS IS, IN EFFECT, A LOW-BACKED VERSION OF THE WINDSOR CHAIR, STILL WITH A SADDLE SEAT BUT RATHER MORE HEAVILY TURNED LEGS.

PRICE GUIDE 5

▲ THIS STANDARD KITCHEN CHAIR WAS MASS PRODUCED, USUALLY IN BEECH OR BIRCH. THE INDUSTRIAL REVOLUTION AND THE NEW MACHINE AGE MEANT GREATER NUMBERS OF AFFORDABLE CHAIRS WERE PRODUCED. ONE LARGE FACTORY IN HIGH WYCOMBE, BUCKINGHAMSHIRE, BOASTED 'A CHAIR A MINUTE'.

PRICE GUIDE 3

▲ THIS KITCHEN CHAIR IS SLIGHTLY MORE DETAILED IN THAT THE CENTRAL SPLAT IS SHAPED AND WITH A CARVED CENTRAL MOTIF.

PRICE GUIDE 3

▼ THIS EARLY 19TH-CENTURY ROCKER WITH A CURVED WOODEN SEAT AND CARVED SPINDLE BACK, IS IN STAINED PINE. **PRICE GUIDE 7**

▼ THIS COUNTRY CHIPPENDALE ROCKER HAS A RUSH SEAT AND INTERESTINGLY CARVED SPLAT. THE JOINTS ARE SECURED BY WOODEN DOWELS. **PRICE GUIDE 6**

▲ THIS COMB-DESIGN, LADDER-BACK ROCKER WITH FINELY-TURNED ARMS, UPRIGHTS AND STRETCHERS IS, IN FACT, A CHILD-SIZE CHAIR. **PRICE GUIDE 7**

▼ THIS BEECHWOOD ROCKER OF C.1840 WAS MADE IN SKANE, IN SOUTHERN SWEDEN, WHERE BEECH TREES GROW. PAINT HAS BEEN SKILLFULLY USED TO SUGGEST A HIGHLY POLISHED FINISH AND STRINGING INLAY. **PRICE GUIDE 6**

▼ THIS NURSING ROCKER, C. 1820, IS IN SIMULATED BAMBOO WITH A LOW RUSH SEAT (THOUGH THE RUNNERS ARE NEW). THE LOW ARMS WERE SO THAT NURSING MOTHERS COULD MORE COMFORTABLY SIT WHEN FEEDING THEIR BABIES. **PRICE GUIDE 5**

▲ THIS UPHOLSTERED, BEECHWOOD ENGLISH CHAIR IS KNOWN AS A SWING ROCKER. THIS KIND OF DESIGN HAD A GENTLE MOTION AND COULD BE TILTED BACKWARDS WITH GREATER SAFETY. **PRICE GUIDE 5**

▼ THE LOWER HALF OF THIS REGENCY CHAIR IS LIKE A SMOKER'S BOW. THE SPLAT CUT WITH HEARTS TIES THE BASE TO A MORE CONVENTIONAL TOP FOR A WINDSOR CHAIR.
PRICE GUIDE 8

▼ THIS WELL-WORN, PAINTED WELSH COMB-BACK CHAIR OF 1780 HAS RATHER SHORT SPLAYED LEGS AND A SOLID, SMOOTH CHESTNUT SEAT.
PRICE GUIDE 7

▼ AN EARLY 20TH CENTURY VERSION OF THE WHEELBACK. SIMILAR TO THE REGENCY CHAIR ON THIS PAGE, IT LACKS THE CONTINUOUS HOOP-BACK OF EARLIER CHAIRS, AS WELL AS THE SUBTLE AND PLEASING PATINA OF OLD AGE.
PRICE GUIDE 4

▲ THIS VERY PLAIN WELSH COUNTRY CHAIR WAS MADE IN THE 1820S. THE THICK ELM SEAT HAS NO SADDLE AND THERE ARE NO STRETCHERS, THOUGH, AS WITH WINDSOR CHAIRS, THE BACK LEGS ARE SPLAYED OUT FOR GREATER RIGIDITY.
PRICE GUIDE 6

▲ THIS REGENCY SIDE-CHAIR IN ELM AND ASH HAS A BACK SUPPORTED BY A BRACE AND BOBTAIL. THE CENTRAL SPLAT IS DECORATED WITH THE PRINCE OF WALES' FEATHERS.
PRICE GUIDE 7

▲ A TYPICAL VERSION OF THE WINDSOR CHAIR FROM THE VERY EARLY VICTORIAN PERIOD. THE LEGS ARE NOT DOWELLED RIGHT THROUGH THE ELM SEAT.
PRICE GUIDE 6

▼ A MAHOGANY CHAIR FROM THE 1870S WITH TURNED AND FLUTED LEGS AND A ROUNDED SEAT COVERED IN BROCADE. THE ADDITION OF CASTORS TO THE LEGS OF SMOKER'S BOWS TURNED A BASIC KITCHEN AND TAVERN CHAIR INTO A PIECE OF DRAWING ROOM FURNITURE.
PRICE GUIDE 5

▼ THIS SOLID CHAIR OF THE 1880S IS MADE OF OAK – NOT USED FOR WINDSOR CHAIRS – AND COVERED IN REXINE (AN ARTIFICIAL LEATHER). THE COMFORT OF THE UPHOLSTERED BOW WAS PERFECT FOR THE SMOKING ROOM OF A VICTORIAN GENTLEMEN'S CLUB.
PRICE GUIDE 6

▼ THIS 1920S BEECH CHAIR HAS SLATS INSTEAD OF SPINDLES ALONG THE BACK AND A GREEN LEATHERETTE DROP-IN SEAT RATHER THAN THE MORE FAMILIARLY SHAPED SADDLE SEAT.
PRICE GUIDE 4

▲ THIS CHAIR FROM THE 1880S, WITH ITS BOW SUPPORTED BY NO LESS THAN 12 SPINDLES, HAS SUBSEQUENTLY BEEN COVERED WITH SYNTHETIC LEATHER. THE UPHOLSTERED BOW WAS A STRONG AND SERVICABLE CHAIR AND, BEING MASS PRODUCED, WAS ALSO RELATIVELY INEXPENSIVE. IT SOON FOUND ITS WAY INTO PUBLIC ROOMS, LIKE BARS AND PUBS.
PRICE GUIDE 6

▲ AN EDWARDIAN VERSION OF THE SMOKER'S BOW IN STAINED BEECH, WITH LIGHT, SIMPLY-TURNED LEGS, SPINDLES AND STRETCHERS.
PRICE GUIDE 4

▲ THIS TYPICAL LATE VICTORIAN SMOKER'S BOW HAS SOLID, SLIGHTLY TURNED LEGS, EIGHT TURNED SPINDLES SUPPORTING THE BACK AND SCROLLED ARM RESTS.
PRICE GUIDE 5

▼ THIS CHAIR FROM 1875 IS A VERSION PHILIP WEBB'S DESIGN FOR AN ADJUSTABLE CHAIR IN OAK. KNOWN AS A 'MORRIS' CHAIR BECAUSE IT WAS MANUFACTURED BY WILLIAM MORRIS' COMPANY, THE BACK OF THIS CHAIR RECLINED BACKWARDS, SUPPORTED ON A BRASS-ENDED RAIL PUSHED THROUGH HOLES IN THE BACK OF THE ARM RESTS.
PRICE GUIDE 8

▲ THIS VICTORIAN EASY CHAIR HAS A CARVED MAHOGANY FRAME AND IS FROM ABOUT 1880. THE UPHOLSTERY OF THIS CHAIR IS RECENT − ORIGINAL UPHOLSTERY WILL ONLY INCREASE VALUE WHEN IN GOOD CONDITION.
PRICE GUIDE 6

▲ OTHER ARTS AND CRAFTS MOVEMENT COMPANIES PRODUCED VERSIONS OF THE ADJUSTABLE CHAIR. THIS PALE OAK CHAIR OF THE 1890S HAS A BACK SUPPORT RAIL THAT DROPS INTO SLOTS IN THE ARM RESTS.
PRICE GUIDE 6

◄ THIS BEECH-FRAMED FOLDING CHAIR WAS MADE IN 1880. PINS LINKING THE FRONT AND BACK LEGS ALLOW THE CHAIR TO HAVE THREE POSITIONS.
PRICE GUIDE 5

► THIS WALNUT, FOLDING CAMPAIGN CHAIR OF THE 1880S HAS A SEAT AND BACK OF BRASS-STUDDED LEATHER. THIS KIND OF CHAIR WAS ORIGINALLY DESIGNED FOR THE COMFORT OF ARMY OFFICERS ON THE CAMPAIGN TRAIL.
PRICE GUIDE 6

▲ IN THIS OAK CHAIR THE UPPER SECTION OF THE ARM REST IS ATTACHED TO A BACK-SUPPORT RAIL. THIS UPPER SECTION THEN SLIDES OVER THE LOWER PART AND IS SAFELY SECURED BY A PEG IN ONE OF FIVE HOLES.
PRICE GUIDE 6

▶ CHILDREN'S-SIZED CHAIRS HAVE BEEN MADE SINCE AT LEAST THE 16TH CENTURY AND THIS LATE 19TH CENTURY CHAIR IS A SCALED-DOWN SMOKER'S BOW.
PRICE GUIDE 4

◀ A LATE VICTORIAN OR EARLY EDWARDIAN PAINTED MECHANICAL HIGH CHAIR. THE FEEDING TRAY IS ON PIVOTED ARMS THAT SWING FORWARDS TO BRING THE TRAY DOWN.
PRICE GUIDE 4

▼ THIS EBONIZED CHILD'S CHAIR WITH A RUSH SEAT AND A SPINDLE BACK IS A PERFECT REPLICA OF AN ADULT'S CHAIR.
PRICE GUIDE 3

▼ THIS ELEGANT FRENCH FRUITWOOD HIGH CHAIR HAS A CANE SEAT AND BACK. WITH NO FORM OF RESTRAINT, THIS CHAIR WAS INTENDED FOR THE MORE WELL-MANNERED CHILD!
PRICE GUIDE 5

▲ THIS EDWARDIAN BAMBOO CHAIR WITH ART NOUVEAU AND ORIENTAL TOUCHES MUST HAVE BEEN A TREASURED CHILDHOOD FRIEND, IMITATING, AS IT DOES, ADULT STYLING RATHER THAN BEING OF CHILDISH DESIGN.
PRICE GUIDE 3

▲ AN EDWARDIAN BENTWOOD CHILD'S CHAIR, PROBABLY OF BIRCH, WITH AN ENGRAVED SEAT.
PRICE GUIDE 3

POINTS TO WATCH

● CHECK THAT ANY CHAIR-BACK MECHANISMS WORK SMOOTHLY AND ARE SECURED EFFECTIVELY.

● ORIGINAL CUSHIONS MAY HAVE BEEN REPLACED. THOSE WHICH NEED IT ARE SIMPLE TO REFURBISH WITH MODERN FABRIC AND CAN QUICKLY GIVE AN OLD CHAIR A SATISFACTORY FACELIFT.

● STAINED WOOD FINISHES THAT APPEAR CLOGGED AND GRIMY CAN BE CLEANED WITH VERY FINE GRADE WIRE WOOL DIPPED IN VINEGAR.

▲ THIS IS PART OF A SET OF FOUR FRENCH WALNUT CHAIRS WITH INTRICATE INLAY, PIERCED SPLAT AND CABRIOLE LEGS. IN 1720, AN EMBARGO WAS PLACED ON THE EXPORT OF NATIVE WALNUT FROM FRANCE. THE TAX ON MAHOGANY IMPORTED TO BRITAIN WAS ABOLISHED IN 1733 AND SO THIS WOOD BECAME FAR MORE WIDELY USED IN THE MANUFACTURE OF CHAIRS AND OTHER FURNITURE.

PRICE GUIDE 8

▲ THE BACK OF THIS HEPPLEWHITE PERIOD CHAIR STANDS CLEAR OF THE SEAT ALLOWING THE SEAT TO BE STUFFED-OVER AT THE BACK AS WELL AS THE FRONT AND SIDES. THOUGH HEPPLEWHITE WAS A PROLIFIC DESIGNER, HE MAY NEVER HAVE MADE ANY CHAIRS HIMSELF. CHAIRS MADE TO HIS DESIGNS ARE DELICATE BUT STRONG AND WELL-PROPORTIONED.

PRICE GUIDE 7

▲ THIS SIMPLE CHIPPENDALE CHAIR HAS SQUARE LEGS, STRETCHERS, AND A SPLAYED BACK SPLAT. MOST 'CHIPPENDALE' CHAIRS REFER TO THE STYLE ONLY, NOT THE MAKER. HOWEVER, FINDING A SIMILAR CHAIR TO THOSE ILLUSTRATED IN THOMAS CHIPPENDALE'S BOOK *THE GENTLEMAN AND CABINET-MAKER'S DIRECTOR* DOES ADD VALUE.

PRICE GUIDE 7

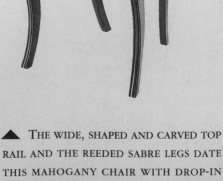

▲ THIS CARVER, OR ELBOW CHAIR, HAS A TRAFALGAR BACK WITH A TURNED 'ROPE' CROSS-PIECE THAT WAS A POPULAR STYLE DURING THE REGENCY PERIOD.

PRICE GUIDE 7

▲ THE WIDE, SHAPED AND CARVED TOP RAIL AND THE REEDED SABRE LEGS DATE THIS MAHOGANY CHAIR WITH DROP-IN SEAT TO 1810.

PRICE GUIDE 6

▲ THIS CHAIR FROM 1785 IS PART OF A SET OF TEN AND HAS AN STUFFED-OVER SADDLE SEAT WITH SILK COVERING.

PRICE GUIDE 8

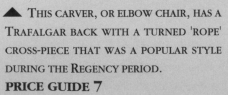

▲ THIS VICTORIAN MAHOGANY DINING CHAIR HAS AN UPHOLSTERED SEAT AND BACK AND THE TURNED BALUSTER LEGS THAT WERE A MOVE AWAY FROM THE CONCAVE SABRE LEGS TYPICAL OF REGENCY PERIOD CHAIRS.
PRICE GUIDE 6

▲ THIS STURDY DINING CHAIR HAS A BUTTONED BACK AND A STUFFED-OVER SEAT WHERE THE UPHOLSTERY IS ATTACHED TO THE CHAIR FRAME AND THEN TRIMMED WITH BRASS STUDS.
PRICE GUIDE 7

▲ THIS IS A MORE ANGULAR VERSION OF THE BALLOON-BACK CHAIR WITH A CARVED CROSS RAIL. THE STUFFED-OVER SEAT IS FILLED WITH THE ORIGINAL HORSEHAIR, COMMON TO THIS KIND OF UPHOLSTERED DINING CHAIR, BUT THE VELVET COVER HAS BEEN REPLACED.
PRICE GUIDE 4

▲ A MAHOGANY CARVER OF THE SHERATON PERIOD WITH SQUARE BACK, TURNED TAPERED LEGS AND THE CHARACTERISTIC ARMS, SET HIGH ON THE BACK UPRIGHTS.
PRICE GUIDE 7

▲ THIS MAHOGANY BALLOON-BACK CHAIR HAS A SERPENTINE CREST RAIL AND BULBOUS TURNED AND REEDED LEGS.
PRICE GUIDE 5

▲ THIS VICTORIAN 'CHIPPENDALE' CARVER HAS CABRIOLE LEGS, BALL-AND-CLAW FEET AND GOTHIC STYLE PIERCED SPLAT. THE UPHOLSTERED SEAT IS DROPPED-IN, SUGGESTING AN EARLY DATE.
PRICE GUIDE 6

▼ VICTORIAN FURNITURE MAKERS OFTEN REVIVED AND ADAPTED TRADITIONAL DESIGNS FOR THEIR OWN PIECES RATHER THAN FAITHFULLY IMITATE PAST STYLES, DIFFERENT MOTIFS WERE TAKEN UP AS IN THIS VARNISHED OAK CHAIR. THE BROAD BACK INCORPORATES STYLIZED BIRDS AND SWIRLING FOLIAGE DESIGN WITH A STURDY, STRONG FRAME.

PRICE GUIDE 5

▲ THE HALL CHAIR HAD BEGUN ITS LIFE AS A HUMBLE SEAT FOR SERVANTS WAITING IN THE PASSAGES OF GREAT ENGLISH HOUSES. BUT BY THE 19TH CENTURY IT HAD BEEN DEVELOPED INTO AN ESSENTIAL PIECE OF FURNITURE FOR THE VICTORIAN HOME. THIS SIMPLE CHAIR IS MADE OF CARVED AUSTRALIAN OAK.

PRICE GUIDE 5

▲ MANY HALL CHAIRS WERE MADE IN PAIRS OR SETS. THIS SQUARE-FRAMED WALNUT CHAIR, FROM A PAIR, DATES FROM C.1900 AND THE BROKEN ARCHITECTURAL PEDIMENT WITH FINIAL AT THE TOP IS DERIVED FROM A DESIGN OF 18TH-CENTURY ORIGIN.

PRICE GUIDE 5

▼ THIS EARLY VICTORIAN HALL CHAIR IS IN MAHOGANY IN A REGENCY STYLE WITH CRESTED BACK — THIS IS A GOOD EXAMPLE OF THE MORE ACCURATE KIND OF REPRODUCTION FURNITURE PRODUCED IN THE 19TH CENTURY.

PRICE GUIDE 5

POINTS TO WATCH

● MATCHING PAIRS OR SETS OF HALL CHAIRS WILL ALWAYS SELL AT A PREMIUM; FOR INSTANCE, EXPECT TO PAY THREE TIMES THE SINGLE CHAIR PRICE FOR A PAIR AND SO ON.

● ALTHOUGH SOME 19TH-CENTURY REPRODUCTIONS MAY BE OF SOME VALUE IN THEMSELVES, BEWARE OF THEM BEING PASSED OFF THE GENUINE ARTICLE.

● MORE HEAVY CARVING IS FOUND IN VICTORIAN REPRODUCTIONS.

● MORTISE AND TENON JOINTS CHARACTERIZE EARLIER CHAIRS AND GIVE A STURDIER STRUCTURE THAN LATER FACTORY-MADE JOINTS.

▲ THE MAIN BODY OF THIS COALBROOKDALE-STYLE CHAIR IS, IN FACT, MADE OF CAST IRON WITH A PLAIN OAK SEAT. IRON ENJOYED A POPULARITY WITH THE NEWLY INDUSTRIALIZED SOCIETY OF THE 19TH CENTURY AND MANY OBJECTS, NOT ONLY FURNITURE, WERE MADE OF THIS VERSATILE MATERIAL.

PRICE GUIDE 6

▼ THE MANUFACTURE OF CHAIRS FOR PURPOSES OTHER THAN DINING GREW IN THE LATE 19TH AND EARLY 20TH CENTURIES. THIS RUSH-SEATED OAK CHAIR WAS BY AMBROSE HEAL AND WAS INTENDED AS A SIDE CHAIR, FOR OCCASIONAL USE IN THE DRAWING ROOM.
PRICE GUIDE 8

▲ THIS HIGH-BACKED CHAIR CLEARY SHOWS THE INFLUENCE OF PROGRESSIVE DESIGNERS, LIKE CHARLES RENIE MACKINTOSH, WHO WERE MAKING THEIR MARK AT THE TURN OF THE CENTURY. THIS CHAIR WAS MADE BY HARRY NAPPER.
PRICE GUIDE 8

▼ E.W.GODWIN WAS A PARTICULARLY INFLUENTIAL DESIGNER WHO WORKED WITH EBONIZED WOOD, AMONGST OTHER MATERIALS, AND WHO CREATED LIGHT AND MODISH FURNITURE IN A STYLE INFLUENCED BY JAPANESE ARTIFACTS. THIS SPINDLY, EBONIZED BEECH FRAME CHAIR WITH WICKER INFILL IS INSPIRED BY GODWIN'S STYLES.
PRICE GUIDE 6

▲ SIDE CHAIRS FOR DRAWING ROOM USE WERE USUALLY SOLD IN SETS — THIS TYPICAL CHAIR HAS A STUFFED-OVER SEAT AND CABRIOLE LEGS.
PRICE GUIDE 3

POINTS TO WATCH

● MANY ANTIQUE CHAIRS STILL HAVE THEIR ORIGINAL UPHOLSTERY. TO CHECK, REMOVE A FEW TACKS — IF THERE ARE OTHER TACK HOLES PRESENT IN THE WOOD THEN THE UPHOLSTERY HAS BEEN REPLACED.

● SIDE CHAIRS WERE NOT BUILT FOR HEAVY USE. CHECK FOR REPAIRS, ESPECIALLY WHERE THE BACK AND LEGS JOIN THE SEAT.

● MANY PROGRESSIVE ARTISTS MADE FURNITURE THAT WAS PART OF A WHOLE ARCHITECTURAL DESIGN — TOP PIECES SHOULD REFLECT THIS.

● TOP DESIGNERS OF FURNITURE AT THE TURN OF THE CENTURY USED TRADITIONAL NATIVE WOODS; LOOK FOR OAK AND YEW AS A CLUE FOR ORIGINALITY OF DESIGN.

▼ THIS MAHOGANY CHAIR HAS ALL THE CHARACTERISTIC FLOWING LINES OF A PIECE OF ART NOUVEAU FURNITURE. RECENTLY UPHOLSTERED, THE CHOICE OF MATERIAL MIGHT HAVE BEEN MORE SUITABLE FOR A REGENCY STYLE.
PRICE GUIDE 4

DESIGN FEATURES

THIS EDWARDIAN WICKER CHAIR IS A VERY GOOD EXAMPLE OF THE LIGHTWEIGHT, YET STURDY, QUALITIES OF WICKER WORK THAT MAKES IT IDEAL FOR SEATING. WICKER AND CANE COULD BE MODELLED INTO MANY EXTREMES OF DESIGN, BUT TRADITIONAL MODELS, SUCH AS THIS EDWARDIAN CHAIR, REMAINED POPULAR. USING BASKET-WEAVING TECHNIQUES THESE PRACTICAL CHAIRS WERE EXTREMELY COMFORTABLE.

INTRICATE WEAVING WAS USED BY THE CRAFTSMEN ON THOSE PARTS, LIKE THE BACK REST AND THE SEAT, THAT REQUIRED THE GREATEST STRENGTH. THE BACK ITSELF WAS LEFT OPEN, TO KEEP THE CHAIR LIGHTWEIGHT AND COOL. THE FOUR LEGS ARE JOINED BY STOUT CROSS-MEMBERS FOR GREATER STABILITY AND THE JOINTS ARE REINFORCED WITH DECORATIVE, BUT PRACTICAL WICKERWORK.

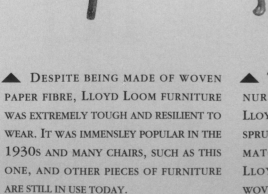

▲ DESPITE BEING MADE OF WOVEN PAPER FIBRE, LLOYD LOOM FURNITURE WAS EXTREMELY TOUGH AND RESILIENT TO WEAR. IT WAS IMMENSLEY POPULAR IN THE 1930s AND MANY CHAIRS, SUCH AS THIS ONE, AND OTHER PIECES OF FURNITURE ARE STILL IN USE TODAY.
PRICE GUIDE 4

▲ THIS KIND OF CHAIR IS DESIGNED FOR NURSING MOTHERS AND THIS 1930s LLOYD LOOM EXAMPLE IS FITTED WITH A SPRUNG SEAT AND PAINTED GREEN WITH MATCHING GOLD HIGHLIGHTS. WITH LLOYD LOOM, LARGE SHEEETS OF PRE-WOVEN PAPER WERE SHAPED OVER FRAMES.
PRICE GUIDE 4

▲ WICKER FURNITURE BECAME INCREASINGLY POPULAR IN THE 19TH CENTURY AS CONSERVATORIES WERE BUILT ON MORE AND MORE VICTORIAN HOMES. THIS BLACK PAINTED ARMCHAIR HAS A WOVEN SEAT AND BACK AND ARM RESTS WITH LOOPED INSERTS.
PRICE GUIDE 5

▼ THIS LOW-BACKED WICKER ARMCHAIR IS EDWARDIAN AND FEATURES A LOZENGE SHAPE MOTIF, IN BOTH BACK AND BASE, ACHIEVED BY ALTERING THE TEXTURE OF THE WEAVE. THOUGH LIGHTWEIGHT, THE CHAIR'S FORM IS SOLID.
PRICE GUIDE 4

▼ THIS SQUARE-BACKED CHAIR DATES FROM THE EARLY 20TH CENTURY. WICKER FURNITURE WAS LIGHTWEIGHT, AS WELL AS DURABLE, MAKING IT EMINENTLY SUITABLE FOR WARMER CLIMATES. MUCH COLONIAL FURNITURE WAS MADE IN THIS MATERIAL.
PRICE GUIDE 4

▼ DURING THE 19TH CENTURY JAPAN AND JAPANESE ART AND DESIGN HAD A WIDER INFLUENCE AROUND THE WORLD. THIS EBONIZED CHAIR WITH A RUSH SEAT WAS MADE BY THE DESIGNER E.W.GODWIN.
PRICE GUIDE 6

DESIGN FEATURES

THIS PLANTER'S CHAIR, SO-CALLED BECAUSE IT WAS TYPICALLY USED BY THE OWNERS OF TEA PLANTATIONS AND THEIR FAMILIES, IS ONE OF THE MOST POPULAR AND ENDURING DESIGNS TO COME OUT OF COLONIAL INDIA. THIS ONE WAS MADE ABOUT 1880, THOUGH THE BASIC DESIGN IS STILL MADE TODAY.

THE FRAME IS MADE OF DOWELLED TEAK. THE BALUSTER-TURNED FRONT LEGS ARE CARRIED THROUGH TO MAKE ARM SUPPORTS. THE BACK LEGS, SHAPED IN AN S-CURVE, ARE JOINED TOGETHER WITH A STRETCHER. BOTH SIDES OF THE SEAT FRAME, MADE FROM INDIVIDUAL PIECES OF TEAK, SWEEP THROUGH TO BECOME THE BACK SUPPORTS. THE SEAT AND BACK ARE FORMED FROM A SINGLE PIECE OF CANING, WOVEN IN THE TYPICAL OCTAGONAL LATTICE PATTERN. THE FLAT ARMS OF THE CHAIR HAVE AN EXTENSION WHICH PIVOTS THROUGH A FULL CIRCLE TO ACT AS A REST FOR DRINKS, PLATES, BOOKS OR FEET.

DESIGN FEATURES

THE VICTORIAN KITCHEN TABLE IS GENERALLY MADE OF SCANDANAVIAN OR NORTH AMERICAN SOFTWOOD, TODAY SIMPLY KNOWN AS PINE. ANY NUMBER FROM THREE TO SIX PARALLEL PLANKS ARE USED TO MAKE UP THE TOP, WHICH IS NEITHER PAINTED NOR STAINED. GAPS CAN FORM BETWEEN THE PLANKS FROM SHRINKAGE OF THE SURFACE WOOD.

LEGS ARE ATTACHED TO THE FRAME WITH MORTISE AND TENON JOINTS: A TENON IN THE FRAME SLOTS INTO A MORTISE IN THE LEG AND THE JOINT IS SECURED WITH DOWELS OR HAND-MADE PEGS DRIVEN THROUGH THE LEG INTO THE TENON.

THERE IS USUALLY A DRAWER AT ONE OR BOTH ENDS. A SIDE DRAWER SUGGESTS THAT THE TABLE WAS FOR USE AGAINST THE WALL. ROUND WOODEN OR WHITE CERAMIC KNOBS ARE CHARACTERISTIC.

▼ THIS SYCAMORE KITCHEN TABLE WITH TAPERING, SQUARE LEGS HAS A CLOSE-FITTING FRONT DRAWER AND BRASS HANDLE. THE JOINERY OF TABLE DRAWERS CAN GIVE A CLUE TO AGE: EARLIER DRAWERS ARE MADE WITH ROUGHER HAND-CUT DOVETAILS OR SIMPLE, NAILED BUTT JOINTS, WHEREAS LATER ONES OFTEN FIT TOGETHER WITH SMALL AND REGULAR MACHINE-CUT DOVETAILS.
PRICE GUIDE 6

▲ THIS STANDARD PINE TABLE HAS TWO DROP-LEAVES AND SHORT STRETCHERS ON THE NARROWEST DISTANCE BETWEEN THE LEGS. THE ADDITION OF DROP-LEAVES SUGGESTS THAT THIS MIGHT BE A 'MARRIED' PIECE; THAT IS VARIOUS PIECES JOINED TO MAKE ONE ITEM.
PRICE GUIDE 3

◀ THE BENCH AND SETTLE ARE PROBABLY THE MOST FUNDAMENTAL FORMS OF FURNITURE. MADE IN A TIME WHEN LEISURE WAS LIMITED, THEY REMAINED UN-UPHOLSTERED. THE HIGH BACK PANELLING OF THIS SETTLE PROVIDES NOT ONLY SUPPORT BUT ALSO PROTECTION FROM DRAUGHTS AND WOULD HAVE BEEN PLACED CLOSE TO THE FIRE.

PRICE GUIDE 8

▼ METAL IS AN IDEAL MEDIUM FOR GARDEN AND CONSERVATORY USE SINCE IT STANDS UP WELL TO THE RIGOURS OF THE ENVIRONMENT. THIS CAST-IRON BENCH IS PROBABLY FRENCH, C.1890.

PRICE GUIDE 7

▲ THIS JACOBETHAN OAK MONK'S BENCH WAS A HYBRID OF REPRODUCTION STYLES. ALTHOUGH PRIMARILY FOR SITTING ON, THE SEAT BACK OF THIS PIECE OF FURNITURE CAN SWING DOWN TO MAKE A TABLE WHILE THE TOP OF THE SEAT LIFTS UP TO REVEAL STORAGE SPACE.

PRICE GUIDE 6

▼ STONE IS ANOTHER MORE DURABLE MATERIAL FOR OUTDOOR AND GARDEN ROOM FURNITURE WHICH CAN ALSO COMPLIMENT STONE CONTAINERS AND STATUARY. THIS STONE BENCH IS A 19TH-CENTURY ITALIAN COPY OF A RENAISSANCE PROTOTYPE.

PRICE GUIDE 8

▲ THIS SMALLER PINE BENCH HAS A NARROW SEAT THAT SUGGESTS IT WAS MADE FOR CHILDREN AND MIGHT HAVE BEEN INTENDED FOR SCHOOL ROOM USE.

PRICE GUIDE 5

DESIGN FEATURES

THIS IS A TYPICAL MASS-PRODUCED EDWARDIAN VERSION OF THE GATELEG TABLE. ALL EIGHT OF THE LEGS HAVE BEEN MACHINE-TURNED TO IDENTICAL BARLEY-SUGAR TWISTS. THE INSIDE OF THE GATELEG HAS BEEN NOTCHED TO CORRESPOND WITH A SIMILAR NOTCH IN THE BOTTOM STRETCHER, SO THAT THE GATE FITS FLUSH WHEN THE FLAPS ARE FOLDED DOWN. EACH LEG ENDS IN A MODIFIED BUN FOOT.

THE OVAL TOP IS EDGED WITH THUMB MOULDING. THE TABLE WAS TREATED WITH A DARK STAIN WHEN NEW TO SIMULATE AGE, BUT USE AND ASSIDUOUS POLISHING HAVE WORN AWAY THE FINISH, REVEALING THE LIGHT WOOD BENEATH, PARTICULARLY ON THE LEGS AND AROUND THE EDGE OF THE TOP WHERE RUBBED BY HANDS AND FEET.

▲ THE GATELEG TABLE WAS AN ESSENTIALLY 17TH-CENTURY SOLUTION TO THE PROBLEM OF SUPPORTING AN EXTRA FLAP ON A TABLE. MOST GATELEGS OF THE 17TH AND 18TH CENTURIES WERE USED AS DINING TABLES. LATER REPRODUCTIONS WERE OFTEN ON A SMALLER SCALE SUCH AS THIS COMPACT OAK TABLE DATING FROM 1900. A CARVED TOP IS USUALLY A GOOD INDICATOR OF A LATER DATE.
PRICE GUIDE 5

▼ THE COMBINATION OF THE MASSIVE AND HEAVILY TURNED UNDER-FRAME AND THE SIMPLE, SQUARE GATELEGS IS AN UNUSUAL FEATURE IN THIS EDWARDIAN OAK TABLE.
PRICE GUIDE 6

▲ THIS VICTORIAN TABLE IS VENEERED IN WALNUT. THE WIDE FRAME IS UNUSUAL, AS IS THE DIFFERENT STYLES OF TURNING ON THE LEGS OF THE FRAME COMPARED WITH THOSE OF THE GATELEGS.
PRICE GUIDE 7

▼ THIS EDWARDIAN SUTHERLAND TABLE IN STAINED OAK HAS FOUR TYPICAL SPINDLE END SUPPORTS AND A SINGLE TURNED STRETCHER. THE GATELEGS HAVE CASTORS, ANOTHER FEATURE COMMON TO THIS TABLE TYPE. THE SUTHERLAND TABLE FIRST APPEARED IN THE 1840S AND ITS MAIN CHARACTERISTIC IS THE NARROWNESS OF ITS TOP: WHEN THE FLAPS ARE BOTH DOWN IT MEASURES NO MORE THAN 9 INCHES (23 CMS) ACROSS.
PRICE GUIDE 5

▲ THIS EDWARDIAN GATELEG TABLE IS IN UNSTAINED LIGHT OAK. AS WELL AS THE BARLEYCORN TWIST LEGS, THIS TABLE ALSO HAS ADDED INTEREST WITH THE CUT CORNERS, THE PIE-CRUST MOULDING ON THE TOP AND THE CURVED STRETCHERS AT THE BOTTOM.
PRICE GUIDE 5

▼ THIS GATELEG FROM THE EDWARDIAN PERIOD HAS BEEN BROUGHT UP TO DATE WITH A SQUARED-OFF STYLE SHOWING MARKED ARTS AND CRAFTS INFLUENCES. THE LEGS AND TOP OF THE FRAME ARE PICKED OUT WITH INLAY.
PRICE GUIDE 6

▼ THIS 1930S EXTENDING DINING TABLE IS MADE OF OAK AND IS A GOOD EXAMPLE OF THE JACOBETHAN STYLE, IMITATING THE BARLEY-TWIST LEGS AND CROSSED STRETCHERS OF AN EARLIER AGE.
PRICE GUIDE 5

▲ THIS JACOBETHAN TABLE IS IN A DARK OAK AND DATES FROM THE 1930S. IT IMITATES AN OLD-FASHIONED REFECTORY TABLE AND THE BULBOUS SUPPORTS DERIVE FROM 17TH-CENTURY STYLES.
PRICE GUIDE 6

▼ THIS SOFTWOOD DROP-LEAF TABLE SHOWS HOW THE GATELEG DESIGN WAS PICKED UP AND ADAPTED IN SWEDEN IN THE LATE 19TH CENTURY.
PRICE GUIDE 8

DESIGN FEATURES

ALTHOUGH IN MANY CASES, VICTORIAN CARD TABLES ARE IN FACT REPRODUCTIONS OF PREVIOUSLY POPULAR STYLES, THE MOST COMMON TYPE HAS A RECTANGULAR SWIVEL TOP SECURED TO A WOODEN UNDERFRAME. TABLE TOPS ARE MOSTLY IN A PLAIN WOOD LIKE WALNUT OR MAHOGANY WITH CARVED EDGES OR ARE INLAID WITH LIGHTER WOODS. A HINGED RECTANGULAR TABLE TOP OPENED UP TO A SQUARE AND COULD BE TURNED THROUGH 90 DEGREES.

THE FOCAL POINT WAS THE LEG SUPPORT – AS A DEPARTURE FROM THE CENTRAL COLUMN OF REGENCY TABLES, VICTORIAN CARD TABLES BOAST A VARIETY OF SUPPORTS. THIS VICTORIAN CARD TABLE HAS A CHEVAL STYLE TABLE BASE WITH TURNED AND CARVED ENDS AND STRETCHER, WITH THE LEGS ENDING IN SCROLL FEET.

▼ THIS SEMI-CIRCULAR TABLE IS KNOWN AS A DEMI-LUNE CARD TABLE. THE TOP FOLDS OUT TO REVEAL THE PLAYING SURFACE. AN ADDITIONAL DRAWER AT THE SIDE HELD CARDS, COUNTERS AND OTHER GAME ACCESSORIES.
PRICE GUIDE 6

▲ THE CARD TABLE HAD A SPECIFIC PURPOSE – FOR PLAYING GAMES ON – BUT WOULD ONLY BE USED OCCASIONALLY. THEREFORE, IT WAS DESIGNED TO BE FOLDED AWAY WHEN NOT IN USE. THIS TYPICAL LATE-VICTORIAN WALNUT CARD TABLE RESTS ON FOUR PILLARS AND FOUR LEGS WITH A CENTRAL FINIAL.
PRICE GUIDE 7

▲ MOST VICTORIAN CARD TABLES HAD A RECTANGULAR SWIVEL TOP THAT TURNED ON A PIVOT AND THEN OPENED OUT INTO A BAIZE-COVERED SQUARE TABLE. THIS WALNUT EXAMPLE HAS DECORATIVE CORNERS AND WAS DESIGNED TO BE PUSHED OUT OF THE WAY, AGAINST THE WALL, WHEN NOT IN USE.
PRICE GUIDE 7

▼ THIS CARD TABLE IS IN THE CHIPPENDALE STYLE AND IS DECORATED WITH BLIND FRETWORK. THE GATELEG AT THE BACK SUPPORTED THE TOP FLAP WHEN DROPPED DOWN. CARD TABLES ARE COVERED IN SOME KIND OF FABRIC, USUALLY GREEN BAIZE, TO PROVIDE A NON-SLIP PLAYING SURFACE.
PRICE GUIDE 7

▼ THIS 1890S CARD TABLE IS DESIGNED IN THE SHERATON STYLE, WITH TAPERING LEGS AND A LARGE DRAWER FOR GAMES ACCESSORIES. RATHER UNUSUALLY, THE SWIVEL TOP FOLDS OUT LIKE AN ENVELOPE.
PRICE GUIDE 7

▲ THIS LATE REGENCY ROSEWOOD CARD TABLE HAS BRASS STRINGING, INLAY AND FINIALS AND A SINGLE CENTRAL COLUMN. SWIVEL-TOP TABLES DID AWAY WITH THE NEED FOR GATELEGS MAKING IT MUCH EASIER FOR PLAYERS TO BE SEATED AROUND THE CARD TABLE.
PRICE GUIDE 7

▶ THIS INDIAN COLONIAL CARD TABLE WAS MADE IN ROSEWOOD, AROUND 1880. THE PEDASTAL AND TOP ARE TYPICALLY HIGHLY CARVED.
PRICE GUIDE 7

▼ THIS EARLY 19TH-CENTURY LIBRARY TABLE HAS, UNUSUALLY, NO DRAWERS. THE LIBRARY TABLE WAS MADE LARGE AND SOLID SO BOOKS AND MAGAZINES COULD BE SPREAD OUT ALONG THE SURFACE.
PRICE GUIDE 7

▼ THIS PARTICULARLY FINE REGENCY LIBRARY TABLE HAS A RIBBED MOULDING AROUND THE TOP. MEASURING ABOUT 4 FEET (1.2 METRES) IN LENGTH, A TABLE LIKE THIS WAS INTENDED FOR A LARGE HOME AND WOULD HAVE STOOD IN THE LIBRARY OR THE HOUSEHOLDER'S STUDY.
PRICE GUIDE 9

▲ THIS EARLY 19TH-CENTURY TABLE IS IN A BEAUTIFUL FADED BRAZILIAN ROSEWOOD. THE TOP IS SUPPORTED ON A FACETED COLUMN, WHICH STEMS FROM THE CARVED BASE. A LARGE DRAWER, THE LENGTH OF THE TABLE TOP, WOULD BE USED FOR KEEPING LARGE PRINTS, MAPS AND OTHER DOCUMENTS.
PRICE GUIDE 8

DESIGN FEATURES

MANY OF THE BEST EXAMPLES OF 1930S FURNITURE DESIGN CAME FROM FRANCE. THIS EXQUISITE WROUGHT-IRON CONSOLE TABLE WITH MARBLE TOP, DESIGNED BY EDGAR BRANDT – REGARDED BY MANY AS THE LEADING METAL-WORKER OF THE TIME – WAS NO EXCEPTION. THE EXTRAORDINARY INTRICATE SCROLLWORK IS TYPICAL OF HIS STYLE.

BRANDT FREQUENTLY USED A MIXTURE OF METAL ALLOYS IN HIS WORK FOR GREATER DECORATIVE EFFECT. IN THIS CASE, HOWEVER, THE TABLE IS EXCLUSIVELY WROUGHT IRON. IT HAS BEEN PAINTED TO GIVE A NATURAL AGEING EFFECT, VERY DIFFERENT FROM THE POLISHED STEEL LOOK THAT WAS COMMON AT THE TIME. BRONZE PAINT HAS BEEN OCCASIONALLY APPLIED TO ADD RELIEF.

▼ THE SOFA TABLE WAS DEVELOPED TO PROVIDE A CONVENIENT WORKING SURFACE DIRECTLY IN FRONT OF A SOFA OR SETTEE. THIS VICTORIAN REPRODUCTION OF A REGENCY DESIGN IS IN CROSS-BANDED MAHOGANY WITH DROP ENDS AND LYRE-ENDED CHEVAL LEGS.
PRICE GUIDE 8

▲ THIS ELEGANT SIDE TABLE WOULD HAVE STOOD AGAINST THE WALL IN POSSIBLY THE DRAWING ROOM OR THE HALL OF A VICTORIAN HOME. MADE IN MAHOGANY, IT HAS CHEVAL LEGS JOINED WITH DOUBLE STRETCHERS.
PRICE GUIDE 6

▲ THIS MID VICTORIAN, DEMI-LUNE SIDE TABLE HAS SQUARED, TAPERING LEGS. THE HALF-MOON SHAPE WAS WELL SUITED TO WALL-STANDING TABLES. MADE IN PINE, THIS TABLE WAS PROBABLY INTENDED FOR USE BELOW STAIRS RATHER THAN IN ANY GRAND ENTRANCE HALL.
PRICE GUIDE 6

▼ THIS MAHOGANY SIDE TABLE HAS INLAY ON THE TOP AND TURNED LEGS AND CASTORS. THERE ARE BRASS HANDLES ON THE DOUBLE DRAWERS. A LARGE 19TH-CENTURY HOUSEHOLD MAY HAVE HAD ANY NUMBER OF DIFFERENT SIDE TABLES, EACH SUITABLE FOR A DIFFERENT ROOM. A TABLE IN THE REGENCY STYLE, LIKE THIS ONE MIGHT HAVE BEEN FOUND IN THE STUDY.
PRICE GUIDE 7

▲ THIS MID-VICTORIAN PITCH PINE TABLE SAW SERVICE IN THE KITCHEN. STANDING AGAINST A WALL IT PROVIDED A USEFUL WORK SURFACE WITH A CONVENIENT DRAWER FOR STORAGE.
PRICE GUIDE 6

▲ THIS DROP-ENDED SOFA TABLE IN ROSEWOOD, IS C. 1835–40. BORNE BY A HEAVY CENTRAL PEDESTAL, THIS TABLE HAS JUST ONE LONG DRAWER WITHOUT HANDLES.
PRICE GUIDE 8

▼ THIS PAINTED PINE AMERICAN PROVINCIAL SOFA TABLE WAS MADE AROUND 1840 TO A PATTERN BASED ON BRITISH REGENCY STYLES.
PRICE GUIDE 8

▼ THE CONSOLE TABLE WITH LEGS WAS A DEVELOPED FORM OF THE SIDE TABLE AND WAS INTENDED FOR USE IN THE HALLWAY. THIS SATINWOOD VENEER CONSOLE TABLE DATES FROM THE 1930s AND WAS ONE OF A PAIR. THE DISTINCTIVE EBONY STRINGING AND SQUARE FEET AND THE SIMPLE HARMONIOUS LINES ARE CHARACTERISTIC OF THE PERIOD.
PRICE GUIDE 7

▲ THE CONSOLE TABLE FIRST MADE ITS APPEARANCE IN 18TH-CENTURY FRANCE WHEN IT WAS SUPPORTED BY A BRACKET ATTACHED TO THE WALL. THE WORD 'CONSOLE' MEANS BRACKET IN FRENCH. THE STYLE WAS REVIVED IN THE 1930s WITH TABLES LIKE THIS FRENCH EXAMPLE, MADE OF MARBLE AND, A MORE MODERNISTIC MATERIAL, POLISHED STEEL.
PRICE GUIDE 8

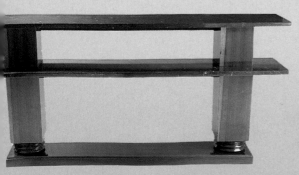

◀ THE CONSOLE TABLE'S FORM DEVELOPED WITH ITS REVIVAL IN THE 20TH CENTURY. RATHER THAN JUST A BRACKET-TYPE, CONSOLE TABLES GREW LEGS AND STOOD AGAINST THE WALL. THIS 1930s TABLE HAS A DISTINCTLY MODERNIST FEEL. IT IS MADE FROM MACASSAR EBONY AND TWO PIECES OF BLACK MARBLE.
PRICE GUIDE 8

DESIGN FEATURES

A PECULIARLY BRITISH PIECE OF FURNITURE, THE DUMBWAITER WAS FIRST MADE DURING THE 1720s. BY THE BEGINNING OF THE 19TH CENTURY, FURNITURE DESIGNERS WERE DEVELOPING NEW FORMS FOR THE DUMBWAITER. ONE OF THE MORE POPULAR HAD TWO TRAYS SEPARATED BY SLENDER COLUMNS AT THE EDGES RATHER THAN BY A SINGLE COLUMN THROUGH THE CENTRE. THIS PIECE IN SOLID MAHOGANY WITH BRASS FITTINGS IS TYPICAL OF REGENCY STYLE.

THE TRAYS ARE GRADUATED IN SIZE AND HAVE MOULDED RAISED RIMS, THOUGH NOT AS RAISED AS IN MANY EARLIER PIECES. THE COLUMNS HAVE TIGHT BARLEY-TWIST MOULDINGS FINISHED IN BRASS WHILE THE BASE HAS THREE SPLAYED LEGS, REEDED ON THE TOP, AND A TURNED BALUSTER SUPPORT. THE FEET ARE CASED IN BRASS, WITH CAST BRASS CASTORS.

▶ THE NEST OF TABLES FIRST APPEARED LATE IN THE 18TH CENTURY AND AS 'PARLOUR-SOCIETY' DEVELOPED IN THE 19TH CENTURY A NEED GREW FOR SMALL TABLES TO PLACE AROUND THE ROOM. THIS 'QUARTETTO', OR NEST OF FOUR TABLES, IS IN PLAIN LACQUERED WOOD.
PRICE GUIDE 8

POINTS TO WATCH

● MANY TUBULAR STEEL TROLLEYS SURVIVE, BUT CHROMIUM PLATE IN PERFECT CONDITION IS UNUSUAL AND MIGHT INDICATE THAT THE FRAME HAS BEEN RECHROMED OR THAT THE TROLLEY IS A MODERN COPY.

● SIGNS OF WEAR ON CHROME WILL APPEAR MAINLY ON THE HANDLES AND WHEELS WHERE THE PLATE WAS AT ITS THINNEST APPLICATION.

● WHEELS ON SERVING TROLLEYS OFTEN DETERIORATE AND IF BUYING A TROLLEY FOR USE RATHER THAN DISPLAY IT MIGHT BE WORTH REPLACING THEM.

▼ EACH OF THESE FOUR TABLES, DESIGNED BY EMILE GALLÉ, HAS A DIFFERENT INLAID TOP. GALLÉ, POSSIBLY MORE FAMOUS FOR HIS GLASSWARE, APPLIED THE SINUOUS AND ORGANIC FORMS OF ART NOUVEAU TO MORE TRADITIONAL FORMS OF FURNITURE.

PRICE GUIDE 8

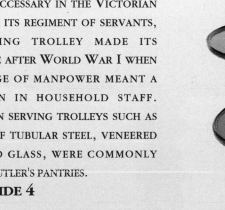

▲ BENTWOOD FURNITURE WAS DEVELOPED IN AUSTRIA AND GERMANY AT THE END OF THE 19TH CENTURY AND SOON BECAME A POPULAR MEDIUM FOR FURNITURE MAKERS. THIS TRIO, OR NEST OF THREE TABLES, WERE MADE BY THE FISCHEL COMPANY IN c.1890. THE LARGEST TABLE HAS A FRET-CUT PANEL TO ADD STRENGTH TO THE SIDES.

PRICE GUIDE 6

▲ THIS TWO-TIERED DUMBWAITER BETRAYS ITS VICTORIAN ORIGINS BY THE SHALLOW CARVING COVERING ITS TRAYS. GEORGIAN TRAYS WERE NEVER CARVED.

PRICE GUIDE 6

▼ UNNECCESSARY IN THE VICTORIAN HOME WITH ITS REGIMENT OF SERVANTS, THE SERVING TROLLEY MADE ITS APPEARANCE AFTER WORLD WAR I WHEN A SHORTAGE OF MANPOWER MEANT A REDUCTION IN HOUSEHOLD STAFF. UTILITARIAN SERVING TROLLEYS SUCH AS THIS ONE OF TUBULAR STEEL, VENEERED WOOD AND GLASS, WERE COMMONLY FOUND IN BUTLER'S PANTRIES.

PRICE GUIDE 4

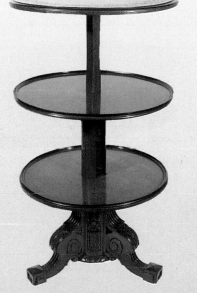

▲ THE JACOBETHAN STYLE WAS A MIXTURE OF MOTIFS DERIVED FROM HISTORICAL FURNITURE AND IS USED HERE FOR THIS SERVING TROLLEY FROM THE 1930s. THE SUPPORTS ARE BARLEY TWIST COLUMNS AND THE SHELVES HAVE CRENATED RIMS.

PRICE GUIDE 4

▲ THIS 1890 DUMBWAITER IS TELESCOPIC AND IT HAS A MECHANISM TO RAISE THE BOTTOM TRAY AND DROP THE TOP ONE – WHICH HAS NO LIP – WHICH CONVERTS IT TO A SIDE TABLE.

PRICE GUIDE 7

◄ IN THE ELABORATE BEDROOMS OF THE 18TH CENTURY THERE WAS A PLACE FOR SMALL CUPBOARDS BESIDE THE BED TO HOLD ALL MANNER OF THINGS. THIS SHERATON DESIGNED BEDSIDE CUPBOARD DATES FROM ABOUT 1820.
PRICE GUIDE 7

▲ THIS GEORGE III COMMODE HAS A TAMBOUR DOOR WITH THE ORIGINAL FITTINGS INTACT. IN THE LARGE HOUSES OF THE 18TH CENTURY THERE WAS NO LAVATORY INDOORS QUITE AS WE WOULD KNOW IT. THEREFORE, THE COMMODE THAT HOUSED THE CHAMBER POT WAS A VITAL PIECE OF FURNITURE, PARTICULARLY DURING THE NIGHT.
PRICE GUIDE 8

◄ THIS SMALL PIECE OF FURNITURE IS IN FACT A MAHOGANY COMMODE, MADE IN BRITAIN DURING GEORGE II'S REIGN. THE LOWER DRAWER PULLED OUT AND A LID WAS LIFTED TO REVEAL A CHAMBER POT. THE TOP OF THIS PIECE COULD ALSO BE USED AS A BEDSIDE TRAY.
PRICE GUIDE 7

▼ NAMED, FOR NO APPARENT REASON, AFTER THE DUKE OF WELLINGTON THIS SATINWOOD WELLINGTON CHEST WAS MADE AROUND 1850. DETAILS ALONG THE PEDIMENT AND THE SIDES AND THE DRAWERS HAVE BEEN EBONIZED.
PRICE GUIDE 8

▲ THIS SMALL PIECE IS A BED STEP AND COMMODE. THE TOP LIFTED UP TO REVEAL A CHAMBER POT AND A STEP PULLED OUT OF THE BOTTOM. BED STEPS CAME INTO USE AS EARLY AS THE LATE 17TH CENTURY WHEN AN INCREASE IN THE HEIGHT OF BEDS MADE GETTING IN AND OUT OF THEM MORE DIFFICULT.
PRICE GUIDE 6

▲ THIS VICTORIAN MAHOGANY SECRETAIRE WELLINGTON CHEST HAS FALSE DRAWER FRONTS THAT FALL FORWARDS TO REVEAL A DESK AND DRAWERS. THERE IS NO RECORD THAT THE DUKE OF WELLINGTON OWNED A WELLINGTON CHEST, OR HAD A HAND IN ITS DESIGN. MAYBE THE NAME DERIVES FROM MILITARY ASSOCIATIONS WITH HIS NAME.
PRICE GUIDE 8

◄ HINGES ON BOTH SHELVES OF THIS FRENCH MAHOGANY COMMODE ALLOWED THEM TO BE RAISED OUT OF THE WAY WHEN THE COMMODE WAS IN USE.
PRICE GUIDE 7

▲ THIS TRAVELLING TRUNK WITH ITS ORIGINAL BRASS HANDLES AND WELL-WORN BRASS CORNERS IS MADE OF CAMPHOR-WOOD. IT WAS IMPORTANT THAT TRUNKS AND CHESTS HAD NO PROTRUDING PARTS TO BREAK OFF OR CAUSE DAMAGE, IF THEY WERE TO BE USED FOR TRAVEL. HANDLES, LOCKS AND HINGES SAT FLUSH TO THE CHEST.
PRICE GUIDE 7

▼ THIS SQUARE OTTOMAN WITH MAHOGANY PLINTH AND FEET HAS A SMALL LOCK. THE SEAT IS UPHOLSTERED IN PAISLEY CLOTH. SOME OTTOMANS HAVE A SOLID WOODEN BODY, BUT MOST HAVE A LIGHT WOODEN FRAMEWORK WITH HESSIAN WEBBING STRETCHED ACROSS THE FRAME TO SUPPORT THE STUFFING.

PRICE GUIDE 6

▲ THE TRUNK MUST BE ONE OF THE MOST BASIC FORMS OF FURNITURE THERE IS. THIS LATE 19TH-CENTURY COFFER LOOKS COMPLEX BUT THE MANY WOOD AND METAL BANDS RUNNING AROUND IT WERE INTENDED TO PROTECT THE TRUNK WHEN TRAVELLING.

PRICE GUIDE 5

▲ ORIGINALLY MADE FROM HOLLOWED-OUT TREE TRUNKS, THE CHEST AS A STORAGE SPACE HAS BEEN AROUND FOR CENTURIES. THIS VERY SIMPLE PINE CHEST FROM 1880 HAS A PLINTH BASE AND AN UNUSUAL HANGING APRON ALONG BOTH SIDES OF THE LID.

PRICE GUIDE 5

DESIGN FEATURES

THE BOX OTTOMAN WAS ONE OF THE MOST VERSATILE PIECES OF FURNITURE IN THE VICTORIAN HOME. GOOD-QUALITY RICHLY UPHOLSTERED EXAMPLES COULD BE USED IN ANY ROOM IN THE HOUSE FROM PARLOUR TO THE SMOKING ROOM.

THIS EXAMPLE WITH ITS ATTRACTIVE CURVED SIDES DATES FROM THE 1850S AND IS UPHOLSTERED ON TOP WITH RED NEEDLEPOINT. A PADDED FABRIC LINING IS USED TO DISGUISE THE WOODEN CARCASE OF THE OTTOMAN. THE HINGED LID AND PLINTH ARE TRIMMED WITH ROSEWOOD AND A BRAID TRIM PROVIDES A NEAT DECORATIVE FINISH TO THE TAPESTRY EXTERIOR FABRIC. SMALL CASTORS FIXED TO THE ROSEWOOD FEET MAKE MOVING EASIER.

POINTS TO WATCH

● CHECK THAT THE HINGES ARE ORIGINAL, ESPECIALLY ON OLDER PIECES.
● MAKE SURE THAT THE FEET ARE ORIGINAL. A LITTLE WEAR IS ACCEPTABLE, BUT CHESTS WITH SPLIT OR UNEVENLY WORN FEET SHOULD BE AVOIDED IF POSSIBLE.
● IF THE CHEST HAS BEEN STRIPPED, CHECK FOR COARSE GRAIN, POSSIBLE SCORCH MARKS AND CAUSTIC DEPOSITS CAUSED BY BAD STRIPPING.
● MANY OAK CHESTS WERE RE-CARVED IN THE 19TH CENTURY. LOOKING AT GOOD MUSEUM PIECES IS THE BEST WAY TO APPRECIATE ORIGINAL WORK.

▼ THIS SMALL OTTOMAN HAS A MAHOGANY PLINTH AND FEET AND A NEEDLEPOINT SEAT. THE INTERIORS OF OTTOMANS WERE OFTEN LINED WITH DARK LINEN OR COTTON, THE TOP EDGES OF WHICH WERE NEATENED WITH A SIMPLE BRAID OR CORD.
PRICE GUIDE 6

▶ THIS COFFER HAS A LOT OF STUDDING ON BOTH THE SIDES AND THE TOP OF THE LID. THIS DOES SUGGEST THAT THE PIECE WAS ONCE COVERED IN LEATHER. VELVET, SHARKSKIN AND EVEN FUR WERE USED TO COVER CHESTS, BUT AT THE END OF THE 19TH CENTURY A NEW MATERIAL CALLED LEATHER-CLOTH, OR AMERICAN CLOTH, BEGAN TO BE USED.
PRICE GUIDE 5

▶ THIS WELL-MADE CHEST HAS BRACKET FEET, A LIPPED LID AND SMALL BRASS ESCUTCHEONS. BEING A PRACTICAL AND CHEAP PIECE OF FURNITURE, THE CHEST WAS A COMMON ITEM IN SERVANT'S QUARTERS AND CHILDREN'S ROOM .
PRICE GUIDE 6

▶ THE BRASS CORNERS OF THIS LATE VICTORIAN CHEST SUGGEST THAT IT WAS ORIGINALLY INTENDED FOR TRAVELLING. THE DOVETAIL JOINTS THAT KEEP THE EDGES TOGETHER HAVE BEEN MADE INTO A DECORATIVE FEATURE.
PRICE GUIDE 5

▶ THIS MASSIVE AMERICAN DOWER CHEST, DATED 1807, HAS PAINTED DECORATION, WHICH WAS A POPULAR ALTERNATIVE TO CARVING AND INLAY. MADE IN THE PENNSYLVANIA DUTCH STYLE, THIS CHEST IS TYPICAL OF THOSE BROUGHT OVER BY EARLY SETTLERS.
PRICE GUIDE 8

▶ THIS SYRIAN TEAK CHEST WAS IMPORTEED INTO EUROPE IN THE LATE 19TH CENTURY. COVERED WITH MOTHER-OF-PEARL DECORATION IN FLORAL PATTERNS, THIS PIECE IS C.1880.
PRICE GUIDE 8

◀ THE TOP OF THIS LONG OTTOMAN, C.1860, IS COVERED IN A GEOMETRIC NEEDLEPOINT PATTERN. THE EXTERIOR FABRIC OF OTTOMAN WAS TACKED TO THE OUTSIDE EDGES OF THE LID AND BOX AND WAS TRIMMED WITH DECORATIVE BRAID OR ORNAMENTAL BRASS TACKS.
PRICE GUIDE 6

DESIGN FEATURES

THE MASS-PRODUCED, VICTORIAN, PINE CHEST OF DRAWERS WAS A CHEAP, FUNCTIONAL PIECE, WITH A SIMPLE FOUR-SQUARE DESIGN AND VIRTUALLY NO DECORATION SAVE FOR THAT PROVIDED BY PAINTS, STAINS AND VARNISHES. THESE FINISHES WERE SUBJECT TO WEAR, AND MOST HAVE SINCE BEEN REMOVED.

THE FIVE DRAWER STYLE, WITH TWO SHORT DRAWERS ABOVE THREE LONG ONES, WAS TYPICAL. MOST FEATURED SIMPLE KNOB HANDLES IN WOOD OR WHITE PORCELAIN.

THIS CHEST TOP IS LIPPED OVER, AND HAS A MOULDED EDGE, WHILE THE FEET ARE ROUNDED, REMINISCENT OF BUN FEET. AS AN ADDED REFINEMENT, THE KEYHOLES ARE INSET WITH BRASS TO CUT DOWN ON WEAR BY THE KEY AGAINST THE SOFT WOOD.

▼ CONTINENTAL MANUFACTURERS WERE MORE INCLINED TO CARVE PINE CHESTS OF DRAWERS. THIS GLASS-HANDLED CHEST WITH BUN FEET IS FRENCH AND DATES FROM 1860.
PRICE GUIDE 6

▼ THIS GEORGIAN CHEST HAS SHAPED BRACKET FEET, BRASS DROP HANDLES AND AN OAK COCK-BEADING AROUND THE DRAWER FRONTS.
PRICE GUIDE 7

▲ THIS LATE-VICTORIAN FOUR-DRAWER CHEST WITH PLAIN BRACKET FEET AND STEEL DROP HANDLES HAS BEEN PAINTED TO IMITATE OAK. PINE WAS A CHEAP MATERIAL AND, THEREFORE, WAS OFTEN DISGUISED IN THIS WAY.
PRICE GUIDE 4

▼ THIS VICTORIAN VERSION OF THE FIVE-DRAWER CHEST HAS WOODEN KNOB HANDLES AND A DECORATIVELY-SHAPED APRON AROUND THE BASE. DURING THE 19TH CENTURY, BEDROOM FURNITURE WAS INCREASINGLY SOLD IN SUITES AND PINE CHESTS OF DRAWERS COULD COME WITH WASHSTANDS, SMALL CHAIRS AND NARROW WARDROBES.

PRICE GUIDE 7

▲ THIS UNUSUAL FOUR-DRAWER CHEST HAS A FANCIFUL, SCROLLED GALLERY TOP. THE FRONTS OF THE TOP TWO DRAWERS ARE SHAPED SO THAT THEY CAN BE OPENED WITHOUT HANDLES.

PRICE GUIDE 5

▼ THIS PLAIN, FOUR-SQUARE CHEST, FROM AROUND 1860, IS IN AN ATTRACTIVE FIGURED WALNUT WITH WOODEN HANDLES AND A PLINTH ON SQUAT BUN FEET.

PRICE GUIDE 6

▼ THIS FRENCH, PINE CHEST OF DRAWERS IN THE LOUIS XVI STYLE, FROM C.1850, HAS BEEN PAINTED WITH DECORATIVE SWAGS AND FLOWERS.

PRICE GUIDE 6

▼ THE CHEST OF DRAWERS WAS AN ESSENTIAL PIECE OF FURNITURE IN THE 19TH-CENTURY BEDROOM. A WELL-FIGURED MAHOGANY VENEER ADDS VALUE TO THIS MID-VICTORIAN SERPENTINE CHEST OF DRAWERS.

PRICE GUIDE 7

▼ DATING FROM 1780, THIS WELL-FIGURED MAHOGANY TALLBOY HAS A DENTIL CORNICE AND FLUTED CORNERS. ORIGINALLY, TALLBOYS WERE MADE WITH A SOLID MAHOGANY CARCASE BUT THIS WAS SOON REPLACED BY MAHONGANY VENEER ON A PINE OR OAK BASE.

PRICE GUIDE 8

▼ THIS SOLID TALLBOY WAS MADE IN THE CHANNEL ISLES IN AROUND 1780. WITH PANELLED SIDES AND A DENTIL CORNICE, THIS EXAMPLE HAS A MUCH SHORTER LOWER CHEST THAN UPPER.

PRICE GUIDE 8

▲ THIS MAHOGANY TALLBOY OF AROUND 1790 HAS HAD ITS HANDLES REPLACED. A BRUSHING SLIDE FEATURES AT THE TOP OF THE LOWER SECTION.

PRICE GUIDE 8

▼ SERPENTINE FRONTS ARE RARE ON 18TH-CENTURY TALLBOYS. THIS PIECE IS A VICTORIAN REPRODUCTION DATING FROM AROUND 1870. THE FAIRLY ORNATE HANDLES ARE MATCHED BY THE BRASS ESCUTCHEONS AROUND THE KEYHOLES.

PRICE GUIDE 8

▼ THIS QUEEN ANNE CHEST-ON-STAND IN WALNUT HAS SWAN NECK DROP HANDLES, CABRIOLE LEGS AND PAD FEET. MANY STANDS WERE MADE WITHOUT STRETCHERS AND WERE, THEREFORE, TOO WEAK TO SUPPORT A HEAVY CHEST AND DO NOT SURVIVE TODAY.

PRICE GUIDE 8

▲ THIS LATE 18-TH CENTURY TALLBOY HAS SATINWOOD STRINGING AND CHAMFERED CORNERS. IT IS SLIGHTLY WIDER THAN USUAL, THOUGH STILL AS TALL — THE TALLBOY DOES SEEM TO BE A INCONVENIENT PIECE OF FURNITURE IN THAT A STEP LADDER WAS OFTEN NEEDED TO REACH THE UPPERMOST DRAWERS.

PRICE GUIDE 8

▼ THIS SMALL CHEST-ON-WHEELS, OTHERWISE KNOWN AS A *KURUMA-DANSU*, HAS TWO DRAWERS AND SLIDING DOORS BELOW THAT. IT WAS MADE IN THE 19TH CENTURY, OF ZELKOVA, A WOOD ALSO KNOWN AS *KEYAKI*.
PRICE GUIDE 8

▲ THE BIEDERMEIER STYLE SPREAD THROUGHOUT GERMANY AND AUSTRIA AT THE BEGINNING OF THE 19TH CENTURY. CHARACTERIZED BY RESTRAINT AND PURITY OF LINE, BIEDERMEIER WAS ADAPED TO MANY CONVENTIONAL FURNITURE DESIGNS. THIS GERMAN BIEDERMEIER TALLBOY, FROM AROUND 1820, IS MADE IN BIRCHWOOD WITH EBONIZED ESCUTCHEONS AS THE ONLY DECORATION ON THE SIMPLE FACADE.
PRICE GUIDE 8

▲ SMALL AMOUNTS OF LACQUERED FURNITURE WERE BEING MADE IN JAPAN FOR EXPORT FROM THE 17TH CENTURY ONWARDS. BY THE MID-19TH CENTURY JAPAN BEGAN TO TRADE MORE FREELY WITH THE WEST AND MORE SUBSTANTIAL AMOUNTS OF FURNITURE WERE MADE. THIS SMALL, PORTABLE 'SEA CHEST', OR *FUNA-DANSU* AS IT WAS CALLED IN JAPAN, WAS MADE AROUND 1850 OF ZELKOVA, A MUCH-PRIZED NATIVE HARDWOOD.
PRICE GUIDE 8

◀ THIS SET OF FREE-STANDING SHELVES, OR *SHODANA*, WERE MADE AROUND 1850, OF A TYPICALLY SIMPLE CONSTRUCTION WITH A TOUCH OF DECORATION AT THE BASE ONLY.
PRICE GUIDE 7

POINTS TO WATCH

● THE TOP OF THE UPPER CHEST OF A TALLBOY SHOULD BE OPEN, WITH ROUGH, UNFINISHED EDGES.

● THE GRAIN AND COLOUR OF THE WOOD ON THE SIDES AND DRAWERS OF BOTH CHESTS SHOULD MATCH TO ENSURE THAT BOTH PIECES ARE A PAIR.

● CHECK INSIDE DRAWERS FOR ANY HOLES THAT WOULD INDICATE ORIGINAL HANDLES HAVE BEEN REPLACED.

● THE SIDES OF WALNUT PIECES WERE NOT ALWAYS VENEERED, BUT WERE OFTEN OAK PAINTED AND GRAINED TO SIMULATE WALNUT.

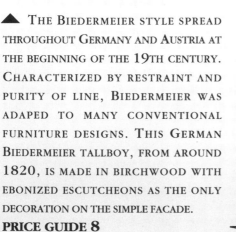

▶ THIS 19TH-CENTURY CHEST-ON-CHEST, A *KASANE-DANSU*, IS MADE OF JAPANESE CYPRESS, KNOWN AS *HINOKI*. THE DOORS ARE SLIDING AND THE HANDLES AND OTHER METAL FINISHES ARE IN IRON.
PRICE GUIDE 8

▲ THIS MID-VICTORIAN, MAHOGANY ROLL-TOP DESK HAS A CYLINDER-SHAPED, TAMBOUR TOP. THE CONTRASTING WOOD IN THE INTERIOR FITTINGS DENOTES A DESK OF GOOD QUALITY.
PRICE GUIDE 8

▲ THIS VICTORIAN, MAHOGANY, CYLINDER ROLL-TOP DESK WITH OPEN KNEEHOLE IS FROM ABOUT 1870. THE SOLID CYLINDER TOP HAS TWO HANDLES TO FACILITATE OPENING AND CLOSING THE RIGID CYLINDER, WHICH IS LESS FLEXIBLE THAN A TAMBOUR TOP.
PRICE GUIDE 8

▲ THIS 1930s ROLL-TOP DESK HAS A SERPENTINE-SHAPED TAMBOUR TOP. MADE IN MAHOGANY AND OAK, THE DESK HAS CUPBOARD SPACE IN THE FRONT AND SIDE OF ONE PEDASTAL, AND DRAWERS IN THE OTHER. THE ROLL-TOP DESKS OF THE 20TH CENTURY ARE OFTEN FAITHFUL COPIES OF EARLIER, ORIGINAL PIECES.
PRICE GUIDE 7

DESIGN FEATURES

THE *BONHEUR DU JOUR* WAS EXTREMELY POPULAR IN THE EDWARDIAN ERA. THIS EXAMPLE HAS A STRIKING CENTRAL FEATURE OF AN OVAL MIRROR. ON SOME EXAMPLES, THE MIRROR WAS SET ON PIVOTS AND ALSO SERVED AS A USEFUL FIRE SCREEN SHOULD THE LADY BE TOO CLOSE TO A WARM FIRE IN WINTER. SOME DESKS HAD THE ADDITION OF A PULL-

DOWN SCREEN AT THE BACK WHICH ALSO ACTED AS A DRAUGHT EXCLUDER.

THE MIRROR IS FLANKED BY TWO SETS OF SMALL DRAWERS IN WHICH PAPER, ENVELOPES AND WRITING UTENSILS WERE STORED. THE DRAWER FRONTS ARE INLAID WITH THIN BANDS OF LIGHT WOOD MATCHING THE INLAY ON THE WIDE DRAWERS OF THE DESK ITSELF.

THE FLAT-TOPPED TABLE HAS AN INSET OF TOOLED LEATHER TO GIVE A MORE COMFORTABLE WRITING SURFACE. DESKS WITH THIS SINGLE SURFACE WERE SOMEWHAT LESS PRACTICAL THAN THOSE WITH THE FLAP-DOWN ADDITION. NOT ONLY WAS THERE LESS DESK SURFACE BUT THE DRAWERS MADE IT AWKWARD FOR LADIES IN LARGE SKIRTS.

▼ THIS VICTORIAN PEDESTAL DESK HAS ORIGINAL HANDLES, A WELL-WORN LEATHER TOP, CHAMPFERED EDGES AND CASTORS BENEATH THE PEDESTALS. THE PEDESTAL DESK WAS A LARGE AND IMPOSING ITEM OF FURNITURE, USUALLY 4–5 FEET (1.2 1.5 METRES) IN WIDTH.
PRICE GUIDE 8

▼ THIS LIGHT OAK PARTNERS' DESK WAS MADE IN ABOUT 1890. THE DESIGN OF DRAWERS AND ROLL-FRONT CUPBOARD IS REPEATED ON THE SIDE NOT VISIBLE. PEDESTAL AND PARTNERS' DESKS COME IN THREE SECTIONS; TWO PEDESTALS AND A DEEP TOP ALSO CONTAINING DRAWERS.
PRICE GUIDE 7

▲ THIS SMALL, TURN-OF-THE-CENTURY HONEY-OAK CYLINDER DESK HAS A LEATHER TOPPED WRITING SLOPE AND TWO SMALLER LEATHER INSET PANELS ON THE DESK SURFACE. THE BRASS DROP HANDLES, INTRICATE INTERNAL FITTINGS AND GALLERY MOULDINGS ARE ALL MARKS OF HIGH QUALITY.
PRICE GUIDE 7

▼ THE SOLID CYLINDER ROLL-TOP OF THIS ROSEWOOD DESK HAS AN ELABORATE FLORAL INLAY OF LIME AND BOXWOOD. SET INTO THE BACK IS A SMALL, DECORATIVE, BEVELLED MIRROR.
PRICE GUIDE 8

▼ THIS UNUSUAL, OVAL-SHAPED, MAHOGANY WRITING TABLE HAS AN ELABORATELY SCROLLED GALLERY ON TOP OF TWO SMALL DRAWERS, THAT CURVES ROUND WITH THE SHAPE OF THE TABLE. THE TOP IS COVERED IN LEATHER AND THE DELICATE TURNED LEGS ARE ON CASTORS.
PRICE GUIDE 8

▲ THIS CYLINDER DESK HAS A SIMPLE LIGHT WOOD INLAY. THE ROLL-TOP REVEALS INNER COMPARTMENTS AND SMALL DRAWERS AND TWO KNOBS PULL OUT AN ADDITIONAL WRITING SURFACE.
PRICE GUIDE 7

DESIGN FEATURES

By the 1930s, bookcases had taken on a smooth streamlined look, and were most often long and low rather than tall and imposing. Glass fronts were no longer compulsory, and the elaborate banding, moulding and cornices of the Gothic or Georgian style had been replaced by simple rectangular shapes and contrasting veneers — in this case maple and walnut. For compactness, shelves were sometimes set at the ends of the case as well as along its length. This example also features compartments whose handles are formed by small metal-lined square recesses.

▼ The bureaux of the 18th century have been long admired as fine examples of furniture design. As a result, 'marriages' combining a new top with a period base, or vice versa, have been around since then. This Victorian example places a contemporary top on an inlaid 18th-century serpentine secretaire base.

PRICE GUIDE 9

▲ The revolving bookstand had been a popular feature in many Regency libraries and drawing rooms but for most of the Victorian period they were not made. Not until 1890 did they reappear. This mahogany bookstand dates from this period and is unusual in that it has three tiers; the bottom tier being slightly wider for larger volumes.

PRICE GUIDE 7

▼ This tall open bookshelf with turned end supports was made in England in about 1890. The heavy supports running across the back of this piece do not add to the decoration of the shelves, but once books were in place, this feature would be hidden.

PRICE GUIDE 8

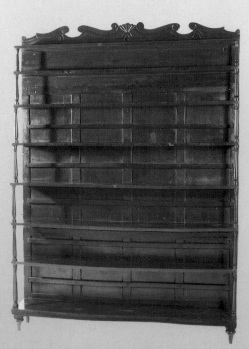

▼ THIS DOUBLE-SIDED REGENCY BOOKCASE IS MADE OF ROSEWOOD AND WOULD HAVE STOOD IN THE MIDDLE OF A LIBRARY. IT HAS BRASS CARRYING HANDLES AT THE SIDES, RATHER THAN CASTORS.
PRICE GUIDE 9

▼ THIS UNUSUAL OCTAGONAL REVOLVING BOOKSTAND DATES FROM C.1880. IT IS IN SATINWOOD AND MAHOGANY, WITH A TOOLED LEATHER TOP. THE SABRE LEGS AND BRASS CASTORS MARK IT AS A REGENCY REVIVAL PIECE.
PRICE GUIDE 9

▲ THIS 'JACOBETHAN' PIECE FROM THE 1920S HAS A REVOLVING DRUM INSIDE AND AN OCTAGONAL FRAME. THE DRUM PIVOTS ON LUGS CONCEALED UNDER THE TABLE TOP AND IN THE BASE.
PRICE GUIDE 6

▼ AS BOOKS THEMSELVES BECAME LIGHTER IN WEIGHT SO TOO DID THE BOOKSHELVES OF THE EARLY 20TH CENTURY. WELL-MADE SETS OF SHELVES WERE THE SIMPLEST WAY OF STORING BOOKS. THIS SET IS IN BIRD'S-EYE MAPLE.
PRICE GUIDE 4

▼ THIS 1930S BUREAU BOOKCASE IN MAHOGANY AND SATINWOOD INCLUDES A FITTED, DROP-LEAF, WRITING CABINET. THIS EXAMPLE ADAPTS THE CLASSIC FORM OF THE BUREAU TO MODERN STYLING.
PRICE GUIDE 6

▲ THIS STURDILY-BUILT, SECTIONED OAK BOOKCASE WAS MADE IN LONDON IN THE 1930S. EACH SHELF HAS ITS OWN GLASS DOOR HINGED AT THE TOP. THERE WERE OBVIOUS ADVANTAGES TO BUYING SECTIONS, OR UNITS, OF BOOKSHELVES. ADDITIONS COULD BE MADE AS MORE BOOKS WERE BOUGHT.
PRICE GUIDE 6

DESIGN FEATURES

VICTORIAN WASHSTANDS WERE MADE TO SUIT EVERY TASTE. THIS PRETTY STAND, MADE IN THE LAST TWENTY YEARS OF THE 19TH CENTURY, SHOWS A STRONG ART NOUVEAU INFLUENCE, ESPECIALLY IN THE CARVED DECORATION. THE TOP IS A SOLID PIECE OF BLACK AND WHITE MARBLE, A COLOUR SCHEME WHICH IS NOT REFLECTED IN THE FLORAL TILES THAT FEATURE ON THE SPLASHBACK.

OTHER UNUSUAL FEATURES ARE THE PANEL-FRONTED CUPBOARD WITH BRASS HANDLE AND HINGES THAT IS SET TO ONE SIDE OF THE LOWER SHELF, AND THE THREE SMALL SHELVES ABOVE THE TILED SPLASHBACK. THIS DISTINCTIVE AND STYLISH STAND IS SET OFF BY ITS ATTRACTIVE TURNED LEGS WITH CASTORS. A RAIL AT ONE END MADE MOVING THE WASHSTAND EASIER.

▶ THE WASHSTAND WAS A VITAL PART OF BEDROOM FURNITURE IN HOMES WITH NO BATHROOM. WASHING COULD BE DONE IN A BOWL OF WATER, FILLED FROM A JUG, PLACED ON THE WASHSTAND. THEREFORE, THE TOP SURFACE IS GENERALLY MARBLE OR SOME OTHER SPLASH RESISTANT MATERIAL. THIS STAND IS PARTICULARLY COLLECTABLE DUE TO ITS EXTRAVAGANT BARLEY-TWIST LEGS.
PRICE GUIDE 6

▶ THIS MAGNIFICENT SATINWOOD WASHSTAND IS DECORATED WITH EBONY BEADING. THE TOP IS COVERED IN A LIGHT MARBLE AND THE WHOLE STAND RESEMBLES A KNEEHOLE DESK.
PRICE GUIDE 7

▶ THIS TWO-DRAWER WASHSTAND WITH BARLEY-TWIST LEGS ON CASTORS IS FINISHED IN SATINWOOD AND HAS AN ATTRACTIVE TILED SPLASHBACK.
PRICE GUIDE 6

▶ THIS DEMI-LUNE WASHSTAND IS IN THE TYPICAL MARBLE AND MAHOGANY THAT CHARACTERIZED THE BEST WASHSTANDS OF THE MID 19TH CENTURY.
PRICE GUIDE 6

◀ THIS PINE WASHSTAND HAS A HOLE IN THE TOP SURFACE INTO WHICH THE WASHING BOWL COULD BE PLACED. THE STAND HAS NARROW TURNED LEGS, A BOTTOM SHELF WITH A DRAWER AND A WOODEN SPLASHBACK. THE STAND HAS BEEN PAINTED TO RESEMBLE BEECHWOOD.
PRICE GUIDE 5

▼ THIS RESTORED SCHOOL DESK HAS, UNUSUALLY, BACK PANELLING AND MIGHT HAVE BEEN USED BY THE TEACHER.
PRICE GUIDE 3

▼ THIS ORDINARY TURN-OF-THE-CENTURY SCHOOLROOM DESK IS SECURED TO ITS STURDY FEET BY WROUGHT IRON LEGS. MANY DESKS ON THE MARKET ARE MISSING THEIR ORIGINAL INKWELLS FROM THE HOLES LEFT IN THE WOOD. IF THEY ARE STILL PRESENT THIS WILL AFFECT THE PRICE OF THE DESK.
PRICE GUIDE 3

▲ DESKS FOR SCHOOL USE TENDED TO BE MADE STRONGLY BUT CHEAPLY USING SCREWS RATHER THAN CABINETMAKER'S JOINTS. THE ROUGH TREATMENT USUALLY GIVEN TO SCHOOL DESKS WILL BE REFLECTED IN THEIR GENERAL CONDITION.
PRICE GUIDE 3

▼ THIS DESK HAS BEEN CLUMSILY REPAIRED AT ONE SIDE WHERE THE DESK LID IS HINGED. HOWEVER, THE DESK IS STILL UNITED TO ITS ORIGINAL STICK-BACK CHAIR, WITH SHAPED SADDLE SEAT, BY WOODEN RUNNERS.
PRICE GUIDE 4

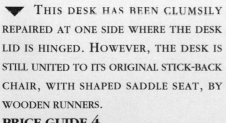

▼ THIS VICTORIAN SINGLE-SEAT DESK IS OF OAK AND WROUGHT IRON AND IS BUILT TO LAST. THE DESK HAS A BOOK LEDGE AT THE TOP, DESIGNED TO PREVENT BOOKS FALLING OFF DURING LESSONS. THE CHAIR HAS A CURVED BACK AND A TILTING SEAT.
PRICE GUIDE 4

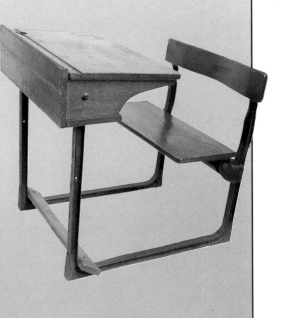

▲ MANY VICTORIANS, AS GREAT TRAVELLERS AND COLLECTORS, DEVELOPED SPECIALIST PORTABLE FURNITURE AND EQUIPMENT. THIS PINE FOLDING DESK IS FROM THE 1890S. IT HAS CARRYING HANDLES IN BRASS, AN INTEGRAL INKWELL AND A SWING OUT CANDLE HOLDER.
PRICE GUIDE 6

POINTS TO WATCH

- PEDESTAL DRESSING TABLES WERE OFTEN CONVERTED TO DESKS BY REMOVING DRAWERS AND MIRRORS. CHECK THAT FITTINGS MATCH THE BASE.
- DRESSING CHESTS WERE OFTEN CONVERTED TO SIMPLE CHESTS OF DRAWERS.
- THE MIRROR MAY BE A LATER REPLACEMENT, SO ATTACHMENTS SHOULD BE CHECKED.

▼ THIS BAMBOO AND RATTAN DRESSING CHEST PICKED UP THE JAPANESE INFLUENCE THAT WAS PREVELANT AT THE END OF THE 19TH CENTURY. A SINGLE, SMALL JEWELLERY DRAWER IS PLACED ON THE TOP, JUST UNDER THE MIRROR.

PRICE GUIDE 6

▲ THE DECORATIVE, TURNED GALLERY AT THE TOP OF THIS CHEVAL MIRROR DRESSING TABLE CONTRASTS WITH THE SIMPLE STRAIGHT LINES CHARACTERISTIC OF ARTS AND CRAFTS STYLING.

PRICE GUIDE 3

▲ THIS DRESSING TABLE IS IN OAK WITH PEWTER HANDLES. THE DELICATE CARVED DETAILS OF THE MIRROR SUPPORTS ARE A CLASSIC EXAMPLE OF ART NOUVEAU STYLING. ALL ITS DRAWERS ARE LOCKABLE.

PRICE GUIDE 4

▼ THIS ORNATE AND HEAVY DRESSING TABLE REFLECTS AN ORIENTAL INFLUENCE. A LARGE CHEVAL MIRROR IS SUSPENDED BETWEEN TWO LARGE PEDESTALS BUT THE EXOTIC PAINTED DECORATION, IMITATING LACQUER, OFFSETS THE HEAVY LOOK.

PRICE GUIDE 7

▲ THIS MORE TRADITIONAL TABLE IN A DARK WOOD IS TYPICAL OF EDWARDIAN TASTE IN FURNITURE. IT HAS A KNEEHOLE AND INLAID DRAWER EDGES.

PRICE GUIDE 6

◄ THE DESIGN OF THIS CHEST IS SQUARE AND SIMPLE BUT THIS IS RELIEVED BY THE OVAL MIRROR AND THE HERRING-BONE PATTERNING IN THE WOOD.

PRICE GUIDE 6

▼ THE FORM OF THIS DRESSING TABLE SEEMS TO COMBINE SOFA AND CABINET DESIGNS IN A TYPICALLY ART DECO ASYMMETRIC STYLE. A LONG PIECE OF WOOD IS CURVED INTO A GONDOLA-LIKE SHAPE AND THEN A GLASS SHELF HAS BEEN DROPPED IN. EVEN THE MIRROR IS UNUSUAL IN ITS FORM.
PRICE GUIDE 7

▲ THIS 1930s DRESSING TABLE HAS PICKED UP ON A VARIETY OF INFLUENCES. DESPITE A MIXTURE OF REGENCY AND VICTORIAN STYLES THIS RETAINS QUITE A CLASSICAL APPEARANCE.
PRICE GUIDE 7

▲ THIS UNUSUAL, EARLY 20TH-CENTURY CHEST IS IN BURNISHED BAMBOO. THE DECORATION IS ORIENTAL WITH DELICATE DESIGNS IN LACQUER ON A BACKGROUND OF RED AND BLACK CHEVRONS.
PRICE GUIDE 7

▼ THIS ANGLED DRESSING TABLE IS MADE UP OF THREE PARTS AND FORMS A STRIKING GEOMETRIC FORM. THE THREE-WINGED MIRROR SUGGESTS THAT THIS WOULD HAVE BEEN INTENDED FOR THE CORNER OF A BEDROOM.
PRICE GUIDE 5

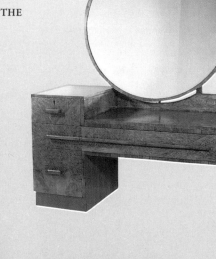

▲ THIS SEMI-CIRCULAR DRESSING TABLE STANDS WITH THE CURVED SIDE AWAY FROM THE SITTER, WHO CAN PLACE THEIR KNEES UNDER THE SPACE LEFT OPEN. A THREE-WINGED MIRROR IS FIXED TO THE BACK AND FLORAL CARVING PICKS OUT DETAILS ON THE DRAWERS. THE UNUSUAL LAYOUT AND SPECIAL FEATURES OF THIS LATE 1920s DRESSING TABLE IN OAK MAKE IT A RARE COLLECTORS'S PIECE.
PRICE GUIDE 6

▲ THIS ASYMMETRIC 1930s DRESSING TABLE SHOWS ALL THE CLASSIC TRAITS OF ART DECO STYLING. A CIRCULAR MIRROR IS SUSPENDED OVER A DROPPED TABLE SURFACE. THIS IS MADE IN BIRD'S-EYE-MAPLE, POPULAR FOR DECO FURNITURE.
PRICE GUIDE 7

DESIGN FEATURES

This magnificent late Regency cot carries a brass trade plate attributing it to the firm of Morgan Sanders, who specialized in patent and convertible furniture. This cot, made around the 1820s, can be readily dismantled for ease of transport and was presumably intended for the children of a family in the colonial service. Two small children could both have fitted in quite comfortably.

All the woodwork, including the slats in the base, is mahogany, and all the metalwork – castors, hinges, corner-pieces, pins, fittings and finials – is brass. The canework panels drop into place and swivel on brass lugs set into the base frame. Each double panel is hinged in the centre. The draped canopy may once have been covered with mosquito netting.

▼ The galleried rails that run along the head and foot boards and that would frame the mattress of this 1840 bed, have been turned and stained to imitate bamboo.
PRICE GUIDE 7

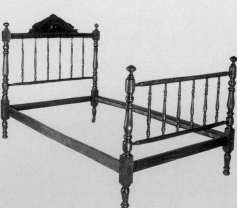

▲ Made entirely of beech, this Spanish bed of around 1900 has a light frame and no castors. Simple designs such as this were increasingly popular in the growing number of suburban villas and houses.
PRICE GUIDE 6

▼ This metal-framed mahogany bed has a simple slatted construction with boxwood stringing. The wooden bed had been ousted in the early 19th century by brass and iron beds but came back later in the century in a variety of guises.
PRICE GUIDE 6

▼ THIS CAST-IRON BEDSTEAD AND MATTRESS BASE HAS BRASS BALL-FINIALS. THIS IS A MID-VICTORIAN EXAMPLE, WITH MORE INTRICATE PLAQUES ON THE FOOT AND HEAD THAN ON LATER BEDS.
PRICE GUIDE 6

▲ THIS FRENCH BED FROM THE 1880S IS GRANDLY STYLED WITH CARVING AND FIGURED PANELS. MADE OF WALNUT, THIS BED HAS SHORT CABRIOLE LEGS.
PRICE GUIDE 7

▲ THIS BURNISHED STEEL BED HAS BRASS TOP RAILS, BALL FINIALS AND FITTINGS. IT DATES FROM AROUND 1870. THE SPINDLES ARE TOPPED WITH BRASS ROSETTES; A POPULAR FEATURE BECAUSE THEY BREAK UP THE STARK, PERPENDICULAR LINES OF METAL BEDS.
PRICE GUIDE 5

▼ THIS 1870S CRADLE IS INSPIRED BY GOTHIC INFLUENCES. THE MAHOGANY FRAME IS FILLED WITH CANEWORK AND THE HOOD IS COVERED WITH GREEN VELVET. THE INTERIOR IS PADDED.
PRICE GUIDE 5

▲ THIS EDWARDIAN BRASS BED HAS MESH PANELS. THE OUTSIDE SUPPORTS ARE SQUARED AND FLUTED, AND THE TOP RAIL IS ENGRAVED. THE FINIALS ARE QUITE ELABORATE TO COUNTERBALANCE THE OVERALL DESIGN.
PRICE GUIDE 8

▲ THIS FRENCH CRIB OF AOUND 1900 HAS A TURNED WILLOW FRAME AND WICKER INFILL WHICH HAVE BOTH BEEN PAINTED DARK BLUE.
PRICE GUIDE 5

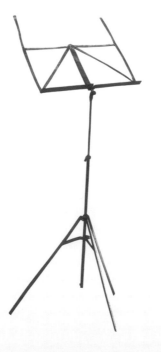

▼ THIS SINGLE-SIDED MAHOGANY MUSIC STAND WITH INTRICATE FRETWORK REST, DATES FROM BETWEEN 1860 AND 1880. IN THE DAYS BEFORE RADIOS AND TELEVISION, THE MUSIC STAND WAS A VITAL PIECE OF FURNITURE IN HOMES WHERE PEOPLE MADE THEIR OWN MUSIC.

PRICE GUIDE 7

▼ A 19TH-CENTURY, FREENCH MUSIC STAND, WHICH, IN CONTRAST TO MANY CONTEMPORARY VICTORIAN EXAMPLES, IS DISTINCTLY PLAIN IN STYLE. AGAIN A DOUBLE STAND, THIS WOULD HAVE BEEN SUITABLE FOR TWO OR MORE MUSICIANS.

PRICE GUIDE 7

▲ DESIGNED FOR THOSE WHO REQUIRED A PURELY FUNCTIONAL STAND, THIS COLLAPSIBLE METAL EXAMPLE WAS A PRACTICAL OPTION. IT WOULD ALSO HAVE BEEN USEFUL WHEN MUSICIANS WERE TRAVELLING BETWEEN CONCERTS.

PRICE GUIDE 7

POINTS TO WATCH

● IT IS NOT ALWAYS EASY TO DISTINGUISH BETWEEN ORIGINAL CANTERBURIES AND SOME OF THE VERY GOOD REPRODUCTIONS MADE, BUT A LACK OF PATINA AND GENERAL WEAR AND TEAR CAN BE DETECTED ON MODERN REPRODUCTIONS.

● TODAY'S COPIES ARE INVARIABLY OF EARLY TYPES AS IT IS MORE DIFFICULT TO COPY VICTORIAN CARVING.

● IN ALL CASES, QUALITY OF DESIGN IS AS IMPORTANT OF QUALITY OF WORKMANSHIP AND A HARMONY OF STYLE AND PROPORTION IS OFTEN THE BEST GUIDE TO A PIECE'S WORTH.

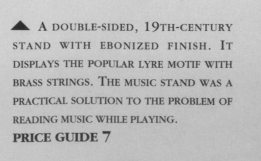

▲ A DOUBLE-SIDED, 19TH-CENTURY STAND WITH EBONIZED FINISH. IT DISPLAYS THE POPULAR LYRE MOTIF WITH BRASS STRINGS. THE MUSIC STAND WAS A PRACTICAL SOLUTION TO THE PROBLEM OF READING MUSIC WHILE PLAYING.

PRICE GUIDE 7

▼ THIS PIECE IS, IN FACT, A MAGAZINE RACK MADE IN BAMBOO AND IT DATES FROM THE EDWARDIAN PERIOD. MANY CANTERBURIES ARE USED TODAY FOR STORING MAGAZINES AND NEWSPAPERS. **PRICE GUIDE 4**

▲ THIS MID-VICTORIAN, WALNUT CANTERBURY WITH LYRE-SHAPED DIVIDERS AND GALLERY ARE ALL RICHLY DECORATED WITH TYPICAL OPEN FRETWORK. DESIGNED TO HOLD SHEET MUSIC, THE CANTERBURY WAS OFTEN KEPT UNDER THE PIANO WHEN NOT IN USE.
PRICE GUIDE 7

▲ THIS WALNUT CANTERBURY FROM THE 1860s IS OF A BASIC DESIGN, WITH BUN FEET TAPERING DOWN TO BRASS CASTORS. THE CASTORS ENABLE THE CANTERBURY TO BE QUICKLY WHEELED TO THE PIANO WHEN A NEW TUNE WAS NEEDED.
PRICE GUIDE 7

▼ THIS WALNUT CANTERBURY DATES FROM THE 1860s. THE ORNATE FRETWORK ON THE DIVIDERS AND THE LOWER DRAWER ALL ADD VALUE. BY THE END OF THE 19TH CENTURY THIS PRACTICAL PIECE OF FURNITURE FEATURED MORE DECORATIVE CARVING.
PRICE GUIDE 7

▲ THIS SPARE, ELEGANT DESIGN IN ROSEWOOD AND MAHOGANY IS TYPICAL OF EARLY CANTERBURIES. THE TOPS OF THE PARTITIONS ARE DIPPED TO MAKE THE MUSIC SHEETS EASIER TO PULL OUT.
PRICE GUIDE 8

▲ THIS SMALL, ROSEWOOD CANTERBURY, WITH ITS DELICATELY-TURNED RAILS AND LEGS AND UNUSUAL BOTTOM SHELF IS FROM ABOUT 1830. THE NAME 'CANTERBURY' IS THOUGHT TO REFER TO AN ARCHBISHOP OF CANTERBURY WHO WAS BELIEVED TO HAVE DEVISED THE ITEM.
PRICE GUIDE 8

was increasingly used for domestic objects. With the advent of steam-powered rolling mills that could produce sheets of the metal, a huge expansion in manufacturing began. As mass production took off many older patterns for brass objects were revived. By the beginning of the 20th century, fire accessories were generally made of brass. Also, a large number of other items were produced in brass at this time for decorative purposes. They ranged from warming pans and oil lamps to horse brasses, hand bells and little brass boxes.

Away from decorative collectable metalware, more practical objects made in the medium have grown in interest to antique collectors. Garden furniture and tools have traditionally been made of metal because exposure to the elements made a hardy material necessary. Many people today prefer to use antique garden accessories as a compliment to their garden or conservatory design. Kitchenware is popular with many buyers and various utensils are available as a feature for a collection. Not all saucepans, kettles or ladles can be used today but their shiny brass and copper surfaces are very pleasing as ornamental additions to the modern kitchen. From gongs to ships fittings, there is a wealth of diverse metalware for the collector.

As with any antique collectable, metal objects need care and attention to preserve their attractive appearance and value, and the different metals have different needs. Silver in daily use may be kept clean by washing in warm soapy water and then rinsed and dried immediately – drips can leave a temporary stain. If attempting to preserve the hallmark on a piece, do not cover the mark with a piece of sticky tape because the adhesive in tape contains a substance that will actually attack the surface of the silver. When storing cutlery, never fasten items together with rubber bands – this can

Unusual in being bronze, rather than silver-plated, this is an example of the famous 'Spirit of Ecstasy' the mascot that sat on the front of Rolls Royce cars.

have much the same effect. Silver should not be rubbed with abrasives to remove salt stains. Such repairs can only be tackled by an experienced silversmith. Some collectors, rather than clean their silver, will have items lacquered, or plated with non-tarnishing rhodium. The first is not advisable because the lacquer deadens the surface of the silver and will discolour it in time. The second is an irreversible process so the antique collector must be sure they want their silver to take on a chrome colouring. The same considerations for cleaning and maintenance should also be taken with plate and electroplate; a good patina can be easily destroyed by rough handling and bad practices, but it can never be recreated.

When cleaning pewter, never use a metal cleaning powder or liquid as these may damage the surface. Stick to warm, soapy water and then dry and polish with a soft chamois or cloth. Bad stains may be removed by gently rubbing with the finest steel wool, dipped in olive oil – the oil will prevent scratching. To clean brass and copper, rub them with a cut raw lemon dipped in fine salt or use a mild polish. Any restoration work should really be tackled by an expert – breakages of metalware are too difficult for the amateur to repair and removing marks or tarnish requires a specialist knowledge of metals and the chemicals of cleaning agents.

Although amongst the more costly of antiques, metalware can be one of the most satisfying of areas for the collector. A wide range of household utensils, ranging from solid silver tureens to garden trowels were made in metal. The very nature of the material means that items will be long lasting, as long as tarnish and wear and tear are guarded against. Sympathetic restoration and careful cleaning and storing will allow the collector to enjoy and appreciate their collection for many years.

▶ THIS SILVER SUGAR BASKET WITH ATTRACTIVE PIERCED DECORATION, HAS A HALLMARK INDICATING THAT IT WAS MADE IN LONDON IN 1769.
PRICE GUIDE 5

▼ THIS ATTRACTIVE PAIR OF TEA CADDIES WERE MADE BY SAMUEL TAYLOR IN 1758. GEORGIAN SILVER TEA ACCESSORIES ARE AMONG THE MOST ATTRACTIVE OF COLLECTABLES.
PRICE GUIDE 8

◀ THIS SILVER SUGAR BOWL IS PART OF A SET WITH THE TEA CADDIES ALSO ILLUSTRATED ON THIS PAGE. ALL THREE PIECES ARE HEAVILY EMBOSSED WITH A DECORATION OF SCROLLS AND FLOWERS.
PRICE GUIDE 8

▼ SUGAR TONGS ARE NOT SCISSOR-LIKE, AS SUGAR NIPS ARE, RATHER, THEY ARE TWO ARMS OF SILVER JOINED AT THE TOP WITH A NECESSARY TENSILE SPRING. THE PAIR AT THE TOP ARE RATHER SHORT AND SQUAT, BUT SIMPLE AND FUNCTIONAL, AND DATE FROM 1814. THE VERY PLAIN PAIR OF SILVER TONGS ON THE LEFT DATE FROM AROUND 1808, THOUGH THE MAKER IS NOT KNOWN. ON THE RIGHT, ARE A PAIR OF LATE REGENCY SUGAR TONGS FROM 1822. THE BOWLS RESEMBLE THOSE FOUND ON SPOONS OF THE PERIOD.
PRICE GUIDE 2

A SILVER PLATE WITH A GADROONED RIM, MADE BY SMITH AND SHARP IN 1787. IT IS ONE OF 12 IDENTICAL PLATES, AND THE PRICE GUIDE GIVEN HERE REFERS TO THE VALUE OF THE SET.
PRICE GUIDE 9

THIS SILVER EGG BOILER, STAND AND HEATER WERE MADE BY EMES AND BERNARD IN 1809. THE BOILER HOLDS FOUR EGGS AND INCOPORATES A USEFUL TIMER ON THE TOP.
PRICE GUIDE 9

A PAIR OF EARLY GEORGE III SILVER WINE COASTERS, WITH VERTICAL SIDES PIERCED WITH SCROLL AND LEAF MOTIFS. THEY WERE MADE BY THOMAS NASH, A SILVERSMITH BASED IN LONDON.
PRICE GUIDE 8

THIS SILVER PEPPER POT WAS MADE BY GEORGE ROUSE IN 1759. IT HAS A PIERCED TOP, BALLON CENTRE AND PEDESTAL BASE. IT WOULD HAVE COME WITH A MATCHING SALT CELLAR.
PRICE GUIDE 7

THIS SILVER SALT CELLAR, WITH A PIERCED DECORATION AND BLUE GLASS LINING, WAS MADE BY THOMAS SHEPHERD IN 1790. IT IS ONE OF A SET OF FOUR SALT CELLARS, AND THE PRICE GUIDE IS FOR THE COMPLETE SET.
PRICE GUIDE 7

THIS SILVER TRUMPET-SHAPED FUNNEL WAS FOR DECANTING WINE. IT WAS MADE IN 1828 BY EMES AND BERNARD. EVEN THE MOST DOMESTIC OF ITEMS COULD BE MADE IN SILVER; THIS PIECE WOULD HAVE BEEN USED BY THE BUTLER ALONE.
PRICE GUIDE 7

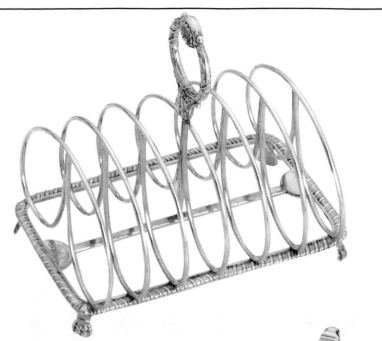

▲ MADE BY WILLIAM SHARP, THIS SILVER TOAST-RACK IS DATED 1818. IT HAS A GADROONED BORDER, LION'S PAW FEET, AND A HANDLE WITH LEAF AND SCROLL MOULDING. THE CENTRAL STRUT AT THE BASE WOULD HAVE PREVENTED THE TOAST FALLING THROUGH.
PRICE GUIDE 7

▼ DESIGNED BY THOMAS WHIPHAM, THIS SILVER SOUP TUREEN IS DATED 1748. IT HAS SPLAYED FEET, DECORATIVE REEDED BORDERS, AND ORNATE HANDLES. A FAMILY CREST IS ENGRAVED ON THE LID.
PRICE GUIDE 9

▲ THIS SILVER MUSTARD POT BY ROBERT HENNELL WAS MADE IN 1789. THE OVAL-SHAPED BODY HAS PIERCED DECORATION, AND THERE IS A BALL FINIAL ON THE LID. A SMALL NOTCH IS CUT AWAY IN THE LID FOR THE SPOON'S HANDLE.
PRICE GUIDE 7

▲ SHEFFIELD PLATE WAS ESTABLISHED IN 1743, WHEN IT WAS DISCOVERED THAT A SHEET OF SILVER AND ANOTHER OF COPPER, WHEN FUSED TOGETHER, COULD BE WORKED AS A SINGLE METAL.
PRICE GUIDE 8

▲ THIS UNMARKED, TWO-BOTTLE DECANTER WAGON, IN PLATE, DATES FROM C.1820. THE COASTERS HAVE CONVEX SPIRAL FLUTES AND BOLD GADROON SHELL AND ACANTHUS MOUNTS APPLIED TO THEIR TOP SURFACES.
PRICE GUIDE 7

▶ ONE OF A SET OF FOUR NEO-CLASSICAL CANDLESTICKS THIS PIECE DATES FROM 1775. THE BASE IS DECORATED WITH DOLPHINS, AND A VINE WINDS ITS WAY ROUND THE STEM OF THE COLUMN. THE PRICE IS FOR THE WHOLE SET.
PRICE GUIDE 8

▼ ONE OF A PAIR, THIS SHEFFIELD PLATE OVAL SAUCE BOAT HAS A BEADED RIM, A DOUBLE SCROLLING BEADED HANDLE, AND THREE BOLD HOOF AND LEAF FEET. THE PRICE GUIDE GIVEN HERE IS FOR THE PAIR.
PRICE GUIDE 7

▶ THIS UNMARKED, TWO-HANDLED SHEFFIELD PLATE TRAY IS FROM 1770. THERE IS AN ENGRAVED CREST IN THE CENTER, AND THE EDGE IS CHASED WITH A SLANTING GADROON BORDER. THERE ARE ROPE-LIKE HANDLES THAT MATCH THE GADROON BORDER.
PRICE GUIDE 5

▼ ONE OF A SET OF FOUR SWEETMEAT
DISHES, THIS WAS MADE IN 1795 BY PITTS
AND PREEDY. A CUT GLASS DISH SITS ON A
PLATE STAND WITH ELEGANT LEAF MOTIFS
AND SPLAYED FEET. THE PRICE GUIDE IS
FOR THE SET OF FOUR.
PRICE GUIDE 9

▲ THIS ÉPERGNE, OF C.1825, CONSISTS
OF CUT GLASS DISHES SUPPORTED BY A
HEAVY SHEFFIELD PLATE STAND. THE
BOWLS WOULD HAVE BEEN FOR FRUIT,
NUTS AND SWEETMEATS.
PRICE GUIDE 8

▼ THIS TOAST-RACK DATES FROM THE 1930S. IT HAS A HEATING TRAY UNDERNEATH THAT WOULD HAVE HELPED KEEP THE TOAST WARM DURING LONG BREAKFASTS OF MANY COURSES.
PRICE GUIDE 4

▲ THIS ELEGANT STAND WOULD HAVE HELD A SODA SIPHON FOR MAKING COCKTAILS. IT DATES FROM THE 1930S AND HAS MACHINE-TURNED DECORATION AROUND ITS BASE.
PRICE GUIDE 4

▲ THIS 1930S EPNS FRUIT BOWL HAS A RATHER TRADITIONAL FEEL. THE SCALLOPED EDGE IS A MODERNIZED AND STREAMLINED VERSION OF A DECORATIVE FEATURE SEEN IN EARLIER SILVER.
PRICE GUIDE 4

▲ CONDIMENT SETS WERE ALSO MADE IN EPNS. THESE INITIALS STOOD FOR ELECTROPLATED NICKEL SILVER; A NEW PROCESS OF PLATING SILVER THAT APPEARED IN THE 1840S. THESE TWIN OCTAGONAL SALT AND PEPPER POTS ARE A FINE EXAMPLES.
PRICE GUIDE 2

◀ THIS VERY PLAIN 1930S EPNS SAUCE BOAT WAS FOR SERVING GRAVY AT THE DINNER TABLE, AND WOULD HAVE BEEN PART OF A COMPLETE ELECTROPLATED DINNER SERVICE.
PRICE GUIDE 3

▶ MUFFINS WOULD HAVE BEEN SERVED AT TEATIME IN THIS CIRCULAR COVERED DISH. DECORATION IS MINIMAL, IN KEEPING WITH MODERNIST TASTE IN THE 1930S.
PRICE GUIDE 3

▲ EPNS CUTLERY CAME IN A VARIETY OF SHAPES, INCLUDING THOSE BASED ON TRADITIONAL SILVER DESIGNS, SO THAT THEY COULD COMPLEMENT BOTH HISTORICAL AND MODERN STYLES OF CUTLERY AND DINNER SERVICES.
PRICE GUIDE 1

▲ THIS EPNS MEAT DISH IS BOTH DECORATIVE AND FUNCTIONAL. IT HAS A RIM ORNAMENTED WITH VINES AND ORNATE FEET. DRAINAGE CHANNELS RUN ALONG THE DISH FOR THE MEAT JUICES.
PRICE GUIDE 5

▼ THIS VEGETABLE TUREEN OF THE 1930s IS THOROUGHLY MODERN WITH ITS CLEAN, SIMPLE LINES AND NO ADDITIONAL ADORNMENT. A SNUG-FITTING LID KEPT THE FOOD WARM.
PRICE GUIDE 3

▶ THE FUNCTION OF THIS LITTLE DISH IS GIVEN AWAY BY ITS DECORATIVE HANDLE IN THE SHAPE OF A FISH. IT WAS USED FOR SARDINES − HENCE ITS SMALL SIZE.
PRICE GUIDE 3

POINTS TO WATCH

• BEFORE BUYING ANY PLATE, EXAMINE THE ARTICLE FOR WEAR, ESPECIALLY ALONG ANY EDGES OR AT THE MAIN CONTACT POINT; FOR INSTANCE, CLOSE TO A FORK'S TINES, WHERE IT HAS BEEN SCRAPED BY A KNIFE.

• CHECK FOR REPAIR WORK BY GENTLY RUNNING A FINGERNAIL OVER ANY SUSPECT AREAS.

DESIGN FEATURES

This 1930s Art Deco tureen successfully blends elements of style from two different eras. Its boat-shape harks back to silver tureens of the 18th century, but its severe angularity and almost total absence of excess decoration also relate it to modern, Deco designs.

The large handles are in a modernistic, geometric style. The lid is trimmed with an octagonal finial that mirrors the shape of the piece and decoration is confined to the raised borders.

▼ This unusual-looking lidded pot, with its strangely positioned handle, dates from the 1930s. This kind of pot would have been used for pouring hot milk into coffee.
PRICE GUIDE 3

▶ Although the octagonal shape of this EPNS coffee pot is reminiscent of 18th-century designs, it is made from modern materials – EPNS and fibre – and dates from the 1930s.
PRICE GUIDE 3

◀ Both these milk jug and sugar bowl are from the same 1920s tea or coffee set. The shapes are pleasingly plain and simple. High quality EPNS is as pleasingly brilliant as silver but only cost a quarter of the price when it was made.
PRICE GUIDE 3

▼ THIS 1930S CHROME-PLATED
SAMOVAR HAS A RING ON TOP TO HOLD A
SMALL TEAPOT. A SAMOVAR IS A RUSSIAN
TEA-URN THAT IS HEATED BY CHARCOAL IN
A TUBE THAT PASSES THROUGH IT. THE
PRICE OF THIS PIECE WOULD BE HIGHER IF
IT WERE ELECTROPLATED.
PRICE GUIDE 5

▲ THIS FOUR-PIECE TEA SET DATES FROM
THE 1920S AND WAS INSPIRED BY THE
DESIGNS OF CHRISTOPHER DRESSER. IT
CONSISTS OF A LARGE TEA KETTLE WITH
SWING HANDLE, A TEAPOT, MILK JUG AND
SUGAR BOWL. THE HANDLES OF THE TEA
KETTLE ARE IN IVORY AND THE INSIDES OF
THE JUG AND BOWL ARE GILT.
PRICE GUIDE 6

▶ THIS SMALL GILT VINAIGRETTE IS DATED 1838. THE SIDES ARE LINED WITH CHASED EDGES AND THE PIERCED GRILLE IS DECORATED WITH A PATTERN OF SCROLLS AND FLOWERS.

PRICE GUIDE 3

▲ A RECTANGULAR VINAIGRETTE WITH CUT CORNERS, c.1818. IT WAS MADE BY THE WELL-KNOWN BIRMINGHAM SILVERSMITH, SAMUEL PEMBERTON. THE PIERCING OF THE STAR GRILLE IS RELATIVELY SIMPLE IN STYLE.

PRICE GUIDE 5

▲ THIS OVAL VINAIGRETTE IN FROSTED SILVER WAS MADE IN 1869. THE TOP OF THE BOX IS PLAIN WHILE THE BASE HAS A STUD-LIKE DECORATION. THE GRILLE IS WORKED IN AN ATTRACTIVE PIERCED SCROLL DESIGN.

PRICE GUIDE 5

◀ A PLAIN SILVER RECTANGULAR VINAIGRETTE WITH STEPPED SIDES AND THE INITIALS 'B.B.' ENGRAVED ON THE TOP. DATED ABOUT 1809, THERE IS A RADIATING, LEAF-PIERCED GRILLE INSIDE.

PRICE GUIDE 4

▼ THIS RECTANGULAR VINAIGRETTE IN SILVER, WAS MADE IN ABOUT 1836. THE LID IS EMBOSSED WITH A PLAQUE OF NEWSTEAD ABBEY AND THE CONVEX SIDES ARE DECORATED WITH FLOWERS. THE GRILLE ALSO INCORPORATES FLOWERS AND SCROLL PATTERNS.
PRICE GUIDE 5

▶ THIS HANDSOME SILVER VINAIGRETTE, C.1841, HAS AN ENGRAVED TOP AND REEDED SIDES. LIFTING UP THE LID REVEALS A SCROLL-DECORATED GRILLE SURROUNDED BY FORMAL LEAF MOTIFS.
PRICE GUIDE 5

▼ THIS SILVER VINAIGRETTE HAS CUT CORNERS AND A TOP ENGRAVED WITH CRISS-CROSS LINES ENCLOSING ENGRAVED ROUNDELS. MADE IN 1809 BY MATTHEW LINWOOD, THE INSIDE REVEALS A PIERCED GRILLE WITH A FLORAL MOTIF.
PRICE GUIDE 4

▲ THOUGHT TO HAVE BEEN MADE IN 1810, THIS IS A GEORGE III OBLONG VINAIGRETTE WITH ROUNDED CORNERS. THE COVER IS ENGRAVED WITH A CLOUD-LIKE MOTIF AND THE SIDES AND BASE ARE DECORATED WITH DOTTED LINES.
PRICE GUIDE 4

▲ THIS CIRCULAR GOLD VINAIGRETTE WAS MADE IN ABOUT 1840. IT IS SHAPED LIKE A WATCH WITH THE SIDES EDGED WITH A BORDER OF SCROLLS AND FLOWER HEADS. VINAIGRETTES WERE DESIGNED SO THAT SWEET-SMELLING SPICES COULD BE CARRIED ON THE PERSON.
PRICE GUIDE 6

DESIGN FEATURES

THIS ELABORATE PIECE IN ART NOUVEAU STYLE INCORPORATES MANY OF THE DECORATIVE FEATURES OF THE WÜRTTEMBERGISCHE METALWAREN FABRIK FACTORY'S WORK. THERE ARE NO STRAIGHT LINES, EVERYTHING IS CURVED. SWIRLING SPAGHETTI-LIKE LINES, WHICH IN THIS PIECE REPRESENT STRANDS OF WATER WEED AND RIPPLES IN WATER, ARE VERY TYPICAL OF WMF. HERE THE LINES ARE PICKED UP IN THE DESIGN OF THE HANDLES AND THE WOMAN'S DRESS.

THE FLOWERS, ESPECIALLY THOSE AT LEFT, RECUR IN MANY ART NOUVEAU PIECES. THE YOUNG LADY AT THE CENTRE, HERE HOLDING A NOTEPAD AND PEN MADE IN CONTRASTING COPPER, IS ANOTHER RECURRENT FEATURE OF ART NOUVEAU. EVEN THE FORM OF THE DISH IS ATTRACTIVELY CURVED IN SHAPE RATHER THAN PURELY FUNCTIONAL IN LINE.

THIS PEWTER DISH MIGHT HAVE BEEN USED PURELY DECORATIVELY OR TO HOLD SWEETS OR OTHER DELICACIES. IT WAS PRODUCED AROUND 1900.

GERMANY WAS VERY MUCH A CENTRE FOR ORNATE ART NOUVEAU METAL WORK AND ALTHOUGH WMF, FOUNDED IN 1864, IS THE BEST KNOWN, THERE WERE MANY OTHER FIRMS AT WORK.

◀ AN UNUSUAL TUREEN IN PEWTER, WITH A LID IN THE SHAPE OF AN OLD HELMET. IT HAS A PARTICULARLY LARGE, PRACTICAL HANDLE. MADE IN 1904, THE TUREEN WAS DESIGN BY ARCHIBOLD KNOX AND WAS INITIALLY SOLD IN LIBERTY'S.
PRICE GUIDE 6

▶ MADE IN 1892, THIS SILVER JUG WITH LID WAS MADE BY ELKINGTON. THE CRUCIFIX ON THE TOP OF THE LID SUGGESTS IT MAY HAVE BEEN FOR CHURCH USE – MAYBE IT WOULD HAVE HELD COMMUNAL WINE.
PRICE GUIDE 6

▼THIS SINGLE CANDLESTICK HAS THREE CURVING STEMS COMING UP FROM A CIRCULAR BASE. MADE OF PEWTER, IT IS ONE OF ARCHIBALD KNOX'S DESIGNS FOR LIBERTY, THE LONDON STORE.
PRICE GUIDE 6

▲ A WALL CLOCK IN PEWTER FROM LIBERTY'S, MADE IN 1905. AT THE TURN OF THE CENTURY, LIBERTY'S WERE PRODUCING EXCELLENT PEWTER ARTIFACTS IN THEIR TUDRIC RANGE, LARGELY DESIGNED BY ARCHIBALD KNOX.
PRICE GUIDE 8

▲ A HIGHLY DECORATED ART NOUVEAU SWEET BARREL, MADE BY WMF AT THE TURN OF THE CENTURY. THE INITIALS WMF STOOD FOR WÜRTTEMBERGISCHE METALWAREN FABRIK, A GERMAN MAKER OF JUGENDSTIL METALWARE. THIS PIECE IS IN PEWTER AND ETCHED GREEN GLASS, A WMF SPECIALITY.
PRICE GUIDE 7

◀ A DOUBLE SWEET DISH IN PEWTER, WITH AN ART NOUVEAU FIGURE RISING FROM THE CENTRE. IT WAS PRODUCED BY WMF, IN GERMANY, AT THE TURN OF THE CENTURY.
PRICE GUIDE 6

▲ A SET OF VICTORIAN KITCHEN SCALES WITH ROUND BRASS TRAY AND SOLID BRASS WEIGHTS. SUCH EXAMPLES, THOUGH POPULAR TODAY, CAN BE SURPRISINGLY COSTLY IN ANTIQUE SHOPS.
PRICE GUIDE 5

▲ DECORATIVE CAST-IRON SCALES IN GOOD CONDITION ARE POPULAR IN TODAY'S KITCHENS. OF THOSE FOUND WITH ORIGINAL WEIGHTS, MANY CONTINUE TO BE SERVICEABLE IN BAKING AND COOKING, AS WELL AS ORNAMENTAL.
PRICE GUIDE 5

▲ A LONG-HANDLED LADLE KEPT THE HANDS CLEAR OF SCALDING STEAM AND WAS IDEAL FOR USE WITH UTENSILS SUCH AS THIS HEAVY, BRASS PRESERVING PAN.
PRICE GUIDE 3 & 5

▲ A LARGE, 19TH-CENTURY, ALL-COPPER KETTLE OF OVAL DESIGN WITH A SOLID FIXED HANDLE AND TYPICAL SERPENTINE SPOUT. A LARGE KETTLE SUCH AS THIS ONE WOULD HAVE SAT ON THE VICTORIAN RANGE ALL DAY, TO PROVIDE A CONSTANT SUPPLY OF HOT WATER.
PRICE GUIDE 4

▲ A HIGH-HANDLED, SQUAT-BODIED EDWARDIAN KETTLE WITH A FIXED ALL-COPPER HANDLE. THE HEMISPHERICAL DESIGN WAS POPULAR.
PRICE GUIDE 5

▶ TRIVETS KEPT KETTLES AND OTHER POTS AND PANS WARM IN FRONT OF THE FIRE. THE ONE WITH TRIPOD LEGS IS FREE-STANDING AND IS ADJUSTABLE. THE OTHER, MORE COMMON TYPES HANG FROM THE BARS OF THE FIRE GRATE.
PRICE GUIDE 1 – 2

▶ THIS POLISHED, CAST-IRON UMBRELLA STAND BEARS A VICTORIAN REGISTRATION MARK ON THE REVERSE, DATING IT TO AROUND 1860. PIECES SUCH AS THIS WOULD HAVE STOOD IN HALLS AND VESTIBULES FOR VISITORS AND RESIDENTS TO PLACE THEIR DRIPPING UMBRELLAS IN.
PRICE GUIDE 5

▼ TWO TURN-OF-THE-CENTURY BOOT SCRAPERS − ONE PAN AND ONE GRID. THESE WOULD HAVE STOOD JUST BY THE FRONT AND BACK DOORS, EITHER INSIDE OR OUT, SO THAT MUD COULD BE SCRAPED FROM BOOTS AND SHOES RATHER THAN WALKED INTO THE HOUSE.
PRICE GUIDE 3

▼ THIS HAND-COLOURED MR. PUNCH IS A DOOR STOP. SUCH PIECES CAN OFTEN BE FOUND WITH THEIR PAIR − JUDY − SINCE THEY WERE MADE IN CONSIDERABLE NUMBERS DURING THE 19TH CENTURY. HIS HAT SERVED AS A CARRYING HANDLE.
PRICE GUIDE 5

▶ THIS SUPERB STEEL PAN-STAND, COMPLETE WITH A SET OF GRADUATED COPPER PANS, WOULD HAVE HAD PRIDE OF PLACE IN A VICTORIAN KITCHEN.
PRICE GUIDE 8

POINTS TO WATCH

- ANTIQUE BATH FITTINGS HAVE BECOME VERY POPULAR FOR INTERIOR DECORATION. REPRODUCTIONS ARE VERY COMMON.
- LOOK AT THE CONDITION OF ENAMEL ON BATHS. IF VERY CHIPPED IT WILL NEED PROFESSIONAL ATTENTION.
- AVOID PAINT-COATED BATHS. SUCCESSIVE LAYERS OF PAINT OFTEN CONCEAL RUST.
- CHECK TAP FITTINGS FOR SIGNS OF METAL CORROSION.
- RUST STAINS CAN EASILY BE REMOVED WITH A WIRE BRUSH.

▼ A BATH SOAP AND LOOFAH RACK, THAT WAS DESIGNED TO GO ACROSS THE BATH. MADE OF BRASS, THIS RACK HAS BOTH THE ORIGINAL SOAP TRAYS SURVIVING. THESE ARE RIDGED AND DETACHABLE FOR CLEANING.
PRICE GUIDE 3

▼ ONE OF THE EARLIEST SYLES OF VICTORIAN BRASS BATH TAPS. ALTHOUGH ONLY HOT AND COLD ARE MARKED ON THE PORCELAIN DISCS, THESE ARE RARE FINDS.
PRICE GUIDE 4

▼ A VICTORIAN BRASS SOAP-HOLDER THAT SCREWS INTO THE WALL BESIDE THE BATH. THE HOLDER SWINGS OUT FROM ITS FRAME TO EMPTY COLLECTED WATER AND TO EASE CLEANING IN GENERAL.
PRICE GUIDE 4

◄ A PAIR OF BRASS HOT AND COLD WATER TAPS. THE TAPS ARE TOPPED WITH PROCELAIN DISCS, MARKING WHICH TAP IS WHICH. THE NAME AND PLACE OF THE MANUFACTURER IS ALSO MARKED.
PRICE GUIDE 3

▲ A BRASS SHOWER FITTING WITH SAUCER-SHAPED SHOWER HEAD AND SEPARATE HOT AND COLD WATER TAPS. THE WALL PIPE AND SHOWER HEAD ARE MADE OF COPPER.
PRICE GUIDE 3

◀ A VICTORIAN HIP BATH MADE FROM TIN WHERE THE METAL HAS BEEN PAINTED TO MAKE IT MORE ATTRACTIVE. NOTE THE ARM RESTS THAT WOULD HAVE HELPED THE BATHER GET OUT OF A BATH THAT WOULD HAVE BEEN SET ON THE FLOOR.
PRICE GUIDE 5

▼ THIS DELICATE STRUCTURE IS A WIREWORK JARDINIERE. RUST SHOWS ON THOSE AREAS WHERE THE PROTECTIVE PAINTWORK HAS PEELED – METAL PIECES, UNCARED FOR, CAN BE PRONE TO RUST.
PRICE GUIDE 6

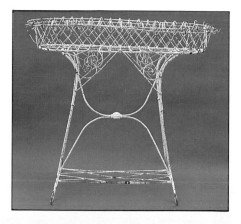

▼ THIS CAST-IRON CHAIR HAS A WOODEN SEAT AND BACK. THE IRONWORK DESIGN SEEN HERE WAS COMMONLY FOUND ON MUNICIPAL PARK AND GARDEN BENCHES.
PRICE GUIDE 7

▲ THIS PAINTED WATERING CAN HAS BRASS TRIMMINGS BUT NO ROSE ATTACHMENT FOR THE SPOUT. DESPITE BEING A VICTORIAN PIECE, THE DESIGN OF THE WATERING CAN HAS CHANGED VERY LITTLE OVER THE YEARS.
PRICE GUIDE 3

▲ THIS SET OF HAND FORK, TROWEL AND SHEARS ALL HAVE POLISHED WOOD HANDLES, WORN BY YEARS OF USE. PIECES SUCH AS THESE ARE OFTEN MADE OF METALS THAT CAN CORRODE AND SHOULD BE PROTECTED BY A THIN LAYER OF OIL.
PRICE GUIDE 3

◀ A MARBLE-TOPPED GARDEN TABLE WITH CAST-IRON AND LYRE-SHAPED SUPPORTS. THE LEGS ARE CAST INTO ORNATE SCROLL PATTERNS. THE EDGE OF THE MARBLE TABLE-TOP IS SCALLOPED.
PRICE GUIDE 7

▶ THIS LARGE RECTANGULAR PORTHOLE FROM AROUND 1930 HAS A BRASS FRAME WHICH WAS SCREWED TO THE WALL. ITS REINFORCED GLASS WINDOW WAS NOT INTENDED TO BE OPENED.
PRICE GUIDE 6

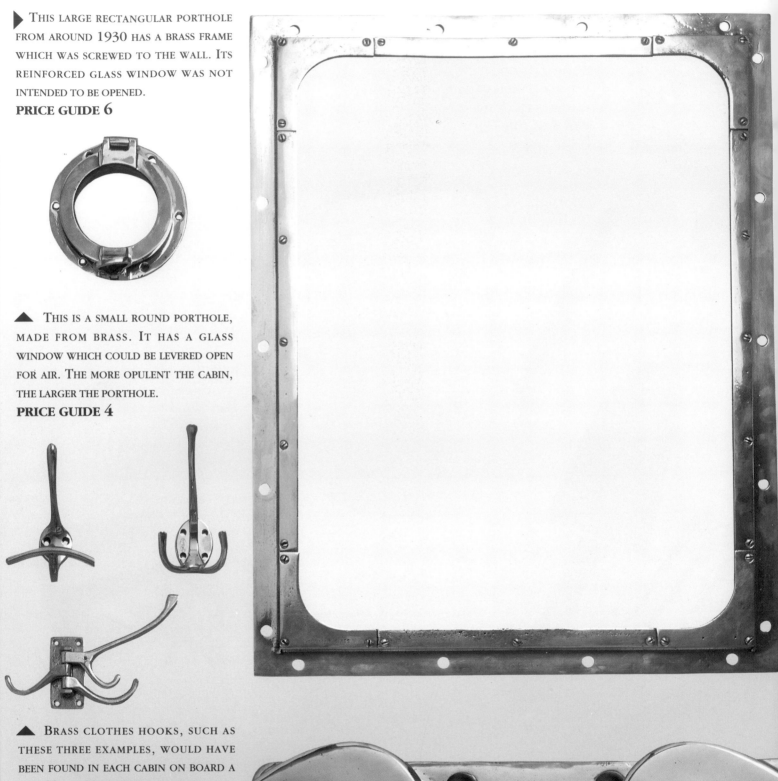

▲ THIS IS A SMALL ROUND PORTHOLE, MADE FROM BRASS. IT HAS A GLASS WINDOW WHICH COULD BE LEVERED OPEN FOR AIR. THE MORE OPULENT THE CABIN, THE LARGER THE PORTHOLE.
PRICE GUIDE 4

▲ BRASS CLOTHES HOOKS, SUCH AS THESE THREE EXAMPLES, WOULD HAVE BEEN FOUND IN EACH CABIN ON BOARD A SHIP. THE PRICE IS FOR EACH HOOK.
PRICE GUIDE 2

▶ A BRASS BOLLARD, MADE IN THE 1930s. ITS FUNCTION WAS FOR TETHERING ROPES IN A FIGURE OF EIGHT FORM. CERTAIN PIECES OF BRASS FITTINGS CAN FETCH GOOD PRICES, ESPECIALLY WITH COLLECTORS WITH SPECIALIST INTERESTS.
PRICE GUIDE 7

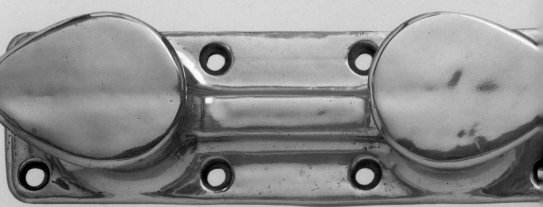

GLASS

The fragility of glass makes it a particularly specialist area for antique collectors. Not only must a collection be protected and cherished, good, undamaged pieces will also be hard to find. Any hand-made glass will fetch a very high price but even early pieces of mass-produced glass can be quite expensive. Much glass was made for use at the table and great pleasure can be found in laying a modern table setting with antique glasses. However, it is certainly advisable to protect glass collectables by reserving their use for special occasions only and it is worthwhile investing in some sort of display case to keep treasured pieces out of dust, and harm's, way.

One of the most common ways of decorating plain glass is by cutting into it to make different facets that catch the light in much the same way that cut gems do. Of necessity, cut glass is made of the thickest material and so can be quite durable. Other techniques of decoration include etched, coloured and moulded glass. During the 19th century, increases in international trade and developments in glass manufacture meant that a wide range of different glasses, jugs and decanters appeared on dinner tables. Mid-Victorian glass is characterized by a great increase in etched ware. Acid etching had been used for some time but only in the 1850s did it become manufactured on a large scale. Glass could also be coloured and purple was one of the commoner colours, though browns, greens, blues and reds are also found. One outstanding design development used coloured glass – a thick glass overlay, usually of a strong colour, was carved away to reveal the clear glass underneath. But the most important advance of this period was the rapid development of press moulding, a technique that was first practised on a large scale in America. The great possibilities of pressed glass meant that it soon became used for all kinds of decorative and practical glassware since shapes varying from sphinxes to fruit baskets could be created.

Despite all the developments in glass manufacture, traditional cut glass remained the most popular for tableware. Heavy mitre cutting was common and these bold shapes were sometimes further decorated with engraving. Deep mitre cutting had become viable due to the use of steam-powered machinery. The removal of excise duty on the weight of glass led to very heavy table glass coming in during the 1850s and 1860s. To compete with cut glass, pressed glass was fire-polished to give some brilliance, but genuine cut glass was, and is, still the preferred glass tableware.

There is such a large range of Victorian glass available that collectors should specialize, either in a particular style of glass, or a theme, such as decanters or sherry glasses. Inexperienced collectors may have some trouble distinguishing a genuine Victorian piece from a later piece made in a Victorian style. The serious enthusiast would be well advised to visit museums and specialist dealers in order to become familiar with the wide range of shapes, colours and decorations prevalent in Victorian glassware.

Victorian blown glass rarely had any identifiable markings. Cheaper pressed glass, however, was marked with a patent office 'lozenge' or registration mark between 1842 and 1883, and individual factories had their own particular impressed mark. Dates of glasses can be roughly estimated by the presence or absence of a pontil mark. This mark is simply a small lump of glass on the base, to which an iron rod or 'pontil' was attached and which the blower held while decorating the piece. Few glasses or decanters after 1850 had this mark – generally, there was just a small hollow where the mark was ground out,

With a solid base and a sturdy stem, this heavy, crystal drinking glass bears an engraved 'N', for Napoleon, surmounted by the French Imperial crown.

was just a small hollow where the mark was ground out, so its presence may indcate a forgery.

When collecting glass, one of the biggest problems is in deciding whether a piece is genuine or a fake. Style is the all-important guide, so it is vital to look at items in shops, museums and catalogues before buying. Contemporary catalogues and magazines are an excellent guide to what was fashionable at the time and these can be bought from dealers or even found in local libraries; good research can pay off for the committed collector. Glassware has an inbuilt rarity factor owing to its fragility and so will always be sought after. Odd glasses displayed randomly will not look particularly interesting so it is always a good idea to try and specialize and to go for matching sets rather than individual pieces. A period, glass-lined display cabinet will set off a collection very well, for instance, a genuine 1920s or 1930s cocktail cabinet.

At the cheaper end of the price scale comes those ornamental glass artefacts produced for the mass market. Pressed glass was produced in imitation of cut glass, though it sold for a fraction of the price, and it had the added attraction of coming in a variety of colours. Particularly striking is Carnival glass, mostly produced in America, where extraordinarily brilliant and iridescent colours were added to pressed glass. These effects were produced by spraying pieces while still hot with a solution of metal oxide. Manufacturers also played with the shapes of their ware, stretching and pulling at pieces when they came out of their moulds. Pressed glass was made in a cast iron mould which had the surface decoration of the piece cut into its inside surface. White-hot, semi-fluid glass was thrust into the mould and a plunger was then pressed into the glass to force it into the mould. This was immediately opened to allow the half-cooled, red-hot piece to be lifted out and

This Jungendstil glass vase is decorated in a swirling lustre pattern that was achieved by coating the glass in metal oxides and then heating it in a furnace.

held at the mouth of the furnace for a few moments to be fire-polished. The variety of shapes and colours that soon became available make this glass a particularly rewarding area for the glass collector today and since this was once the poor-man's glass, prices are more easily affordable.

When buying any glass it is best to avoid damaged pieces since any cracks or knocks will weaken the item considerably and it may break totally. It is possible to have small chips polished out by an expert, though if the chip is too deep, the damaged portion will have to be ground down considerably and the height of the piece will alter. Small chips can be repaired at home by using a diamond file available from specialist suppliers. Heavily cut glass is susceptible to this kind of damage and it is advisable to check a piece before buying by running a finger round the rim and over the cut decoration. Any defects in the glass or the design can mean a cheaper buy and sometimes add to the character of the piece. But only experience and handling of good pieces will enable the collector to spot a bad example or a bad buy.

The glass collection should, naturally, be handled with care and it is a good idea to wash pieces thoroughly every once in a while rather than dust regularly which can result in accidental breakages. Some methylated spirits can help with cleaning glass but it should then be washed in plain soap and water – never in a dishwasher. A little jewellers rouge on a cloth or chamois leather when polishing can give glass an added sparkle. The inside of decanters can be damaged by condensation so when washing it is vital to dry items carefully either with tissues or soft cloth, or with a hair dryer on a low setting. If these tips are followed and great care is taken in use or display, then collectors

▼ THIS VICTORIAN PORT GLASS (LEFT) IS A COPY OF AN EARLIER 18TH-CENTURY DESIGN. IT IS DELICATELY ENGRAVED WITH A CREST AND IS SUPPORTED BY AN ELEGANT, FACETED STEM.
PRICE GUIDE 4

▼ THIS PORT GLASS (BOTTOM) WAS PRODUCED IN 1890 AND HAS A CUP-SHAPED BOWL WITH A FINELY-CUT STEM AND BASE. THE ENGRAVING AROUND THE RIM SHOWS A RIBBON DESIGN.
PRICE GUIDE 2

▲ THIS SIMPLY-DESIGNED TANTALUS, DATING FROM THE EARLY 1900S, IS MADE IN MAHOGANY AND SILVER AND CONTAINS THREE HOBNAIL CUT CRYSTAL DECANTERS WITH MANY-FACETED BALL STOPPERS. THE WOODEN BASE MOUNTS AND HANDLE ARE FASHIONED IN ELECTROPLATED SILVER.
PRICE GUIDE 7

◀ THIS CUT GLASS DECANTER DATES FROM 1850 AND HAS THE HIGHLY ELABORATE PATTERNS AND HEAVILY DECORATED STOPPER THAT WERE TYPICAL OF MANY VICTORIAN PIECES PRODUCED THEN.
PRICE GUIDE 5

◀ MADE IN 1870, THIS PORT GLASS IS A VICTORIAN IMITATION OF AN 18TH-CENTURY DESIGN. THE OPAQUE, TWIST PATTERN SEEN ON THE STEM WAS VERY POPULAR IN ENGLAND FROM 1760 ONWARDS AND OFTEN INCORPORATED COLOURED STRANDS.
PRICE GUIDE 3

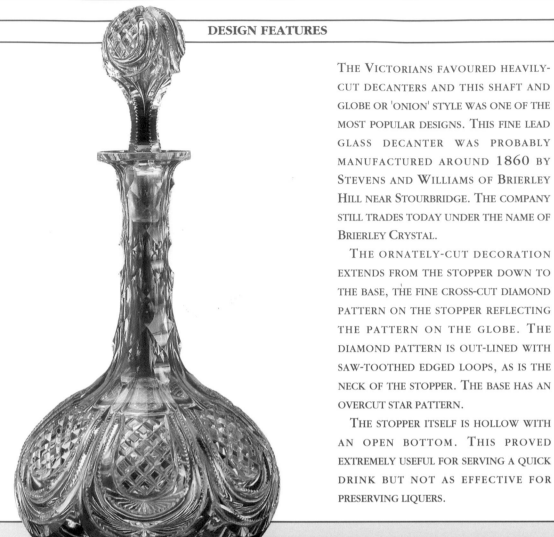

DESIGN FEATURES

THE VICTORIANS FAVOURED HEAVILY-CUT DECANTERS AND THIS SHAFT AND GLOBE OR 'ONION' STYLE WAS ONE OF THE MOST POPULAR DESIGNS. THIS FINE LEAD GLASS DECANTER WAS PROBABLY MANUFACTURED AROUND 1860 BY STEVENS AND WILLIAMS OF BRIERLEY HILL NEAR STOURBRIDGE. THE COMPANY STILL TRADES TODAY UNDER THE NAME OF BRIERLEY CRYSTAL.

THE ORNATELY-CUT DECORATION EXTENDS FROM THE STOPPER DOWN TO THE BASE, THE FINE CROSS-CUT DIAMOND PATTERN ON THE STOPPER REFLECTING THE PATTERN ON THE GLOBE. THE DIAMOND PATTERN IS OUT-LINED WITH SAW-TOOTHED EDGED LOOPS, AS IS THE NECK OF THE STOPPER. THE BASE HAS AN OVERCUT STAR PATTERN.

THE STOPPER ITSELF IS HOLLOW WITH AN OPEN BOTTOM. THIS PROVED EXTREMELY USEFUL FOR SERVING A QUICK DRINK BUT NOT AS EFFECTIVE FOR PRESERVING LIQUERS.

▶ A LATE VICTORIAN CUT-GLASS CLARET JUG WITH A HALLMARKED SILVER LID. THE LID, WHOSE LEVER IS JUST VISIBLE, SITS WITHIN THE SPOUT, KEEPING DUST OFF THE WINE.

PRICE GUIDE 7

▶ AN ATTRACTIVE EXAMPLE OF A CASED-GLASS WINE DECANTER IN THE SHAPE OF A WINE BOTTLE. ITS GLASS-TOPPED CORK STOPPER IS SILVER-MOUNTED.
PRICE GUIDE 5

▼ A FLASHED WINE DECANER WITH A MUSHROOM STOPPER, A HOOPED NECK AND GRAPE AND VINELEAF DECORATION. THE CLEAR GLASS WAS DIPPED INTO MOLTEN RED GLASS AND THE DESIGN WAS THEN CUT OUT TO REVEAL THE CLEAR GLASS BENEATH.
PRICE GUIDE 5

◀ A WINE DECANTER WITH A CUT-GLASS NECK AND ENGRAVED VINELEAF DECORATIONS ON THE BODY. THE STOPPER HAS BEEN MOULD-BLOWN. DECANTERS BECAME USED WHEN WINE WAS DECANTED FROM CASKS IN ORDER TO LEAVE THE SEDIMENT BEHIND.
PRICE GUIDE 5

POINTS TO WATCH

- LOOK OVER THE GLASS CAREFULLY – CRACKS ARE OFTEN CONCEALED BY THE DEEP FACETING AND BRILLIANT CUTTING, AND RELIEF DIAMONDS ARE PRONE TO CHIPPING.
- CHECK THE RIMS OF WINE GLASSES. IF THEY ARE TOO FLAT AND STRAIGHT THEY MAY HAVE BEEN GROUND DOWN TO ELIMINATE CHIPS.
- THE STOPPER SHOULD FIT THE DECANTER PERFECTLY AS EACH WAS GROUND INDIVIDUALLY TO ENSURE AN AIRTIGHT SEAL. A LOOSE STOPPER IS NOT ORIGINAL.

▼ A SIMPLY DESIGNED WATER GOBLET (LEFT) WITH CUT INDENTATIONS ON THE GLOBULAR BOWL. THE WAISTED, HOLLOW GLASS STEM – BLOWN FROM A SECTION OF GLASS ROD – IS TOPPED AND TAILED WITH SLIM BALUSTERS OF SOLID GLASS.
PRICE GUIDE 3

▲ A LARGE WINE GLASS DESIGNED FOR DRINKING RED BURGUNDY. THE TALL, OVOID BOWL RESTS ON A THICK, FACETED, CUT-GLASS STEM AND A SOLID FOOT. THE HEAVINESS OF THE GLASS COMBINED WITH THE BOWL'S LOW CENTRE OF GRAVITY ENSURES STABILITY.
PRICE GUIDE 3

▲ A THIN AND MORE DELICATE DESIGN OF BURGUNDY GLASS WITH A GLOBULAR BOWL ON A SLIM STEM ABOVE A BROAD, BUT LIGHT, FOOT. THE BOWL IS ETCHED WITH A SERIES OF GEOMETRIC DESIGNS.
PRICE GUIDE 3

◀ A HIGHLY DECORATED WINE GOBLET (CENTRE) WITH A RIOT OF THE POPULAR GRAPES AND VINELEAVES DESIGN ENGRAVED ON THE BOWL, ABOVE A BULBOUS STEM.
PRICE GUIDE 4

◀ A CUT-GLASS WATER GOBLET (RIGHT) WITH AN ENGRAVED HERALDIC IMAGE ON THE BOWL ABOVE THE BAND OF DIAMOND CUTTING. THE STEM HAS A BULBOUS LOWER PORTION AND IS ALSO SHAPED BY A METHOD OF FACET CUTTING.
PRICE GUIDE 4

▲ THESE FOUR MATCHING PORT GLASSES WERE MADE IN 1830 BY VONECHE OF BELGIUM AND ARE ELABORATELY CUT WITH UNUSUAL GEOMETRIC PATTERNS.
PRICE GUIDE 5

▼SHERRY GLASSES COME IN A VARIETY OF SHAPES, FROM TALL FLUTES DOWNWARDS. THE SIMPLE DESIGN OF THIS PARTICULAR GLASS HAS AN OVOID BOWL ENGRAVED WITH GRAPES AND VINELEAVES.
PRICE GUIDE 2

▼THE GLOBULAR BOWL OF THIS PORT GLASS IS ENGRAVED WITH A TYPICAL GRAPE MOTIF. THERE ARE FINGER-SHAPED INDENTATIONS, OR 'PRINTIES', AT THE BASE AND THE CUT-GLASS STEM IS FACETED.
PRICE GUIDE 3

◀ THIS THISTLE GLASS WAS INTENDED FOR DRINKING LIQUEURS. DELIGHTFULLY MADE, THE LOWER HALF OF THE WAISTED BOWL IS DIAMOND-CUT, WHILE THE UPPER HALF OF THE BOWL HAS AN ENGRAVED THISTLE DESIGN.
PRICE GUIDE 3

POINTS TO WATCH

- **Many decanters have lost their stoppers in the course of time; make sure that the stopper matches the decanter in style and age.**
- **Check the glass for minute cracks and chips and any scratches in the colour decoration.**
- **Watch out for highly collectable items not normally made of glass, such as cocktail shakers and swizzle sticks.**

▼ A LEMONADE OR WATER JUG AND MATCHING CONICAL GLASSES IN FROSTED GLASS, WITH RED AND WHITE SPOTS AND CONCENTRIC RED RINGS.
PRICE GUIDE 4

▼A WINE DECANTER SET DECORATED WITH AREAS OF PINK ETCHING AND DELICATE ETCHED LINES. THE GLASSES HAVE ELEGANT SLIM STEMS AND THE DECANTER HAS A GROUND GLASS STOPPER.
PRICE GUIDE 4

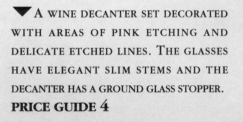

▼ A STYLISH DECO LIQUEUR SET. DESIGNED THREE-DIMENSIONALLY, THE HEART-SHAPED DECANTER AND GLASSES ARE DECORATED WITH ABSTRACT PATTERNS.
PRICE GUIDE 7

▼ A TALL, STRAIGHT-SIDED LEMONADE OR WATER SET IN TINTED GLASS ENLIVENED BY BANDS OF GOLD IN VARYING WIDTHS. SETS SUCH AS THIS WERE CONSIDERED AN IDEAL GIFT IN THE 1930S AND WERE OFTEN PUT ON DISPLAY.
PRICE GUIDE 4

▼ THESE THREE GLASSES AND DECANTER ARE PART OF A CLASSIC SHERRY SET DECORATED WITH A LIGHT ENGRAVED PATTERN REMINISCENT OF FOUNTAINS. EACH PIECE IS SIGNED BY THE DESIGNER, CLYNE FARQUHARSON.
PRICE GUIDE 8

▼ A COLOURFUL, HARD-WEARING DECO LEMONADE OR WATER SET IN PLAIN GLASS, WITH BANDS OF COLOUR AND A PEPPERMINT GREEN BASE AND RIM. COLOUR WAS INTRODUCED TO DECO GLASS BY A MIX OF TRANSFER-PRINTING AND ENAMELLING.
PRICE GUIDE 4

▼ A 1930s CHROME AND CUT CRYSTAL COCKTAIL SHAKER. PADDLES INSIDE THE SHAKER WERE USED TO STIR THE COCKTAIL INGREDIENTS TOGETHER.
PRICE GUIDE 3

▼ THESE CLASSICALLY-SHAPED 1930s COCKTAIL GLASSES HAVE BLACK GLASS STEMS AND BASES. THEY ARE LABELLED FOR PINK LADY COCKTAILS.
PRICE GUIDE 3

▼ AN ELEGANT ENGLISH-MADE COCKTAIL SHAKER. THE STOPPER, IN THE SHAPE OF A COCKEREL'S HEAD, SITS INSIDE A GLASS STRAINER WHICH IS SEPARATE FROM THE ETCHED BODY.
PRICE GUIDE 5

▼ A SET OF SIX UNUSUAL COCKTAIL GLASSES. MADE OF GLASS, THEY ARE SILVERED INSIDE AND OUT, WITH BLACK DECORATION, AND THIS GIVES THEM THE APPEARANCE OF BEING MADE OF METAL. THESE GLASSES MAY RESEMBLE TRADITIONAL WHISKY TUMBLESRS BUT THEIR DESIGN IS QUINTESSENTIALLY DECO.
PRICE GUIDE 5

▼ A FROSTED GLASS DECANTER AND MATCHING GLASSES. THE GLASSES ARE SILVER RIMMED AND THE DECANTER IS DECORATED WITH IRREGULAR SPOTS.
PRICE GUIDE 5

▼ A COCKTAIL SET IN YELLOW GLASS, MADE BY JAMES POWELL AND SONS LTD AT WHITEFRIARS GLASS WORKS. AS COCKTAIL DRINKING BECAME A FASHIONABLE PASTIME, SO FASHIONALBE ACCESSORIES WERE DEVELOPED. WHEN COCKTAILS WERE INTRODUCED IN THE 1920S, THE GLASSES DESIGNED FOR THEM CAME IN A WIDE VARIETY OF SHAPES. THE DRINKS WERE NEW AND GLASSES EVOLVED TO ACCOMODATE THEM. AT FIRST THEY WERE BASED ON EXISTING LIQUER GLASSES AND TUMBLERS, DECORATED WITH CONTEMPORARY DESIGNS. BUT EVENTUALLY THE TYPICAL COCKTAIL GLASS DESIGN OF AN INVERTED CONE ON A CYLINDRICAL STEM AND CIRCULAR BASE, AS HERE, BECAME MOST POPULAR
PRICE GUIDE 5

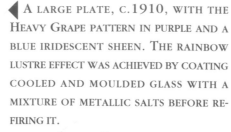

◀ A LARGE PLATE, C.1910, WITH THE HEAVY GRAPE PATTERN IN PURPLE AND A BLUE IRIDESCENT SHEEN. THE RAINBOW LUSTRE EFFECT WAS ACHIEVED BY COATING COOLED AND MOULDED GLASS WITH A MIXTURE OF METALLIC SALTS BEFORE RE-FIRING IT.
PRICE GUIDE 5

▶ THIS FENTON DISH, C.1910, WITH 'CANDY RIBBON' EDGE HAS A BLACKBERRY DESIGN. PATTERNS WERE ACHIEVED BY PRESSING GLASS BETWEEN TWO MOULDS, AN INNER AND AN OUTER.
PRICE GUIDE 4

▼ A PIECE OF LATER CARNIVAL GLASS PRODUCED IN CZECHOSLOVAKIA IN ABOUT 1920. MADE IN AMBER-COLOURED GLASS, THIS POWDER BOWL AND LID HAS A FRIEZE WHICH HAS BEEN STAINED GREEN TO GIVE AN ANTIQUE EFFECT.
PRICE GUIDE 4

▲ GREEN WAS A POPULAR COLOUR IN THE MANUFACTURE OF EARLY CARNIVAL GLASS. MADE AT THE BEGINNING OF THIS CENTURY, THIS NORTHWOOD COMPORT, OR FRUIT BOWL, HAS AN INTERESTING FRUIT AND FLOWERS PATTERN ON A BASKET-WEAVE BACKGROUND.
PRICE GUIDE 3

▲ A ROSE BOWL IN AMETHYST-COLOURED GLASS WITH A BEADED CABLE PATTERN AND AN EXAGGERATED INWARD-FACING CRIMPED EDGE. IT STANDS ON THREE FEET AND WAS MADE BY THE NORTHWOOD GLASS COMPANY, WEST VIRGINIA, IN THE EARLY 1900S.
PRICE GUIDE 4

A GOLDEN AMETHYST VASE, SHAPED LIKE A TROPHY, MADE IN AROUND 1910. THE DESIGN OF STYLIZED FLOWERS, KNOWN AS MARY ANN, WAS INSPIRED BY DELICATE EMBROIDERY WORK. THIS IS A FINE EXAMPLE OF CARNIVAL GLASS.
PRICE GUIDE 3

THIS FLUTED BOWL IS IN A SOFT PEACH COLOUR AND HAS AN INTERLOCKING STARFISH PATTERN FORMED BY SCULPTED RAISED BEADS. MADE IN 1910, BY THE DUGAN COMPANY, THE SEMI-OPAQUE MILKINESS OF THE OPALESCENT COLOUR OF THE BOWL STARTS FROM THE EDGE AND SHADES INTO THE CENTRE.
PRICE GUIDE 5

A PEDESTAL-STEMMED BOWL DESIGNED TO HOLD SUGAR MADE IN AN ELEGANT AQUA BLUE GLASS. PRODUCED IN 1920, IT IS DECORATED WITH A PINEAPPLE AND BOW PATTERN.
PRICE GUIDE 4

DESIGN FEATURES

THE FENTON COMPANY OF OHIO WAS THE FIRST TO PRODUCE CARNIVAL GLASS AND STAYED AS THE MARKET LEADER FOR SOME TIME. FRANK LESLIE FENTON WAS RESPONSIBLE FOR THE MANY AND VARIED DESIGNS OF CARNIVAL GLASS PRODUCED BY HIS FACTORY WHICH, WHEN IRIDIZED, BOTH DAZZLED THE EYE AND STIMULATED THE IMAGINATION. AS MOST OF THE GLASS OBJECTS WERE SO DECORATIVE, MANY OF THEM WERE NEVER USED FOR THE VARIOUS FUNCTIONS FOR WHICH THEY WERE ORIGINALLY CREATED.

THE QUICKEST SHAPE TO PRESS WAS A SHALLOW BOWL AS THIS COULD BE EASILY PUSHED DOWN INTO A FLAT PLATE OR PULLED UP INTO A DEEP BOWL, ALTHOUGH SOME BOWLS STARTED AS FLAT PLATES. AS ALL CARNIVAL GLASS MAKERS WERE KEEN TO INDIVIDUALIZE THEIR OBJECTS, ITEMS WERE OFTEN CRIMPED, PLEATED AND PULLED TO GIVE DIFFERENT AND ORIGINAL FINISHES.

THIS MARIGOLD-COLOURED HAIR TIDY MADE BY THE FENTON COMPANY IN 1910, STARTED OFF AS A FLAT PLATE WHICH WAS ROUNDED INTO A BOWL. THIS WAS THEN SQUARED OFF AT THE TOP AND EDGED WITH AN ORIGINAL FENTON PATTERN OF STYLIZED FLOWERS.

▲ AN ICE-GREEN DISH, MADE IN AROUND 1910 BY THE FENTON COMPANY, WEST VIRGINIA, IN THE BASKET-WEAVE DESIGN WITH OPEN-EDGED BASKET WORK AROUND THE OUTER RIM.
PRICE GUIDE 4

◀ KNOWN AS SECONDARY CARNIVAL GLASS BECAUSE IT WAS MADE DURING THE SECOND 'WAVE' OF PRODUCTION, THIS BLACK DISH FROM AUSTRALIA, c.1920, HAS A KINGFISHER DESIGN.
PRICE GUIDE 4

▲ A RADIUM-FINISHED GREEN BOWL MADE BY THE MILLERBURG GLASS COMPANY IN OHIO, c.1910, WITH A CENTRAL FLOWER DESIGN KNOWN AS THE MAYAN PATTERN.
PRICE GUIDE 4

◀ MADE BY THE NORTHWOOD GLASS COMPANY IN WEST VIRGINA IN 1910, THIS AMETHYST-COLOURED BOWL HAS A HAND-FINISHED FRILLED EDGE AND A PATTERN KNOWN AS NIPPON.
PRICE GUIDE 3

▲ ALL SHADES OF BLUE WERE PRODUCED, BUT PARTICULARLY IMPRESSIVE WAS THE RICH COBALT BLUE FOUND ON THE PEACOCK PATTERNS, AS SEEN IN THIS DISH WHICH WAS MADE IN 1910.
PRICE GUIDE 3

◀ ALTHOUGH FLOWERS PREDOMINATED IN CARNIVAL GLASS DESIGNS, THE OCCASIONAL ANIMAL WOULD SOMETIMES APPEAR AMONG THE UNDERGROWTH AS ON THIS ORNATE MARIGOLD PLATE. THIS FENTON DESIGN DATES FROM 1910 AND THE PATTERN IS CALLED HORSES' HEADS.
PRICE GUIDE 4

POINTS TO WATCH

- Look for vessels with an overall harmony of design, subject and technique, and a poetic conception typical of the era.
- Hand made pieces are a more worthwhile investment than mass-produced ware.
- Stick to a reputable dealer and ask for advice on damage, repair and signatures.

▼ This Daum vase from c.1900 has been acid-etched with orange and green flowers. The firm of Daum was established in 1875, but only moved into glass production in 1887.
PRICE GUIDE 8

▼ An unusual Daum vase with gold and white mistletoe overlay and a gold rim. Daum had developed a techinque whereby a surface was carved to reveal further multiple layers of engraved, etched and enamelled glass.
PRICE GUIDE 6

▲ A Muller Frères vase with characteristic mottled background overlaid with purple and yellow crocuses and a grass hopper. Vases composed of several different layers of glass were a feature of the Muller brothers work.
PRICE GUIDE 8

▶ A Daum bowl with enamel-painted apple blossom set against cream and peach background. The mottled background was achieved by mixing powdered glass and additives into the glass during smelting.
PRICE GUIDE 8

▶ This squat rectangular Daum vase shows a panoramic landscape with trees along a river bank reflected in the water. The delicate orange tinge of the body of the vase has been used to suggest a sunset.
PRICE GUIDE 7

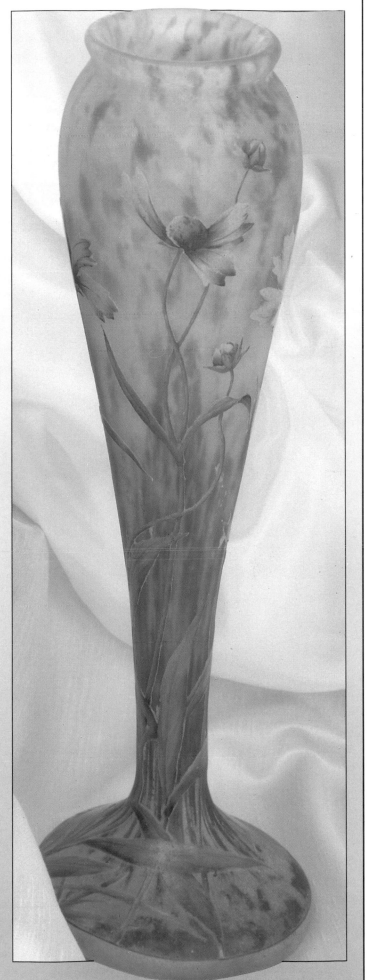

▲ A MULLER FRÈRES BALL-SHAPED VASE FROM C.1900, DECORATED WITH AN ALPINE LANDSCAPE SHOWING A LAKE FRAMED BY MOUNTAINS AND TREES.
PRICE GUIDE 9

◀ AN OBLONG DAUM VASE WHOSE SHAPE BETRAYS A JAPANESE INSPIRATION. THE FUCHSIAS HAVE BEEN DELICATELY HAND-PAINTED ON TO THE VASE WITH AN ENAMEL PAINT.
PRICE GUIDE 7

▶ THIS ELONGATED DAUM VASE HAS A TANGLE OF YELLOW FLOWERS PAINTED ON TO A YELLOW AND MAUVE STREAKED BACKGROUND.
PRICE GUIDE 8

▶ A PINK AND GREEN GALLÉ VASE FROM 1910, DECORATED WITH ACORNS AND LEAVES. EMILE GALLÉ HAD REVOLUTIONIZED THE ART OF GLASS MAKING WITH HIS INTEREST IN THE EFFECTS OF OPACITY, IRIDESCENCE AND SURFACE TEXTURE.
PRICE GUIDE 7

▼ A VERY LARGE BOWL FROM 1906–07, WITH A BROWN OVERLAY ON AN OPALINE GROUND THAT DEPICTS A TRANQUIL RIVERSCAPE. GALLÉ EVEN MANAGED TO TRANSFORM IMPURITIES THAT APPEARED DURING MANUFACTURE INTO PARTS OF HIS AESTHETIC DESIGN.
PRICE GUIDE 8

▶ A ROUND GLASS VASE, C.1900, WITH AN OPALINE BASE OVERLAID WITH YELLOW DAFFODILS SET AGAINST A LANDSCAPE. THE LAYERS AND TEXTURES GALLÉ ACHIEVED WERE REMINISCENT OF METALS, MINERALS AND NATURAL STONES.
PRICE GUIDE 8

▼ A DELICATE TRACERY OF YELLOW HONEYSUCKLE FLOWERS WITH BROWN STEMS AND LEAVES, PLAYS OVER THE SURFACE OF THIS VASE. THIS PIECE IS SIGNED NEAR THE BASE.
PRICE GUIDE 8

▶ A SLENDER VASE FROM C.1900 WITH
GALLÉ'S MANY LAYERED 'MARQUETRY'
DECORATION THAT BLENDS IN TONALLY
WITH THE BACKGROUND. THIS TECHNIQUE
RIVALLED PAINTING IN THE EFFECTS IT
COULD ACHIEVE.
PRICE GUIDE 9

◀ SOME GALLÉ GLASS WAS MOUNTED IN
METAL: THIS VASE HAS SILVER HANDLES
WITH LEAFY FINIALS THAT ECHO THE
DECORATIVE GLASS OVERLAY OF
SYCAMORE SEEDS.
PRICE GUIDE 8

▼ THREE EXAMPLES OF POPULAR 1930S SCENT BOTTLES IN CLEAR GLASS WITH DECORATIVE LABELS. BOTTLES CONTAINING THEIR ORIGINAL PERFUME FETCH A HIGHER PRICE.
PRICE GUIDE 3

▼ A SEALED BOTTLE OF 1930S 'EMIR' PERFUME COMPLETE WITH ITS ORIGINAL CARDBOARD BOX AND STAND. THE STANDARD OF THE PACKAGING OF PERFUME IN THE 1930S MATCHED THE QUALITY OF THE BOTTLE DESIGN.
PRICE GUIDE 5

▼ PINK AND BLUE GLASS DECO-STYLED SCENT ATOMIZERS. BOTH ARE OPERATED BY A SILK PUMP DECORATED WITH A THICK TASSEL. THEY WERE OFTEN SOLD EMPTY TO BE FILLED WITH A CHOICE OF PERFUME.
PRICE GUIDE 4

▶ A SELECTION OF PAPERWEIGHT DESIGNS FROM DIFFERENT FACTORIES. CLOCKWISE FROM BOTTOM RIGHT: WHITEFRIARS CONCENTRIC MILLEFIORI, C.1850; CLICHY SCRAMBLE MILLEFIORI, C.1850; CLICHY CHEQUER WEIGHT WITH A CENTRAL ROSE, C.1850; CLICHY SPACED MILLEFIORI ON BLUE GROUND, C.1850; ENGLISH ROUND BUBBLE WEIGHT, C.1880; NORTHERN ENGLISH GREEN GLASS STUMP, C.1880.
PRICE GUIDE 3 – 6

▼ THIS ATTRACTIVE BLUE GLASS THREE PIECE TABLE SET HAS BLACK ENAMEL DECORATION AND WAS MADE IN BOHEMIA. SETS SUCH AS THESE USUALLY FETCH HIGHER PRICES THAN SINGLE PIECES.

PRICE GUIDE 6

▼ THIS CLEAR GLASS SCENT BOTTLE HAS A ROLLED GOLD TOP AND BRIGHT YELLOW SILK TASSEL. THIS BOTTLE STILL HAS ITS ORIGINAL LEATHER CASE.

PRICE GUIDE 5

▲ THIS 1920S CLEAR AND FROSTED GLASS SCENT BOTTLE HAS A 'BLUE MOTH' STOPPER. THOUGH INTENDED AS A CONTAINER TO SELL PERFUME IN, THE WORKMANSHIP OF PIECES LIKE THIS, MEANT THAT THE BOTTLE WAS KEPT AFTER THE SCENT WAS USED.

PRICE GUIDE 5

▲ TWO QUAINT FROSTED GLASS SCENT BOTTLES WITH 'GOLLIWOG' STOPPERS – THE SAME NAME GIVEN TO THE PERFUME THEY CONTAINED.

PRICE GUIDE 7

▶ GLASS PRODUCED IN MOULDS WAS IDEALLY SUITED TO COMMEMORATIVE WARE. RAISED LETTERING, PORTRAITS, FLAGS AND OTHER MOTIFS COULD ALL BE ENGRAVED IN A CAST-IRON MOULD. ONCE THIS SKILLED WORK HAD BEEN CARRIED OUT — USUALLY IN ADVANCE OF THE EVENT — COUNTLESS THOUSANDS OF PLATES, DISHES, BASKETS AND OTHER ITEMS COULD BE RAPIDLY TURNED OUT.

PRICE GUIDE 3

▼ A SELECTION OF PRESSED GLASS FROM EARLY 20TH CENTURY. MANY DESIGNS HAVE BEEN PRODUCED SINCE THE 1820S AND THOSE SHOWN HERE GIVE AN IDEA OF THE WIDE RANGE OF PATTERNS AND SHAPES THAT CAN EASILY AND, FOR THE MOST PART, BE CHEAPLY OBTAINED AT FLEA MARKETS AND ANTIQUE STALLS.

PRICE GUIDE 1 – 3

Toys have only come to the attention of antique collectors in recent years and are now very much in fashion. Tin toys, toy, cars and dolls are perhaps among the most sought after of toy collectables but there is a wide range available to the interested collector.

Doll collecting is one of the most popular areas in the antique scene, resulting in high prices and keen competition. Experienced collectors buy at specialist auctions, but the beginner is advised to purchase from a reputable dealer, as damage and faults are not always stated in catalogues, and the inexperienced could be misled by reproductions. Doll fairs, at which many dealers exhibit, are regularly held and both reproductions and antiques are shown. There are collectors' clubs where knowledge, as well as price guides are passed on to the new collector. At first, however, as with any toy collectables, more can be gained by visiting museums and consulting specialist books.

It is important to look after old dolls with great care, though bisque head dolls are among the easiest as they are not affected by light and will not suffer in normal conditions. However, extreme cold can cause heads to crack, so if dolls are to be left in an unheated room in winter their heads should be wrapped up for protection. Extremes of heat can make composition bodies crack or warp and wax bodies will melt, so it is advisable to keep dolls out of the sun. Minor damage can be repaired but it is always a good idea to ask a dealer's advice before commencing and there are good professional restorers around. With dolls in original costume, damage is more likely to occur to the clothes, which should be kept out of direct light to prevent the colours from fading. Antique silk and satin clothes should not be washed, as the colours may run and the fabrics disintegrate. Ideally a doll collection should be stored in glass-fronted

This brightly-painted, wooden horse on wheels would have been the toy of a young child. Without pedals, it would have been pushed or pulled by an attendant adult.

cabinets with sachets of moth and insect repellent.

Teddy bears, made of cloth, need much the same love and care as dolls – it is just as important to protect their fabric covering and stuffing or the bear might disintegrate. As with dolls, teddies are today one of the most sought after of collectables and can fetch extraordinary prices. Any bear with a history or associated with a famous owner will be of particular value, but there are numerous more affordable bears on the market. An American toy maker, Morris Michtom, first made toy bears in 1902, and it was he who named them after the American president, Theodore, 'Teddy', Roosevelt. A bear from this early period will probably fetch a high price so collectors on a budget should look out for those dating from after 1925. Added extras, like turning heads or mechanical growlers, can increase a bear's worth and an unusual colour, such as black or red, can also arouse more interest.

Mechanical toys are a specialist collectors' area in their own right and consequently the market is large and prices high. Hand-painted items may indicate an early model and this was usually reserved for the more expensive toys. With any metal toy it is vital to check all parts for signs of rust. Established rust is difficult to eradicate and, if left unchecked, can lead to serious deterioration, destroying the value of a piece. Looking at the paintwork can give the collector clues. While minor, almost invisible scratches may be acceptable, serious blemishes and signs of bubbling are an indication that the piece has already been attacked by rust from below. If operated by a key, test the mechanism carefully and if the key does not turn then the motor has been overwound or has rusted solid. While this fault can be corrected, it is expensive and the cost of the piece should be proportionately less.

Metal was used for many toys such as soldiers, cars,

planes and trains; toys intended for the mass market. So it should be remembered that though metal is durable in the short term, these toys were not designed to last forever. The most common problems are metal fatigue and chipped paintwork. The former is likely to affect toy soldiers which were cast from an alloy of lead and tin. Metal suffering from corrosion will have a grey, powdery surface and will be extremely brittle. Collectors are advised to avoid toys affected this way and to protect their own models by ensuring that they are not stored in a damp place. Probably the most enduringly popular of toys is the train set, especially with grown-up 'children' but there is a growing interest in planes and toy cars.

Puzzles and games, for indoors and out, would have made up a considerable part of the toy trunks of the past, and today these are quite easily found at very reasonable prices. Early in this century, new and exciting board games were developed offering a greater variety than old-fashioned draughts, dominoes or card games. 'Monopoly' and 'Cluedo' both appeared but all sorts of different games were also invented that have now slipped into obscurity. Jigsaws and games of skill were equally popular and, as with all these kinds of toys, are more valued if they are in their original boxes. However, 20th-century games are usually mass-produced and are generally made of less durable materials such as flimsy paper. They will not necessarily have survived under the wear and tear of constant play.

The indoor games of the Victorian and Edwardian periods were made of more hard-wearing materials and so toys lasted much longer than some modern versions will. However, this also means they are more expensive collectables today. Indoor versions of outdoor games were made for both adults and children; games like parlour croquet or carpet bowls could be played in a

Dolls are a perenially popular toy and this classic example from the 1930s, with her shoulder-length blonde hair, is lovingly dressed in a glamorous evening gown.

relatively small area, though indoor tennis and table tennis did require a larger room. Parlour croquet was played on a cloth-lined mahogany board equipped with adjustable screws to ensure a level 'green'. Another version featured hoops supported by flat metal stands that did not interrupt the run of the ball. Carpet bowls were normally two to four inches (five to ten centimetres) in diameter and made of stoneware. They came in sets of six with the smaller white ball called the jack. Whole sets of the less vigorous indoor games are sometimes found, usually known as compendiums. These sets might include chess, draughts, dominoes, dice, solitaire and cribbage boards and any compendium that remains complete today will be of great interest to collectors and this will be reflected in the price.

Some collectors specialize in particular games and one of the most popular of these is chess. There is no shortage of chess men today but, as with anything, they vary in quality and value. A complete set still with its board is obviously ideal but board and men have often parted company. If collecting chess pieces it is most important that all the men match, preferably both white and black. Faced with the bewildering variety of chess sets produced over the last two centuries, collectors may wish to restrict the field in which they buy. Some may decide to collect playing sets rather than decorative ones, but any enthusiast will often be attracted to entertaining oddities, where the pieces are animals, opposing armies or political parties, or even abstract modern designs. If collectors are purely interested in the decorative quality of the pieces then they may be satisfied with collecting odd individual men in as many styles as they can find. Most of the time collectors and dealers are faced with incomplete sets. Unless they are of a strikingly unusual design, sets with the odd pawn and knight's head missing are best avoided. Better one complete set than three or four with pieces from other sets substituted for the originals. Many sets are made in ivory and collectors should familiarize themselves with the different qualities of ivory so they can identify the country of origin of their potential purchases, and tell faked ivory. Other materials have been used and these include bone, wood, porcelain and pottery.

Apart from playing games, children have always been encouraged to read to pass the time and both fictional and educational books and comics for children have become increasingly valuable to collectors. Any well-read books will have suffered considerable wear and tear and badly damaged examples, though still of interest, will be of little investment value. Serious collectors should look for first editions in mint condition and anything signed by author or artist will be of particular worth. Books should always be kept under the right conditions, preferably in glass-fronted book cases. The correct humidity level is most important and should ideally be between 50 and 65 per cent. Any higher and glues, pastes, leather, linen and paper will start to rot and attract fungi and insects. Traces of mould, or foxing, first appear as tiny, pinhead-sized brown or orange spots and this can be kept at bay with a proprietary impregnated paper inserted between every eighth page. Dust books regularly, carefully and thoroughly, particularly along the tops and edges.

The equipment for all sorts of outdoor games and sports is very popular and there is a growing market for antique cricket bats, tennis rackets and golfing accessories. Cricket has been a well-loved and frequently-played sport since the 18th century and by the Edwardian era the game was played in those

This blue biplane is made from a Meccano kit of the 1930s. It is a model of the Westland Wapiti; the real-life plane came into production in 1934.

countries, all around the world, under British influence, and in schools throughout the United Kingdom. Still popular today, the game of cricket has given rise to a large souvenir industry. Apart from the equipment and dress used in the actual game, the collector can choose from a vast array of cricketing memorabilia in silver, porcelain, pottery and metal. Photographs and printed ephemera – like cartoons, cigarette cards showing famous players, and copies of Wisden's Almanack – are highly sought after. Second-hand cricketing equipment and clothing is usually well within the price range of most sports enthusiasts. Bats, stumps, blazers and caps are relatively plentiful and inexpensive, and there are now a few specialists who deal in this field. Bats can be dated roughly by looking at their shape. Earliest bats were, in effect, long, heavy clubs which curved outwards towards the bottom. This shape reflected the conditions and style of play then; underarm bowling and unscientific slogging. As the game grew in finesse, however, the bat evolved to its present well-balanced and standardized shape. Until about the middle of the 19th century, cricket bats were made all in one piece, but then the spring handle was introduced, acting as a shock absorber. The familiar rubber covering of the twine binding on the handle was introduced towards the end of W.G. Grace's career, but some batsmen still preferred the feel of the bat without it. The traditional material for cricket bats was, and still is, English willow that combined lightness with durability and springiness.

The value and collectability of a cricket bat depends largely on its associations. Signed bats are reasonably commonplace, but the status of a player, or the significance of the event commemorated are generally much more important than the condition of a bat. A well-cared-for example will still be more desirable than one that is falling apart. Much the same can be said for all other kinds of sporting equipment and memorablilia, such as tennis and golfing accessories.

Lawn tennis was increasingly played in the 1920s and 1930s, particularly by young women, recently liberated from the confines of restrictive clothing. Real tennis, played on an indoor, enclosed court, had been played since the 16th century, but it was not until the late 19th century that the outdoor version of the sport appeared. Lawn tennis rackets have never been completely standardized, but by the 1930s most rackets were similar in general appearance. The design of early rackets had been strongly influenced by those used in real tennis. These had long shafts and heads that were not oval but curved away to one side to make it easier for the real tennis player to scoop up and control the heavy ball used. An alternative design – with a head that was flattened at the end – was far longer lived, although it disappeared by the 1920s. However, other interesting features persisted, notably the curiously designed 'fish-tail' butt, shaped to give a surer grip. Another feature was the double main – a set of extra strings strung across the centre of the mesh in order to strengthen it. Up until the 1930s, tennis racket frames were made from steam-bent, rendered ash, but this method of manufacture gradually gave way to a new process involving the bonding together of strips of different laminated woods, which gave the racket additional strength. Steel and aluminium frames were also made in the 1930s, but they failed to take off at that date and did not pass into general use until the 1960s. The earliest rackets had uncovered wooden handles, but leather grips became more popular after the turn of the century and were universal by the 1930s. Some rackets had additional gadgets such as scoring mechanisms in their handles and ways of adjusting the

These wet salmon flies are kept in a wallet to protect their dressings from being crushed. Flies such as these would have been prize possessions.

tension of the strings, but these unusual gimmicks never became widespread. Strings were made from 'catgut' until cheaper modern nylon versions began to replace them. Catgut strings are actually made from sheep's intestines, and have nothing to do with cats. The name arose from a corruption of 'kit' – the word used to denote a violin in the 17th century – as the gut used to make early rackets was adapted from that found in stringed instruments. As with cricket bats, ordinary rackets and other tennis ephemera is not hard to come by and can be quite cheap. Any equipment that was once the property of a famous player or that was used at a famous match or tournament will be of greater value and interest than the ordinary racket.

Sporting collectables should be treated with as much respect as any other form of antique and care should be taken to preserve the wood, leather, rubber and metal that they may be made from. Proprietary wood and leather polishes are available that can both protect and rejuvenate older materials. Wood should be guarded against drying out and leather should be kept at an even temperature and humidity to prevent the material rotting away. Any metal parts, such as golf club shafts, should be kept rust-free and clean. Repairs are, as always, are best undertaken by a specialist restorer.

Collectable toys and games are so varied that anyone interested in this field of antiques has a wide range from which to chose. It is advisable to pick a specialist area rather than just buying any toys or games that take the eye, and to read around or visit any of the excellent toy or sporting museums will give the collector invaluable tips and ideas. Whether collecting dolls or toy soldiers, books or chess sets, boats or cricket bats, toys and pastimes can prove a rewarding and satisfying subject for the antiques enthusiast.

▼ ALTHOUGH RATTLES WITH WHISTLES AND BELLS WERE VERY POPULAR, A NUMBER OF SIMPLER DESIGNS WERE ALSO MADE, LIKE THIS SILVER MODEL OF A BABY ON AN IVORY TEETHING RING.
PRICE GUIDE 5

▲ A SMALL SILVER RATTLE AND TEETHING RING DATING FROM ABOUT 1850. BEARS, OTHER ANIMALS AND MINIATURE FIGURES WERE POPULAR ADDITIONS IN VICTORIAN TIMES.
PRICE GUIDE 5

▲ ORIGINALLY THIS SILVER RATTLE WOULD HAVE HUNG FROM A RING. A RIBBON TIED TO THE RING WOULD HAVE BEEN ATTACHED TO THE MOTHER'S GIRDLE OR BELT SO SOMETHING WAS ALWAYS AT HAND TO AMUSE BABY.
PRICE GUIDE 4

▼ A RATHER ELABORATE EARLY REGENCY SILVER RATTLE WITH BELLS AND A WHISTLE. THE CORAL TEETHING STICK WAS A COMMON FEATURE OF RATTLES OF THIS PERIOD, PARTIALLY BECAUSE CORAL WAS THOUGHT TO WARD OFF EVIL SPIRITS.
PRICE GUIDE 7

▲ MADE IN 1877, THIS SILVER RATTLE IS ELABORATELY DECORATED WITH MANY TRINKETS TO AMUSE THE BABY. BELLS HANG AROUND THE CENTRE, THERE IS A WHISTLE TOO, AND A MOTHER-OF-PEARL TEETHING STICK AT THE BOTTOM.
PRICE GUIDE 7

▲ A SILVER REGENCY RATTLE DATING FROM ABOUT 1815. THIS PARTICULAR EXAMPLE HAS A PAIR OF BELLS AND A PATTERNED IVORY TEETHING STICK WHICH IS LONGER THAN MOST.
PRICE GUIDE 6

POINTS TO WATCH

- BISQUE HEADS ARE SUSCEPTIBLE TO DAMAGE, SO REPLACEMENT HEADS WERE COMMON. THIS CAN DRASTICALLY REDUCE THE VALUE.
- INSPECT POTENTIAL PURCHASES CAREFULLY – EVEN THE FINEST HAIRLINE CRACK REDUCES THE VALUE OF A DOLL BY HALF.
- SLEEPING EYES ARE SOMETIMES REPLACED WITH GLUED-IN FIXED EYES – CHECK THAT THE EYES AND MECHANISMS ARE RIGHT FOR THE PARTICULAR MODEL.
- MANY REPRODUCTIONS HAVE BEEN TAKEN FROM ORIGINAL MOULDS AND THESE ARE OF EXCELLENT QUALITY, ALTHOUGH THE BISQUE IS GENERALLY SMOOTHER. BEWARE OF UNSCRUPULOUS DEALERS WHO SOMETIMES PASS OFF REPRODUCTIONS AS ORIGINALS.
- RESTORATION OF A DOLL CAN OFTEN BE DETECTED BY A SMOOTHER AREA OF THE BISQUE THE BODY IS MADE OF.

◀ A CHARACTER DOLL MADE BY JD KESTNER; ITS MOULD NUMBER IS NO.260. THE BISQUE HEAD IS MADE WITH SLEEPING EYES AND AN OPEN MOUTH WITH TEETH.
PRICE GUIDE 6

▶ A GERMAN BENT-LIMBED BABY DOLL WITH A BLONDE WIG. THE DOLL IS DRESSED IN A WHITE CHRISTENING ROBE WITH A WHITE LACE BONNET. A TREND FOR DOLLS WITH LIFE-LIKE FACES GREW IN GERMANY WHEN DOLL ARTISTS BEGAN TO TIRE OF CREATING IDEALIZED FACES.
PRICE GUIDE 6

▶ THIS CHARACTER TODDLER WAS MADE BY GEORGE BORGFELDT, AND IS MOULD NO.327, MADE IN C.1920. THE BISQUE HEAD WAS MOULDED BY ARMAND MARSEILLE. SOME CHARACTER DOLLS WERE SAID TO HAVE BEEN MODELLED ON REAL CHILDREN.
PRICE GUIDE 6

▼ THIS KAMMER AND REINHARDT TODDLER DOLL HAS MOULD NO.122 AND WAS MADE IN ABOUT 1912. THIS GERMAN COMPANY WAS THE MARKET LEADER WHEN IT CAME TO QUALITY CHARACTER DOLLS.
PRICE GUIDE 7

▶ THIS BABY DOLL WAS MADE IN ABOUT 1910 BY GERBRUDER HEUBACH. A BENT-LIMBED COMPOSITION BODY, THIS DOLL HAS MOULDED HAIR. MANY FACTORIES DEVELOPED CHARACTER DOLLS THAT BECAME SPECIALIZED RANGES.
PRICE GUIDE 8

▼ AN IDEALIZED DOLL MADE BY THE FIRM OF JD KESTNER OF WALTERSHAUSEN, GERMANY. THE BISQUE HEAD IS MODELLED WITH A PARTIALLY CLOSED MOUTH AND SLEEPING EYES, AND IS IMPRESSED WITH THE MOULD NUMBER 192.
PRICE GUIDE 7

▼ THIS SIMON AND HALBIG DOLL WITH A COMPOSITION BODY IS DRESSED IN WHITE VOILE WITH A PINK RIBBON TRIM. THE FACE IS MODELLED WITH SLEEPING EYES AND A PARTIALLY CLOSED MOUTH.
PRICE GUIDE 6

▶ A SMALL BLONDE KAMMER AND REINHARDT DOLL WITH A COMPOSITION BODY. THE DOLL IS DRESSED IN WHITE COTTON WITH A BRODERIE ANGLAISE BONNET AND SATIN SLIPPERS.
PRICE GUIDE 7

▼ A SIMON AND HALBIG DOLL WITH A COMPOSITION BODY. THE PARTIALLY OPEN MOUTH HAS MOULDED TEETH AND THE SLEEPING EYES HAVE REAL LASHES. SOME DOLLS CAN BE FOUND WITH PIERCED EARS FOR EARINGS. THIS DOLL HAS A LILAC COSTUME WITH A MATCHING HAT.
PRICE GUIDE 7

◀ A LARGE DOLL BY SIMON AND HALBIG WITH A COMPOSITION BODY. THE FACE IS MODELLED WITH BLUE, SLEEPING EYES AND A PARTIALLY CLOSED MOUTH WITH TEETH. THE CLOTHES ARE MADE IN A POPULAR EDWARDIAN STYLE.
PRICE GUIDE 6

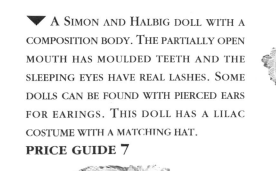

▲ A SMALL KESTNER DOLL WITH BLUE EYES AND A CLOSED MOUTH. THE DOLL IS DRESSED IN A LONG PINK FROCK WITH A MATCHING HAT PINNED ON TO HER ELEGANT BLONDE COIFFEUR.
PRICE GUIDE 5

▲ EDWARDIAN BEARS COME IN ALL SHAPES AND SIZES FROM VERY SMALL ONES OF A FEW INCHES HIGH TO THOSE OF SEVERAL FEET. FEATURES ARE OFTEN MORE DETAILED THAN ON THE CONTEMPORARY BEAR. PADS ARE MADE MORE REALISTIC WITH BLACK STITCHING FOR CLAWS AND FUR IS CLIPPED TO IMITATE LIVE BEARS. POINTED SNOUTS DISTINGUISH THE EARLIEST TEDDY BEARS FROM LATER VERSIONS, AS, INITIALLY, IMITATION OF THE REAL ANIMAL WAS ADHERED TO MORE STRICTLY. SOME TEDDIES HAVE, IN RECENT YEARS, FETCHED EXCEPTIONAL PRICES WHEN COMING UP FOR SALE, PARTICULARLY THOSE WITH ANY UNUSUAL FEATURES OR MECHANICAL MOVEMENTS.

PRICE GUIDE 3 – 5

POINTS TO WATCH

- AFTER SOUNDNESS OF CONSTRUCTION, ONE OF THE MOST IMPORTANT FEATURES OF A ROCKING HORSE IS A GOOD HEAD; THE EYES SHOULD BE WELL DEFINED, THE EARS PRICKED AND THE NOSTRILS FLARED.
- THE MANE AND TAIL, SHOULD BE LUXURIANT RATHER THAN STRAGGLY, AND SHOULD BE REAL HORSE HAIR. CHECK THEY ARE FIRMLY SECURED.
- IDEALLY, PAINTWORK SHOULD BE ORIGINAL, AS SHOULD THE SADDLE, BRIDLE STRAPS AND STIRRUPS.

▼ DATING FROM 1880, THIS ROCKING HORSE IS MADE IN WOOD AND IS COVERED IN REAL PONY HIDE TO GIVE A LIFE-LIKE EFFECT. AS WITH THE EARLIEST MODELS, THIS ROCKING HORSE SITS ON THE SIMPLEST OF SEMI-CIRCULAR ROCKERS.
PRICE GUIDE 7

▲ AN UNUSUAL DAPPLED GREY PATTERN DATING FROM THE 1890s. THE HORSE IS CARVED FROM PINE AND IS BASED ON A TRESTLE ROCKER. THIS KIND OF ROCKING MECHANISM IS MUCH SAFER THAN THE TRADITIONAL BOW ROCKER.
PRICE GUIDE 6

▲ DATING FROM 1890, THIS ROCKING HORSE IS A SMALL DAPPLE GREY AND IS ATTACHED TO A WOODEN SAFETY ROCKER. ROCKING HORSES, IN THEIR MOST BASIC FORM, ARE THOUGHT TO HAVE FIRST APPEARED IN THE EARLY 17TH CENTURY.
PRICE GUIDE 6

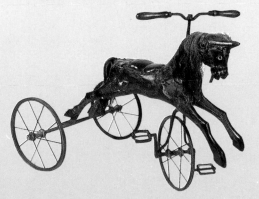

▲ THIS FINELY CRAFTED WOODEN TRICYCLE HORSE WAS DESIGNED FOR A SMALL CHILD IN THE 1870s.
PRICE GUIDE 7

▲ A LATE VICTORIAN WOODEN ROCKING HORSE IN DAPPLED GREY WITH A BROWN MANE AND AN ORNATELY DESIGNED SADDLE AND BRIDLE. THESE DAPPLED MARKINGS MUST HAVE BEEN THE MOST POPULAR OF DESIGNS FOR ROCKING HORSES — MAYBE BECAUSE THEY ARE MORE INTERESTING THAN A PLAIN COAT.
PRICE GUIDE 6

▼ THIS WOODEN ROCKING HORSE DATES FROM THE LATE 19TH CENTURY AND IS MOUNTED ON A TRADITIONAL BOW ROCKER. THE BLACK MANE AND FORELOCK ARE EXTRAVAGANTLY LONG.
PRICE GUIDE 7

◀ MAGNETIC GAMES OF SKILL WERE ALWAYS POPULAR. THIS GAME, JUNIOR SPILLI WOBBLE, CLAIMED TO BE A GAME OF FUN AND DEXTERITY.
PRICE GUIDE 2

▼ THIS SET OF WALL QUOITS HAS BEEN WELL USED. THREE OF THE PEGS ARE MISSING AND THE ORIGINAL BOX IS LOST – GREATLY REDUCING THE VALUE.
PRICE GUIDE 1

◀ THE JIGSAW PUZZLE HAS BEEN AROUND FOR MANY YEARS, IN VARIOUS LEVELS OF COMPLEXITY. THIS EXAMPLE IS FROM A 'FAMOUS ARTIST SERIES' THAT FEATURED PAINTINGS BY OLD MASTERS.
PRICE GUIDE 2

POINTS TO WATCH

● KEEP ALL BOXES AND ORIGINAL PACKAGING MATERIAL. DO NOT ATTEMPT TO REPAIR THEM WITH ANY GLUE OR STICKY TAPE, NO MATTER HOW WORN.

● AVOID ANY METAL TOYS SUFFERING FROM CORROSION. A ROUGH, POWDERY SURFACE IS A TELL-TALE SIGN.

● BEWARE OF ANY REPAINTING THAT MIGHT HIDE PAST REPAIRS.

▲ DOMINOES HAVE EITHER HAVE WHITE DOTS OR COLOURED DOTS, AND THESE CAN SHOW SIGNS OF WEAR OVER THE YEARS. AS WITH ANY GAME WITH MANY PIECES, IT IS HARD TO COME BY A FULL SET.
PRICE GUIDE 2

▶ THIS TABLE GAME, A FORM OF QUOITS, STILL HAS ITS ORIGINAL BOX. AS CAN BE SEEN FROM THE PICTURE ON THE LID, THIS GAME WAS INTENDED TO BE USED ON THE TABLE, AS AN AFTER-DINNER GAME.
PRICE GUIDE 2

▲ THIS IS A MECCANO NO.8 SET.
THOUGH THE BOX IS WORN AND
DILAPIDATED, ALL THE PARTS ARE STILL
THERE AND MOST ARE AS GOOD AS NEW. A
POPULAR TOY FOR YEARS, MECCANO
PROVIDED AN ENJOYABLE INTRODUCTION
TO MECHANICS FOR MANY CHILDREN.
PRICE GUIDE 5

▲ THIS IS A GAME OF FIDDLESTICKS —
THE IDEA BEING TO DROP A HANDFUL OF
THE STICKS ON TO A SURFACE AND THEN
EXTRACT THEM, ONE-BY-ONE, WITHOUT
MOVING THE REMAINING PILE.
PRICE GUIDE 2

◀ BY THE 1920s, JIGSAWS BECAME MUCH
MORE FUN AND LESS RESTRICTED TO
EDUCATIONAL SUBJECTS. THIS EXAMPLE IS
SLIGHTLY DAMAGED BY THE PICTURE
PEELING AWAY FROM THE BACKGROUND.
PRICE GUIDE 1

DESIGN FEATURES

THIS CHILDREN'S STORY, *SHOCK-HEADED PETER* OR *STRUWWELPETER*, WAS A VICTORIAN FAVOURITE. PART OF A COLLECTION OF CAUTIONARY TALES THAT FIRST APPEARED IN GERMANY IN 1845, THIS RAPIDLY BECAME ONE OF THE BEST-SELLING NURSERY BOOKS OF ALL TIME. ITS AUTHOR HEINRICH HOFFMAN, A MEDICAL DOCTOR IN FRANKFURT, FRUSTRATED BY THE OVER-MORALISTIC STORIES ON OFFER IN PICTURE BOOKS, PRODUCED IT IN AN EXERCISE BOOK TO AMUSE HIS FOUR-YEAR-OLD SON. A YEAR LATER, HE WAS PERSUADED TO PUBLISH HIS COLLECTION OF GRUESOME STORIES, SUBTITLED WITH DELIBERATE IRONY: 'PRETTY STORIES AND FUNNY PICTURES FOR LITTLE CHILDREN.' THE RESULT WAS INSTANT SUCCESS.

THERE FOLLOWED NUMEROUS EDITIONS IN MANY LANGUAGES, INCLUDING ENGLISH. ALTHOUGH ORIGINALLY WRITTEN AS A TYPE OF SPOOF, IN ITSELF IT INSPIRED PARODIES, SUCH AS THE *EGYPTIAN STRUWWELPETER* (1899), CREATED ON BROWN PAPER TO RESEMBLE ANCIENT EGYPTIAN PAPYRUS BY THREE CHILDREN OF A VIENNESE DOCTOR, AGAIN, ORIGANALLY WITH NO THOUGH OF SERIOUS PUBLICATION.

INSET HERE IS AN EARLY DEPICTION OF STRUWWELPETER IN THE FIRST ENGLISH VERSION OF THE STORY. THE LATER VERSION ON THE RIGHT IS DATED 1894–5 WITH A MUCH MORE REFINED ILLUSTRATION THAN THE EARLIER BOOK.

ONE OF THE HALLMARKS OF RANDOLPH CALDECOTTS ILLUSTRATIONS WAS A GREAT SENSE OF FUN COMMUNICATED THROUGH LIVELY CHARACTERS. THE VICTORIANS DELIGHTED IN HIS BOOKS FOR CHILDREN AND COPIES SOLD IN GREAT NUMBERS.
PRICE GUIDE 1

BY THE 1840s, COLLECTIONS OF FAIRY TALES WERE WIDELY PUBLISHED. SOME OF THE MOST DECORATIVE ILLUSTRATIONS AND COVER DESIGNS WERE INSPIRED BY STORIES OF FANTASY AND MAGIC.
PRICE GUIDE 2

◀ ADVENTURE STORIES ARE COLLECTABLE FOR THEIR FINE, OFTEN COLOURFUL, COVERS DESIGNED TO ATTRACT YOUNG 19TH-CENTURY READERS. FREQUENTLY THEY WERE ILLUSTRATED WITH LAVISH COLOUR PLATES AND DRAMATIC FRONTISPIECES WHICH SERVED TO BRING THE GRIPPING TALES TO LIFE.

PRICE GUIDE 1

DESIGN FEATURES

A LARGE NUMBER OF TINPLATE MODEL BOATS WERE MADE RANGING FROM STEAMERS AND SPEEDBOATS TO GUNBOATS AND SUBMARINES. OFTEN MADE AS EXACT REPLICAS OF FULL-SIZED MODELS, MANY HAD CLOCKWORK OUTBOARD MOTORS AND SOME EVEN HAD ENGINES THAT EMITTED CLOUDS OF STEAM FROM FUNNELS AND EXHAUSTS.

BATTLESHIPS AND SUBMARINES HAVE ALWAYS FASCINATED CHILDREN, AND ALL EDWARDIAN TOY BOAT MANUFACTURERS INCLUDED DESTROYERS IN THEIR CATALOGUES. TOY SUBMARINES WERE ESPECIALLY APPEALING AS THEY RAN UNDERWATER, FOR A TIME, BEFORE RE-EMERGING ON THE SURFACE. THEY WERE ALWAYS CLOCKWORK DRIVEN — WOUND UP BY A KEY — AND WERE FITTED WITH SCREW-IN PLUGS TO KEEP THE WATER OUT OF THE KEYHOLES.

◄ WITH THREE SAILS AND SPECIAL PASSENGER SEATING, THIS DEEP-HULLED WOODEN MODEL YACHT WAS MADE IN THE 1920s. DELICATELY STITCHED, THE SAILS WORKED AS ON A REAL BOAT.
PRICE GUIDE 4

◀ MADE IN WILLOW, THIS EDWARDIAN TOY YACHT HAS RIGGING UP THE MAIN MAST, FOUR SAILS AND A BRIGHT RED HULL. THIS BOAT HAS THE NAME 'ST.MALO' AND A DELICATE LITTLE ANCHOR HAND-PAINTED ON TO ITS SIDE.
PRICE GUIDE 6

▶ THIS MODEL YACHT, MADE FROM OAK, C.1910, CAME WITH A STEERING MECHANISM SO THAT ITS DIRECTION COULD BE CONTROLLED FROM THE SHORE.
PRICE GUIDE 5

▲ THIS WOOD AND METAL REPLICA SHOWS AN OCEAN-GOING SCHOONER FROM THE EARLY 19TH CENTURY IN A PRESENTATION CASE. THIS MODEL HAS ONE FUNNEL AND TWO MASTS WITH AUXILIARY SAILS. CAREFULLY MADE, THIS BOAT IS FAITHFULL DOWN TO THE LAST DETAILS.
PRICE GUIDE 9

▲ MADE IN THE 1930s, THIS FINELY CRAFTED MODEL YACHT HAS A WOODEN DECK COMPLETE WITH A SCREW-TOP HATCH, RUDDER AND TWO SAILS.
PRICE GUIDE 7

POINTS TO WATCH

● ALWAYS CHECK THAT A MODEL SHIP HAS BEEN RESTORED ACCURATELY.
● NEVER ATTEMPT TO REPAIR A SHIP YOURSELF – CONSULT AN EXPERT.
● PROTECT MODEL SHIPS AND BOATS FROM DUST BY DISPLAYING THEM IN A GLASS CASE.
● DAMAGED MODELS WILL NOT BE WORTH AS MUCH AS THOSE IN PRISTINE CONDITION.

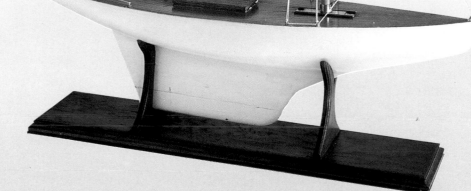

▶ FAIRLY SIMPLE IN DESIGN, THIS DEEP-KEELED MODEL YACHT HAS A VARNISHED WOODEN DECK AND TWO SAILS. IT IS SECURELY DISPLAYED ON A SPECIALLY DESIGNED SUPPORT.
PRICE GUIDE 6

▼ EXQUISITELY MODELLED WITH NO SPARING OF DETAILS, THIS TWO-FUNNELLED AND THREE-MASTED, EARLY 19TH-CENTURY, WOODEN AND METAL SCHOONER IS DISPLAYED IN A GLASS CASE FOR SAFEKEEPING.
PRICE GUIDE 7

◀ A POPULAR DISNEY TOY WAS THIS PROJECTOR. IT CAME WITH SETS OF COLOUR SLIDES THAT STARRED FAVOURITE DISNEY CHARACTERS.
PRICE GUIDE 5

▼ DONALD DUCK, WITH A SLIGHTLY ANXIOUS PLUTO AS PASSENGER CROUCHING IN THE BACK SEAT, GOES FOR A SPIN IN A BLUE RUBBER CAR.
PRICE GUIDE 3

◀ THIS MINIATURE CHINA TEA SET IS DECORATED WITH TRANSFER-PRINTED DISNEY CHARACTERS. THIS PARTICULAR SET SHOWS PINOCCHIO AND HIS FRIENDS. IT HAS A TEAPOT, MILK JUG, SUGAR BOWL AND TWO CUPS AND SAUCERS.
PRICE GUIDE 5

▲ THIS POCKET WATCH FEATURES MICKEY MOUSE ON THE WATCHFACE. HIS HANDS AND ARMS ACT AS THE HOUR AND MINUTE HANDS. MICKEY, AND OTHER DISNEY CHARACTERS, FEATURED ON BOTH POCKET AND WRIST WATCHES.
PRICE GUIDE 6

▼ A METAL HANDCAR WORKED BY
DONALD DUCK AND MICKEY MOUSE,
MAKES ITS WAY ALONG TRACKS. STILL IN
EXCELLENT WORKING ORDER, THE BODY
OF THE HANDCAR IS DECORATED WITH
PLUTO, ANOTHER DISNEY FAVOURITE.
PRICE GUIDE 6

▼ SNOW WHITE AND THE SEVEN
DWARFS ARE AMONG THE MANY DISNEY
CHARACTERS AND FILMS THAT FEATURED
ON JIGSAW PUZZLES.
PRICE GUIDE 3

▼ NUMEROUS BOOKS WERE PUBLISHED
AND ILLUSTRATED BY WALT DISNEY
STUDIO ARTISTS. THIS ANNUAL TELLS THE
TALE OF THE *THREE LITTLE PIGS*. THE
FIRST DISNEY ANNUAL WAS *THE MICKEY
MOUSE BOOK* OF 1930.
PRICE GUIDE 5

◀ THIS EARLY 19TH-CENTURY HORN CHESS SET IS SUPRISINGLY MODERN-LOOKING AND IS MADE IN FRANCE. HORN WAS A POPULAR, AND MUCH CHEAPER, ALTERNATIVE TO IVORY.
PRICE GUIDE 6

▶ SEVEN PIECES FROM AN EARLY 19TH-CENTURY, BLACK AND WHITE, ROYAL WORCESTER CHESS SET BASED ON AN ORIGINAL WEDGWOOD SET DESIGNED BY THE SCULPTOR JOHN FLAXMAN. THE FIGURES ARE INSPIRED BY SHAKESPEARE'S PLAY *MACBETH*.
PRICE GUIDE 8

▲ SIX PIECES FROM A LIGHT BLUE AND BLACK, GLAZED CERAMIC, CHESS SET MADE BY THE CASTLEFORD POTTERY IN THE 1820s. THE FIGURES ARE SHOWN WEARING CONTEMPORARY COSTUME.
PRICE GUIDE 8

▼ SIXTEEN PIECES FROM AN IVORY CHESS SET MADE IN CANTON IN THE 1820S THAT WAS PROBABLY IMPORTED TO BRITAIN BY THE EAST INDIA COMPANY. **PRICE GUIDE 8**

▼ THIS CHESS SET WAS MADE BY THE LONDON FIRM, LUND. OCCASIONALLY LUND DID COMMISSION INDIAN CRAFTSMEN TO PRODUCE CHESS PIECES. **PRICE GUIDE 7**

◀ TABLE BADMINTON PROVED POPULAR BECAUSE IT COULD BE PLAYED INDOORS IN ANY WEATHER. IN EARLY BADMINTON SETS RACKETS CAME COMPLETE WITH PROTECTIVE PRESSES AND SHUTTLECOCKS HAD REAL FEATHER FLIGHTS.
PRICE GUIDE 4

▼ THIS CHARMING SEPIA PHOTOGRAPH DATED 1904 SHOWS A GROUP OF AMATEUR PLAYERS AT THE OAKFIELD CRICKET CLUB. THOUGH AN AMATEUR TEAM, ALL PLAYERS ARE NEATLY KITTED OUT IN WHITES, BLAZERS AND CAPS.
PRICE GUIDE 4

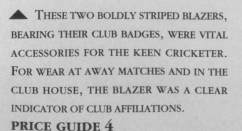

▲ THESE TWO BOLDLY STRIPED BLAZERS, BEARING THEIR CLUB BADGES, WERE VITAL ACCESSORIES FOR THE KEEN CRICKETER. FOR WEAR AT AWAY MATCHES AND IN THE CLUB HOUSE, THE BLAZER WAS A CLEAR INDICATOR OF CLUB AFFILIATIONS.
PRICE GUIDE 4

▲ THESE TWO CRICKET CAPS ARE MADE OF DIFFERENT MATERIALS. ONE IS OF A SOFT VELVET AND IS EMBROIDERED WITH THE DATE 1926; NO DOUBT THE CAP WAS PRESENTED TO A TEAM AFTER A SPECIFIC MATCH OR EVENT. THE OTHER IS IN A WOOL CLOTH WITH A REMOVABLE METAL BADGE BEARING A COAT OF ARMS.
PRICE GUIDE 2

▼ THIS COMPLETE SET OF WISDEN'S CRICKET BALLS ARE STILL IN THEIR PRESENTATION BOX. BALLS STILL FOUND TODAY IN SETS LIKE THIS WILL BE VALUED AT A SLIGHTLY HIGHER PRICE THAN THOSE SOLD SINGLY.
PRICE GUIDE 3

▼ DURING THE EDWARDIAN ERA, BOATERS, SUCH AS THESE TWO, WERE OFTEN WORN BY THE SPECTATORS RATHER THAN THE PLAYERS. LIGHTWEIGHT AND COOL, THE BOATER SHIELDED THE EYES ON HOT SUMMER AFTERNOONS.
PRICE GUIDE 3

▼ THIS PAIR OF CRICKET PADS ARE STILL IN A FAIR CONDITION, ALTHOUGH MAYBE A LITTLE WORN. THE LEATHER STRAPS THAT WOULD HAVE BUCKLED BEHIND THE KNEE TO HOLD THESE VITAL SHIN GUARDS ON, ARE STILL INTACT.
PRICE GUIDE 2

▲ THESE TWO EDWARDIAN CRICKET BATS ARE IN REASONABLE, BUT NOT PERFECT, CONDITION. ONE SHOWS SIGNS OF REPAIR TO THE BLADE. BATS SIGNED BY FAMOUS CRICKET PLAYERS CAN FETCH SEVERAL HUNDRED POUNDS, DEPENDING ON THE CELEBRITY OF THE PLAYER.
PRICE GUIDE 3

◀ THE BASIC SHAPE OF TENNIS RACKETS MAY NOT HAVE CHANGED MUCH IN THE 1920s AND 1930s, BUT THE PRESSES THAT THEY WERE STORED IN CAME IN SEVERAL DIFFERENT STYLES, AS WITH THE THREE EXAMPLES SHOWN HERE.
PRICE GUIDE 3

DESIGN FEATURES

AT THE BEGINNING OF THE 19TH CENTURY, GOLF CLUB HEADS WERE MADE FROM LOCAL HARDWOODS SUCH AS APPLE, PEAR AND BOXWOOD, USUALLY IN THE POPULAR LONG-NOSED SHAPE. WITH THE ADVENT OF HARDER, GUTTA-PERCHA BALLS IN 1848, BEECH, WHICH WAS MORE RESILIENT, WAS INTRODUCED AND HEADS BECAME SHORTER IN LENGTH.

EARLY SHAFTS WERE MADE FROM ASH OR HAZEL, BUT BY THE TURN OF THE CENTURY HICKORY WAS ALMOST EXCLUSIVELY USED.

THE CLUB HEAD, AS HERE, WAS CONNECTED TO THE SHAFT BY MEANS OF A SCARED JOINT, HENCE THE TERM 'SCARED HEAD'. THE SHAFT WAS SPLICED TO THE HEAD AND GLUED, THEN FURTHER STRENGTHENED WITH A BINDING SUCH AS FISHING LINE. THE GRIP AT THE TOP OF THE HANDLE WAS MADE BY WRAPPING SUEDE TIGHTLY AROUND IT.

THE SCARED JOINT WAS REPLACED BY THE SOCKET METHOD OF JOINTING AT THE TURN OF THE CENTURY.

▶ EDWARDIAN CADDY BAGS WERE CONSTRUCTED OF CANVAS AND LEATHER, USUALLY AROUND A WOODEN FRAME. THIS EXAMPLE, MADE IN 1910, CAN STILL BE USED TO CARRY CLUBS.
PRICE GUIDE 3

▲ THIS 1920s CADDY TROLLEY IS MADE OF A RELATIVELY MODERN MATERIAL, ALUMINIUM. LIGHT, BUT STURDY, THIS MADE AN IDEAL CADDY TROLLEY, POPULAR WITH AMATEURS CARRYING THEIR OWN BAGS, AND PROFESSIONAL CADDIES.
PRICE GUIDE 6

◀ THESE EDWARDIAN GOLFING TROPHIES ARE MADE OF PEWTER AND SILVER AND ARE ENGRAVED WITH THE DETAILS OF SPECIAL COMPETITIONS. THESE AFFORDABLE PIECES MAKE A GOOD BASIS FOR AN INTERESTING AND REWARDING COLLECTION.
PRICE GUIDE 4

▲ THIS WOOD AND ALUMINIUM PUTTER WAS DESIGNED BY WILLIAM MILLS IN 1910. LIGHT, STRONG AND WELL MADE, THIS TYPE OF CLUB WAS POPULAR WITH BRITISH GOLFERS EARLY THIS CENTURY.
PRICE GUIDE 5

▲ THIS LATE 18TH-CENTURY, WOODEN SHAFT CLUB WAS MADE BY BUSSEY, MAKERS OF GOLF CLUBS TO THE BRITISH ROYAL FAMILY. IT HAS A SPECIAL PATENTED STEEL HEAD.
PRICE GUIDE 5

▲ THIS IS ALSO A LATE 18TH-CENTURY, BUSSEY GOLF CLUB. A PATENT BRASS HEAD IS FIXED TO A HANDMADE WOODEN SHAFT. GOLF CLUBS COULD BE MADE TO ORDER, TO SUIT ANY HEIGHT AND SWING.
PRICE GUIDE 5

◀ THIS LATE VICTORIAN SPLIT REED CREEL IS BOUND IN LEATHER AND IS IN NEAR PERFECT CONDITION AND, THEREFORE, EXPENSIVE. IT WAS OFTEN USED TO HOLD SPARE TACKLE. THE BROWN LEATHER AND CANVAS WADERS THAT PROTECTED THE FEET DATE FROM THE SAME PERIOD.
PRICE GUIDE 5 & 3

▶ THIS LEATHER FLY WALLET FROM AROUND 1900 CONTAINS GUT-EYED FLIES. THE WALLET USUALLY HELD THE ANGLER'S PERSONAL SELECTION OF HAND-MADE, TRADITIONAL FLY PATTERNS.
PRICE GUIDE 5

▶ THIS BRASS AND CORDING LANDING NET, DATED 1880, IS BOTH ATTRACTIVE AND PRACTICAL. EASIER TO CARRY, THE TELESCOPIC HANDLE CAN BE DETACHED FROM THE NET WHEN NOT IN USE.
PRICE GUIDE 4

▲ THIS METAL FLY TYER'S VICE AND PRICKER ARE BOTH LATE VICTORIAN. BOTH WERE USED IN THE MANUFACTURE OF FLYS. THE PRICKER HAS A CHERRY WOOD HANDLE AND THE NEEDLE WAS USED FOR PRICKING OUT THE EYES.
PRICE GUIDE 3 & 5

▶ THIS SHARP HOOK IS A SALMON LANDING GAFF MADE OF BRASS AND ROSEWOOD AND DATING FROM AROUND 1860. THE BANDED HANDLE WAS TO MAKE IT EASIER TO HOLD ON TO.
PRICE GUIDE 4

▶ THIS IS A HAND-CRAFTED BRASS FISH SCALE DATING FROM THE LATE 19TH CENTURY. THE MEASURES, NUMBERED UP TO TEN, ARE IN POUND WEIGHTS.
PRICE GUIDE 3

◀ THE TWO WOODEN SALMON REELS HERE WERE AMONG THE MOST COMMON TYPES AVAILABLE AT THE END OF THE 19TH CENTURY. THE IVORY-HANDLED BRASS REEL IS OF AN EARLIER DATE.
PRICE GUIDE 5

This chapter covers that wide and varied range of antiques that do not happily fit into the other categories. Either because these pieces are made of unusual substances or combinations of material, or because they seem to fall into a category of their own, they have been grouped together under the loose term, collectables. To anyone contemplating collecting antiques, especially first-time buyers, the diversity of collectables available offers a rich source of inspiration.

At the top end of the market, jewellery is a very popular area for collectors since not only can pieces be of high investment value, they are also attractive to own and wear. The value alone of gems and metals used can make a piece of jewellery highly desirable and pieces made by famous artists or renowned companies have added appeal. Precious stones in gold or platinum settings will fetch the top prices but even this will vary according to the cut of the gems and the design of the setting. Collectors, therefore, need to be aware of the craftsman's intentions and priorities before making any judgements on the value of jewellery. Genuine flaws or bad condition should always be avoided by anyone buying as an investment. Watch out for pearls that have lost a layer of nacre, for stones darkened by perfume and body oils, for cracked opals, and common faults like bad repairs, lead solders, damaged enamel and missing or replacement stones.

Away from the more valuable pieces, there is a vast amount of high quality jewellery in more modern and affordable materials. Many collectors specialize in costume and Art Deco jewellery that skilfully uses plastics, paste, and chrome, sometimes in combination with more precious gems and metals. More modern jewellery can prove a safer bet than Victorian or Edwardian pieces since older items have often lost

This Ernemann camera was known as 'The Bob' when it was put on sale in about 1906. The bellows for focusing are mounted on brass tracks.

stone or been repaired. However, some materials have certain problems. Enamel is notoriously hard to repair and it is best to avoid buying badly chipped or cracked pieces. If silver is scratched then it is not advisable to try and remove scratches; this is best left to professionals. All jewellery should be polished with a cloth and not immersed in liquid, particularly in the case of foil-backed paste which will lose its sparkle forever.

Antique clothing has become an increasingly popular field for collectors. The main challenge for the enthusiast is the scarcity of good clothing available; in the past garments had to last and were worn until they could be worn no longer. However, they were made of sturdy and durable fabrics and the clothing that was looked after remains well-preserved today. The best places to look for antique costume are specialist dealers and outdoor clothes markets. Some collectors focus on single items, such as blouses, nightwear, hats or underwear, but entire costumes can make a much better display. In caring for antique clothing, it is important not to wear valued items. They should be kept out of light when they are not on display, and they should not be out on display for very long periods. Tailor's dummies are an ideal way to exhibit pieces in a collection. Alterations to antique clothing should not be carried out, and mending should only be attempted with great care. Cleaning should only be done extremely carefully, and preferably only after advice from an expert. When garments are not on display they should be folded carefully, laid between sheets of acid-free tissue paper with some kind of moth repellent that does not touch the fabric, and put in a box in a cool, dark room.

Prices of clothing collectables are unpredictable, though generally not astronomical. They vary with quality and attractiveness. A blouse in really fine

often short-lived, but they are worth investigating, since they will have items of interest that cannot be purchased elsewhere. Fortunately, most advertising ephemera is still inexpensive for even the most impecunious of collectors. When looking for this kind of paper ephemera it is worth making sure that the advertisement is genuine; reproductions of famous posters are quite common, and some of these are carefully 'aged' to simulate originals. Work by well-known artists is bound to be more valuable and posters are the most costly form of advertising art; collectors on a budget should look to packaging and newspapers for the cheaper items. Collecting ephemera is so well-organized to day that there are clubs for every conceivable kind of material, from cheese labels to adverts for limousines.

One of the most enduringly popular collectables for many years has been stamps, a subject so extensive as to warrant its own name, philately. There are also letters, postcards and covers to be collected, either with stamps or as a field on their own. Stamp collections today fall into one of four types. First there is the general collection, which, as its name implies, ranges widely but cannot by its nature be comprehensive in any area. Then there is the selective, which narrows the focus somewhat to a particular time or place. There are also thematic collections where a particular subject of stamp design is focused on, such as art, sport, birds or flowers. All these kinds of collections fall under the umbrella of philately and, as such, can be an expensive form of antique for the average enthusiast. Equally rewarding to anyone interested in stamps and the postal system is the collecting of letters and postcards bearing period stamps and postmarks. They have the added interest of being reasonably cheap and quite widely available in markets and junk shops, as well as from

Books, such as these 19th-century volumes of Robert Burns and Sir Walter Scott, have long been a popular antique collectable and certain editions can fetch high prices.

specialist dealers. When beginning a collection of stamps and covers it is worth first considering how to keep and display the items. The printed album is ideal for the general collector, but for anyone making a collection of stamps and associated ephemera as the record of an era, a blank album, in which the collector can construct his own story or theme, is more appropriate. Antique stamp albums themselves can make an interesting focus for a collection, either with or without stamps enclosed.

Such popularity makes the field of philately prone to forgery and anyone seriously considering investing in stamps should read round the subject extensively if they want to avoid disappointment. There are three kinds of forgery with stamps. Firstly, there are postal counterfeits that were intended to defraud the post office of revenue and these can now command higher prices than the stamps they were meant to imitate. Secondly, there are philatelic forgeries, designed to deceive collectors and these have been around since the 1860s. Lastly, there are fakes, or genuine stamps which have been altered in some way to make them appear more rare and valuable and these can be hard to spot.

Too numerous to mention in entirety here, there is a diverse and fascinating wealth of collectables to be found in both shops and markets. With such a wide range of subjects available, there is no shortage of themes from which to chose. But whatever field the collector becomes interested in, there will be certain specialist books and magazines, and dealers and museums that can offer practical advice on cost, maintenance and restoration. As well as awakening an interest in a particular subject, the literature available can guide the enthusiast through both the perils and the joys of buying collectable antiques.

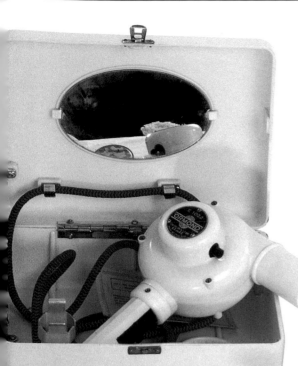

◀ A WELL-KEPT EXAMPLE OF A BAKELITE ELECTRIC HAIRDRYER, AVAILABLE IN THE 1930s, WITH ITS ORIGINAL FLEX AND STORAGE BOX. THE SMALL MIRROR SET IN THE LID MADE THIS DRYER AND CASE SUITABLE FOR TRAVELLING.
PRICE GUIDE 3

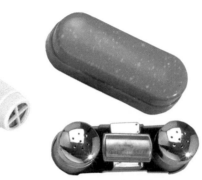

▲ THIS SMALL CASE CONTAINS A ROLLS RAZOR, NO.3 IMPERIAL MODEL. THE RAZOR HAS A SINGLE-EDGED BLADE AND ALSO INCLUDED IN THE SET ARE STROPPING AND HONING SURFACES.
PRICE GUIDE 3

▼ THESE ARE A VARIETY OF STROPS FOR SHARPENING RAZORS – SOME ARE RIGID AND HAVE WOODEN HANDLES. THE HANGING STROP, WITH A LOOP TO ATTACH IT TO THE WALL, HAS LEATHER ON ONE SIDE AND CANVAS ON THE OTHER.
PRICE GUIDE 1

▲ A NEAT, GREEN BAKELITE SHAVING SET – ITS COMPACT DESIGN MADE IT IDEAL FOR TRAVELLING. IT INCLUDES ALL THE ORIGINAL PARTS; A RAZOR, BRUSH AND SHAVING STICK HOLDER.
PRICE GUIDE 3

▲ THESE TWO TRAVELLING SHAVING SETS DATE FROM THE 1930s. THE LARGER BOX STILL CONTAINS A PACKAGED SET OF GILLETTE BLADES. PRIOR TO 1921, GILLETTE HELD THE PATENT ON THE BLADES FOR SAFETY RAZORS; AFTER THAT DATE THEY HAD TO COMPETE WITH OTHER RAZOR BLADE MANUFACTURERS.
PRICE GUIDE 1

▲ THESE TWO CUT-THROAT RAZORS BOTH HAVE STAINLESS STEEL BLADES. THE RAZOR IN THE CASE HAS A BLADE GUARD INCORPORATED TO PREVENT ACCIDENTS.
PRICE GUIDE 1

▲ A SERPENTINE, SILVER CLOTHES BRUSH ADORNED WITH SCENES OF DRINKING AND MERRYMAKING SET IN THE COUNTRYSIDE. DATING FROM 1883, THIS BRUSH IS DECORATED WITH A HIGH RELIEF.
PRICE GUIDE 5

▶ THIS IS A RARE EXAMPLE OF TWO SILVER-TOPPED SCENT BOTTLES IN A SILVER-PLATED STAND. THE VICTORIAN LADY'S DRESSING TABLE WOULD HAVE FEATURED MANY DIFFERENT LITTLE GLASS BOTTLES FOR VARIOUS DIFFERENT SCENTS AND BEAUTY PREPARATIONS.
PRICE GUIDE 5

▲ A BLUE GLASS BOTTLE IS CONTAINED WITHIN THIS PIERCED SILVER MOUNTING. THE EDWARDIAN LADY COULD FILL A BOTTLE LIKE THIS THAT WOULD FIT INTO A BAG WITH THE PERFUME OF HER CHOICE.
PRICE GUIDE 5

▲ AN EDWARDIAN SILVER TRINKET BOX DECORATED IN A RAISED PATTERN IN THE ART NOUVEAU STYLE. LITTLE BOXES LIKE THIS ONE WOULD HAVE CONTAINED SMALL PIECES OF JEWELLERY OR HAIR ORNAMENTS, PINS AND RIBBONS.
PRICE GUIDE 5

▲ THIS SMALL SILVER PHIAL WOULD HAVE BEEN SUITABLE FOR CARRYING PERFUME IN AND WOULD HAVE BEEN FOUND ON BOTH DRESSING TABLE AND IN THE HANDBAG. THE SILVER HALLMARK DATES THIS PIECE TO 1890.
PRICE GUIDE 5

▲ THIS TINY GLASS POT WOULD PROBABLY HAVE BEEN USED FOR ROUGE OR SOME OTHER BASIC BEAUTY PREPARATION. THE SILVER LID, HALLMARKED AT 1889, IS LIGHTLY DECORATED WITH A CIRCLE OF ROCOCO SCROLLS.
PRICE GUIDE 3

▲ THIS PRETTY CERAMIC POT WOULD PROBABLY HAVE BEEN USED TO HOLD SOME TYPE OF HAIR OIL OR CREAM, AS THE DECORATION OF A WOMAN DRESSING HER HAIR SUGGESTS.
PRICE GUIDE 5

▼ A VICTORIAN, DIE-STAMPED, SILVER HAND MIRROR, WITH TYPICALLY FLORID DECORATION. MOST MIRRORS OF THIS KIND WERE PART OF A SET WITH MATCHING HAIR AND CLOTHES BRUSHES. **PRICE GUIDE 7**

▼ MATCHING DRESSING TABLE SETS COULD INCLUDE AN EXTRAORDINARY NUMBER OF ITEMS. SHOWN HERE ARE PARTS OF A MANICURE SET AND A SHOE HORN FINISHED IN TORTOISE-SHELL THAT WERE, IN TURN, PART OF A LARGER SET OF POTS, MIRROR AND BRUSHES. **PRICE GUIDE 5**

▲ THIS LONG-BRISTLED BRUSH WITH ROCOCO, SILVER HANDLE HAS A SPECIALIZED USE. DESIGNED AS A BRUSH FOR LADIES' BONNETS, THE LONG, SOFT HAIRS COULD BRUSH AWAY DUST WITHOUT DISTURBING EXTRAVAGANT MILLINERY. **PRICE GUIDE 3**

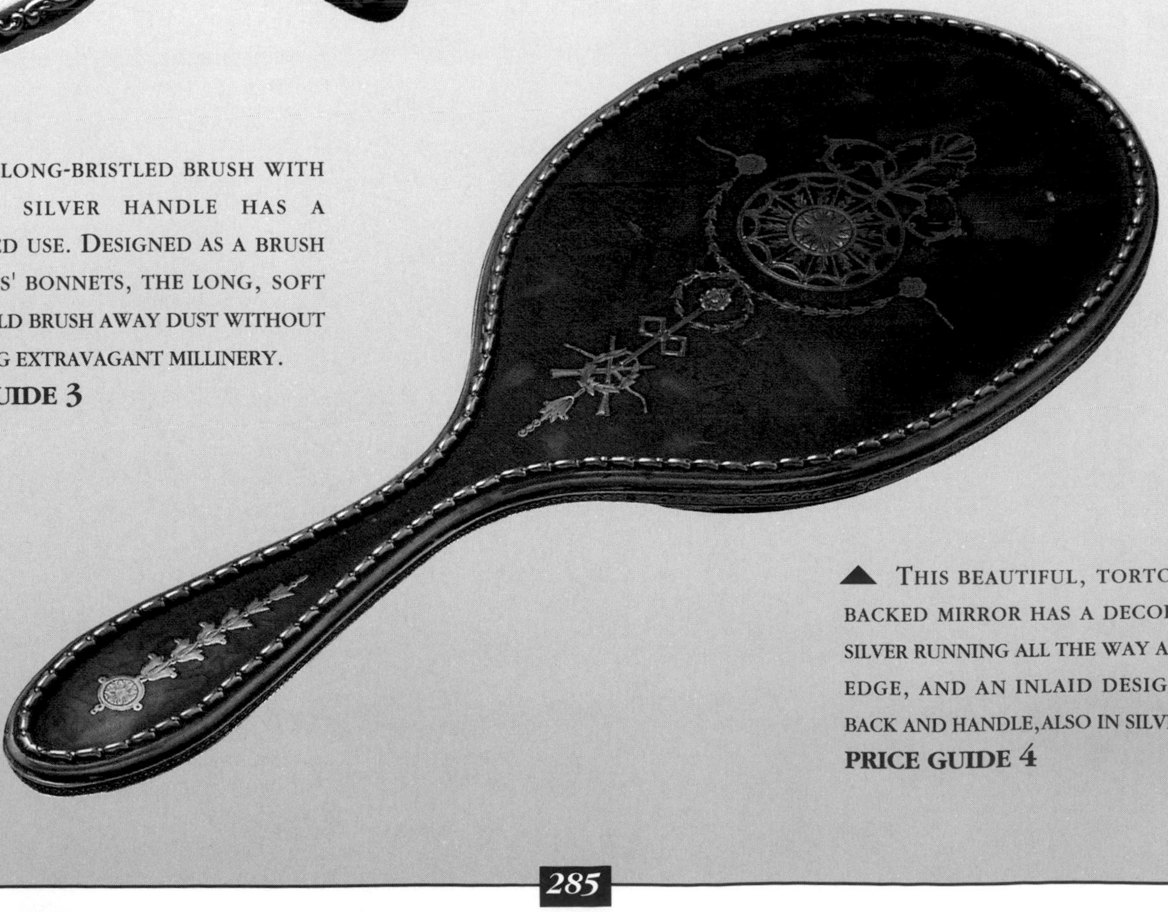

▲ THIS BEAUTIFUL, TORTOISESHELL-BACKED MIRROR HAS A DECORATION IN SILVER RUNNING ALL THE WAY AROUND ITS EDGE, AND AN INLAID DESIGN ON THE BACK AND HANDLE, ALSO IN SILVER. **PRICE GUIDE 4**

▼ THESE TWO SILVER AND CRYSTAL POTS WOULD HAVE MADE UP PART OF A SET OF GROOMING ACCESSORIES. ONE POT CONTAINED POMADE, A DRESSING MEN USED ON THEIR HAIR, AND THE OTHER WAS FOR A SHAVING BRUSH.
PRICE GUIDE 4

▲ A SILVER MATCH CONTAINER AND STRIKER, WITH A STAND FOR THE LIGHTED MATCH. THIS SMALL ITEM WOULD HAVE BEEN KEPT ON THE GENTLEMAN'S DRESSING TABLE OR DESK TO LIGHT CANDLES, LAMPS, FIRES, CIGARS AND PIPES.
PRICE GUIDE 5

◀ THIS SILVER CLOTHES BRUSH, FROM AROUND 1900, WOULD HAVE COME FROM A SET THAT INCLUDED HAIR BRUSHES AND MATCHING POTS. THE DECORATION CONSISTS OF A SIMPLE BORDER.
PRICE GUIDE 3

▶ WHEN TRAVELLING, THE VICTORIAN GENTLEMAN WOULD HAVE BEEN ABLE TO CARRY COLOGNES AND OTHER GROOMING PREPARATIONS IN A CONTAINER LIKE THIS. THREE GLASS BOTTLES, DECORATED WITH GOLD LEAF, ARE CARRIED IN A SOLID, LOCKABLE WALNUT CASE.
PRICE GUIDE 5

◀ DATING FROM 1792, THIS TRAVELLING TOOTBRUSH SET ARE VERY WELL PRESERVED. THE BRUSH COMES WITH ITS OWN SILVER HOLDER AND BOTH THEN FIT INTO A PROTECTIVE LEATHER CASE.
PRICE GUIDE 7

▲ THIS SMALL, ROUND IVORY POT, BOTH SIMPLE AND FUNCTIONAL, WOULD MOST LIKELY HAVE BEEN USED TO STORE HAIRDRESSING OR SHAVING LOTIONS.
PRICE GUIDE 4

▼ THESE TWO TORTOISESHELL-BACKED HAIR BRUSHES DATE FROM 1820. HAIR BRUSHES HAVE BEEN COMMONLY USED SINCE THE 18TH CENTURY – INCREASING IN POPULARITY AS WIGS WENT OUT OF FASHION. HIGH QUALITY BRUSHES WERE MADE FROM HOG'S BRISTLE WHICH CAME PRINCIPALLY FROM RUSSIAN WILD BOAR.
PRICE GUIDE 4

▲ THIS SILVER-HANDLED SHAVING BRUSH CAME IN ITS OWN SILVER SCREW-TOP CONTAINER. SHAVING BRUSHES WERE INTRODUCED TO BRITAIN FROM FRANCE IN THE 1750S, BUT WERE NOT WIDELY USED UNTIL A CENTURY LATER. THIS BRUSH DATES FROM 1838.
PRICE GUIDE 5

▲ THIS SMALL WOODEN CONTAINER WITH ITS SCREW TOP LID WHICH SPORTS A MOTHER-OF-PEARL INSET, WOULD HAVE BEEN USED TO STORE SMALL ITEMS OF DRESS SUCH AS BUTTONS OR COLLAR STUDS. IT DATES FROM AROUND 1830.
PRICE GUIDE 6

▶ THIS BONE SHOE HORN, DATING FROM 1830, IS IDENTICAL IN STYLE TO THE MODERN VERSION WHICH WOULD BE MORE LIKELY TO BE MADE OF PLASTIC.
PRICE GUIDE 3

◀ INTRICATE FESTOONS OF GOLD FILIGREE ARE USED TO MOUNT THE GEMS THAT EMBELLISH THIS THREE-PIECE SET WHICH IS STILL IN ITS ORIGINAL CASE.
PRICE GUIDE 9

▼ THIS IMPRESSIVE BRACELET AND NECKLACE SET IS A COMBINATION OF LARGE PERIDOTS (A GREEN MINERAL) AND SMALL CLUSTERS OF DIAMONDS LINKED BY A GOLD CHAIN IN ORNATE SCROLLWORK.
PRICE GUIDE 9

▼ THIS SET CONSIST OF SEVEN PIECES: NECKLACE, BROOCH, EARRINGS, PINS, CLIPS, PENDANTS AND BRACELET. EACH HAS A SPARKLING PINK TOPAZ SET IN A TEXTURAL GOLD FILIGREE.
PRICE GUIDE 9

▼ THIS BRASS INLAID JEWEL BOX WITH CENTRAL MONOGRAMMED PLATE HAS MATCHING LION'S HEAD CARRYING HANDLES AND ROUND BRASS FEET. IT IS DATED AT ROUGHLY 1810.
PRICE GUIDE 9

DESIGN FEATURES

EDWARDIAN JEWELLERY IS RENOWNED FOR ITS DELICATE, BEAUTIFULLY CREATED DESIGNS. IN CONTRAST TO VICTORIAN JEWELLERY, MANY PIECES WERE MADE IN A VERY FEMININE FASHION, USING SMALLER STONES AND VERY LIGHT SETTINGS THAT WERE MADE POSSIBLE BY USING PLATINUM.

THIS SAPPHIRE AND DIAMOND BOW-SHAPED BROOCH IS A PERFECT EXAMPLE OF SUCH WORK AND HAS AN ELEGANT, ALMOST LACY SETTING, CRAFTED IN PLATINUM. THE DELICATE, OPENWORK SETTING IS FORMED INTO LACY FEATHERS OF ROSE DIAMONDS. THE BAND OF SMALLER, SQUARE SAPPHIRES ARE DEFTLY PLACED INTO GROOVES TO CREATE AN INVISIBLE SETTING. A LARGE SQUARE-CUT SAPPHIRE IN THE CENTRE IS FRAMED BY A CLUSTER OF DIAMONDS.

THE EXPERT CRAFTSMEN WHO MADE PIECES LIKE THESE SOUGHT TO DISPLAY THE PRIZE GEMS TO THEIR BEST ADVANTAGE AND STROVE TO MAKE THE SETTINGS BECOME ALMOST INVISIBLE. THIS VERY NEAT LOOK IS MUCH SOUGHT AFTER TODAY.

▼ THIS OVAL, GOLD LOCKET IS DECORATED WITH WHITE AND BLUE ENAMEL. THE BLUE, CENTRAL BOSS IS SURMOUNTED WITH A STAR OF TINY SPLIT SEED PEARLS.
PRICE GUIDE 6

▲ LOCKETS BEARING PORTRAITS OF LOVED ONES HAVE BEEN POPULAR FOR YEARS. THE PORTRAIT OF A CHILD, HERE, IS ENCLOSED IN A CIRCULAR PENDANT LOCKET OF PINCHBECK (AN ALLOY OF COPPER AND ZINC) THAT DATES TO ABOUT 1880. THE SEPIA-TONED PHOTOGRAPH IS HELD IN AN OVAL, GOLD PENDANT LOCKET FROM AROUND 1890.
PRICE GUIDE 3

▼ THIS LARGE, OVAL PENDANT LOCKET IS MADE OF PINCHBECK AND IS ENGRAVED ALL OVER, INCLUDING THE LINK AT THE TOP, WITH A FLORAL DESIGN. IT IS HINGED FOR OPENING AT THE SIDE.
PRICE GUIDE 4

▶ THESE HEXAGONAL CUFF LINKS FROM C.1925 ARE MOUNTED IN PLATINUM. ALSO SET WITH DIAMONDS AND SQUARE-CUT BURMESE RUBIES THEY ARE VALUED AT A HIGH PRICE TODAY.
PRICE GUIDE 8

▼ THIS LARGE OVAL LOCKET WAS MADE IN AROUND 1880. IT CONTAINS AN ARTISTICALLY ARRANGED CURL OF HAIR WHICH IS READILY VISIBLE. A POPULAR WAY TO DISPLAY A LOVED-ONE'S LOCKS OF HAIR WAS TO WEAVE THEM TOGETHER.
PRICE GUIDE 4

▼ THIS PAIR OF BROOCHES TAKE ON THE DESIGN OF A BASKET OF FLOWERS. THESE PASTE VERSIONS WERE PROBABLY INSPIRED BY THE DIAMOND-ENCRUSTED FLOWER BASKETS PRODUCED BY FABERGÉ AT THE END OF THE 19TH CENTURY.
PRICE GUIDE 5

▲ THESE EXTRAVAGENTLY DESIGNED EARRINGS DATE FROM THE 1900s. THE PASTE GEMS ARE SET IN SILVER AND THE HOOKS FOR PIERCED EARS ARE IN GOLD.
PRICE GUIDE 6

▲ THE FINELY-CARVED, GOLD FLORAL DESIGN OF THIS BROOCH WAS MADE IN FRANCE IN ABOUT 1900. SET WITH DIAMONDS, THERE IS AN OVAL OPAL IN THE CENTRE WITH A ROSE DIAMOND SURROUND AND DECORATED WITH GREEN ENAMEL.
PRICE GUIDE 8

▼ THIS ENAMEL AND PASTE PENDANT DATES FROM AROUND 1905. PASTE JEWELLERY WAS, AT FIRST, USED TO COPY MORE VALUABLE PIECES THAT OWNERS WANTED TO HIDE AWAY FOR SAFE-KEEPING BUT THE BRILLIANCE AND ATTRACTIVENESS OF PIECES SOON MADE IT A POPULAR FORM OF JEWELLERY IN ITS OWN RIGHT.
PRICE GUIDE 5

DESIGN FEATURES

BROOCH BUCKLES, WHICH BECAME POPULAR IN THE 1920S, USUALLY CONSISTED OF AN INNER RING OR ELLIPSE OF SEMI-PRECIOUS STONES SUCH AS ONYX OR CORAL, SURROUNDED BY AN OUTER, CONTRASTING RING OF DIAMANTÉ, PEARLS OR SAPPHIRES.

THIS ATTRACTIVE EXAMPLE WAS MADE IN PARIS IN 1929, AND IS IMPRESSIVE IN ITS SIZE – 5 INCHES (12.5 CM) ACROSS. IT HAS A CENTREPIECE OF GREEN BAKELITE AND AN OUTER BORDER OF PASTE. THE BLACK BAKELITE STRIPS AT THE CENTRE ARE HINGES THAT ALLOW THIS PIECE TO CURVE AROUND THE BODY.

IT WAS WORN ATTACHED TO A BELT OR SASH WHICH WAS PASSED THROUGH THE SLOTS IN THE GREEN BAKELITE.

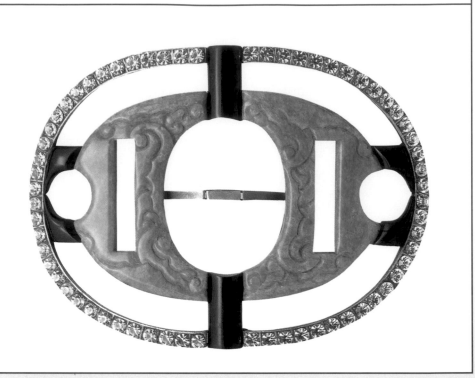

▼ THE DECORATION OF THIS BAKELITE BANGLE IS DELIBERATELY KEPT TO A MINIMUM TO EMPHASIZE THE BOLD GEOMETRIC SHAPE AND COLOUR OF THIS PARTICULAR PIECE.
PRICE GUIDE 2

◀▶ BOTH THE CHAIN AND CUBES OF THE NECKLACE ON THE LEFT ARE MADE OF A YELLOW CLEAR PLASTIC. THE ONE ON THE RIGHT, OF CIRCLES AND TRIANGLES OF DIFFERENT SIZES, IS MADE OF A RED, SOLID AND OPAQUE PLASTICS. THE MODERNIST FORMS POPULAR WITH ART DECO ARE CLEARLY INFLUENTIAL HERE.
PRICE GUIDE 3 & 5

▼ This Art Deco necklace made up of geometric shapes with abstract colour designs clearly shows the influence of an Egyptian revival. The coloured sections are separated by small paste rondels.

PRICE GUIDE 7

▼ Geometric and mechanical forms were highly influential in Art Deco jewellery design. The 'machine aesthetic' can easily be seen in this typical 1930s brooch.

PRICE GUIDE 4

▼ No fashionable flapper of the 1920s was without her compact. The small dress watch here comes in a matching case — both could easily be slipped into a handbag.

PRICE GUIDE 4

▲ The raised oblong pieces on this bracelet that appear to be of a blue marble are, in fact, made of Bakelite. The rest of the piece is made of chrome and brass.

PRICE GUIDE 5

▲ These pyramid-shaped earrings are made in yellow Bakelite. Designed to sit close to the ear, these would have been clip-ons.

PRICE GUIDE 1

▶ Women in the 1920s and 1930s had, for the first time, taken to shorter haircuts, often dramatic and bold. These Deco paste earrings and the silver and blue Bakelite examples would have been suitably complimentary to modern styles.

PRICE GUIDE 5 & 4

◀ THIS SMALL, BRUSSELS, PRINCESS LACE HANDBAG HAS A DRAWSTING OPENING AND A PINK LINING. A BAG LIKE THIS WOULD PROBABLY HAVE BEEN CARRIED BY A BRIDE, THOUGH DRAWSTRING BAGS WERE ALSO POPULAR FOR EVENING USE.
PRICE GUIDE 3

▶ THIS BLUSH-PINK WEDDING DRESS IS MADE OF SATIN WITH LACE AND COTTON EMBROIDERED PANELS. IS HAS A HIGH WAIST AND A CROSS-OVER BODICE WITH THE SAME LACE AND EMBROIDERED PANELS AS THE SKIRT. A CORSAGE OF SATIN AND COTTON FLOWERS TRIMS THE WAISTBAND.
PRICE GUIDE 6

◀ THIS CREAM COTTON AND LACE DRESS, MADE IN 1900, IS A WEDDING DRESS. THE HIGH NECK IS MADE OF LAYERED LACE AND LARGER PANELS OF A BROAD-PATTERNED LACE TRIM THE BODICE. SLEEVES OF RUCHED COTTON FALL GENTLY OVER SPOTTED NET UNDERSLEEVES.
PRICE GUIDE 6

◀ THE CAMISOLE TOP WAS ONE OF THE MANY PIECES OF UNDERWEAR THAT THE VICTORIAN LADY HAD TO WEAR AS WELL AS THE CONFINING CORSET. THIS TOP IS MADE IN WHITE COTTON LAWN WITH LACE INSERTS, FINE PINTUCKS AND TINY MOTHER-OF-PEARL BUTTONS.
PRICE GUIDE 4

◀ THESE WHITE, COTTON LAWN CAMIKNICKERS DATE FROM AROUND 1865. THE TOP HALF OF THE KNICKERS ARE MADE UP OF BANDS OF LACE AND THE LEGS ARE SET WITH STRIPS OF THE SAME LACE. A PALE, GREEN RIBBON IS ALSO THREADED THROUGH.
PRICE GUIDE 4

▼ DATING FROM AROUND 1870, THIS LADY'S CORSET IS MADE FROM COTTON, BONE AND LACE. DECORATED WITH TINY, EMBROIDERED ROSEBUDS, THIS CORSET IS FASTENED WITH PALE PINK LACES.
PRICE GUIDE 4

▶ THIS CREAM WEDDING DRESS WAS MADE IN AROUND 1900. IT IS IN THREE PIECES: A LONG COTTON SKIRT, AN OVER-BODICE AND A BLOUSE WITH GATHERED SLEEVES AND LACE YOKE AND NECK.
PRICE GUIDE 6

▶ THE VICTORIAN GENTLEMAN'S HANDKERCHIEF WAS ON A MUCH LARGER SCALE THAN ITS FEMALE COUNTERPART. THIS COMMEMORATIVE HANDKERCHIEF SHOWS QUEEN VICTORIA IN THE CENTRE AND HER FOUR SONS IN THE CORNERS.

PRICE GUIDE 3

▼ THIS SQUARE VEIL FROM C.1900 IS MADE OF LIMERICK LACE. IT IS ELABORATELY DECORATED ALL OVER WITH ATTRACTIVE FOLIAGE MOTIFS. MANY TOWNS AND AREAS HAVE SPECIALIZED IN LACE MANUFACTURE, NOTTINGHAM IN ENGLAND, AND BRITTANY IN FRANCE, ARE AMONG THE MOST FAMOUS.

PRICE GUIDE 6

▼ THIS SIMPLE LACE VEIL WAS MADE AROUND 1910. THE MAIN BODY OF THE VEIL IS DECORATED WITH OCCASIONAL SPRIGS OF DOG ROSES AND THE BORDER IS MADE UP OF THE SAME FLOWERS. THE VEIL WOULD HAVE BEEN HELD IN PLACE BY A CIRCLET OF WAX AND PAPER FLOWERS, USUALLY ORANGE BLOSSOMS.

PRICE GUIDE 5

▼ THOUGH APPEARING TO BE AN ORDINARY SUITCASE WHEN SHUT, THIS CASE WAS ESPECIALLY FITTED TO TAKE SIX PAIRS OF SHOES. MADE IN ENGLAND, IT DATES FROM THE 1930S.
PRICE GUIDE 4

POINTS TO WATCH

● GOOD FAKE CROCODILE LUGGAGE CAN BE DIFFICULT TO DISTINGUISH FROM THE REAL THING.

● BEWARE OF IMITATION LOUIS VUITTON LUGGAGE; OBVIOUS SIGNS OF AGE AND THE 'L V' MONOGRAM ON DETAILS AND BODY OF THE LUGGAGE ARE GOOD INDICATORS OF AUTHENTICITY.

● WORN STRAPS, HANDLES AND FASTENINGS MAY HAVE TO BE REPLACED, BUT IT IS NOT PROHIBITIVELY EXPENSIVE.

▼ ITS COLLECTION OF TRAVEL STICKERS HAVE INCREASED THE VALUE OF THIS ENGLISH VELLUM SUITCASE. VELLUM IS A FINE KIND OF PARCHMENT PRODUCED BY SPECIALLY TREATING THE HIDE OF CALVES OR KIDS THAT WAS COMMONLY USED FOR ILLUMINATED MANUSRIPTS.
PRICE GUIDE 5

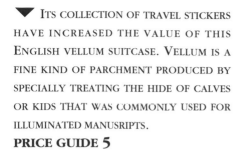

▲ THIS CROCODILE SKIN SUITCASE WITH CORNER STRENGTHENERS DATES FROM AROUND 1920 AND REMAINS IN EXCELLENT CONDITION. INITIALS ARE OFTEN FOUND ON LUGGAGE.
PRICE GUIDE 6

▼ THIS CANVAS AND LEATHER SUITCASE IS MADE BY GOYARD OF PARIS AND DATES FROM THE 1930S. THE CANVAS IS STYLISHLY PATTERNED WITH A LATTICE-WORK DESIGN AND THE WHOLE CASE IS MADE STURDY AND SECURE WITH LEATHER AND BRASS TRIMMINGS.
PRICE GUIDE 6

▼ THIS VELLUM-COVERED TRUNK WITH CORNER REINFORCEMENTS AND BRASS STUDS WAS MADE BY BENJAMIN OF MAYFAIR IN ABOUT 1930. THE SEVERAL DIFFERENT STURDY BRASS LOCKS WOULD HAVE KEPT THE TRUNK'S CONTENTS SECURE DURING TRAVELLING.
PRICE GUIDE 6

▲ HAT-WEARING BY BOTH MEN AND WOMEN WAS STILL THE NORM IN THE EARLY 20TH CENTURY AND SPECIAL CASES WERE VITAL TO PROTECT HATS WHEN TRAVELLING. THIS LEATHER AND CANVAS BOX WITH BRASS FITTINGS, FROM AROUND 1910, IS BIG ENOUGH FOR TWO HATS.
PRICE GUIDE 5

DESIGN FEATURES

DURING THE SECOND HALF OF THE 19TH CENTURY, THE 'MARQUISE' PARASOL WAS REINTRODUCED. THIS WAS A PARASOL WITH A FOLDING STICK THAT WAS SMALL IN SIZE. THE INVENTION WAS VERY POPULAR FOR USE IN OPEN CARRIAGES.

THE STEM OF THIS PARASOL IS MADE OF TURNED ROSEWOOD AND THE HINGE IN ITS CENTRE IS MADE OF METAL. THE MATERIAL COVERING IS MADE OF A BLACK SILK MOIRÉ FABRIC WITH A SEWN-ON SILK FRINGE. AT THE VERY TOP IS A CARVED, BELL-SHAPED FERRULE IN IVORY.

▶ THIS CHARMING, SATIN PARASOL IS DECORATED WITH A PINK FABRIC DELICATELY SPRIGGED WITH ROSES AND TRIMMED WITH A FRILLED EDGE. A PARASOL LIKE THIS WAS PROBABLY MADE TO ORDER TO MATCH THE FABRIC OF A FAVOURITE SUMMER DRESS.

PRICE GUIDE 4

◀ THIS ELEGANT, LATE-VICTORIAN, SATIN PARASOL IS TRIMMED WITH A HEAVY BLACK LACE AND HAS AN EBONIZED WOODEN HANDLE. THE PARASOL WAS A VITAL ACCESSORY TO PROTECT THE COMPLEXION OF THE VICTORIAN LADY.

PRICE GUIDE 4

▶ THE SIMPLICITY OF THIS UMBRELLA HANDLE SUGGESTS AN EARLY DATE BUT, IN FACT, IT DATES FROM THE 1930s. A BAKELITE TOP IS INSET INTO A DECORATIVE SILVER MOUNT.
PRICE GUIDE 3

▶ THIS PARTICULARLY FINE EDWARDIAN UMBRELLA HANDLE IS MADE OF THREE DIFFERENT MATERIALS. THE CARVED HORN HANDLE IS JOINED TO THE BAMBOO STEM BY AN EMBOSSED SILVER BAND.
PRICE GUIDE 3

▶ THIS QUIRKY UMBRELLA HANDLE FROM THE 1920s IS SOMETHING OF A NOVELTY. IMITATION IVORY IS USED TO MAKE THE STEM WHICH THEN TURNS INTO A KNOT TO MAKE THE HANDLE.
PRICE GUIDE 3

▶ THIS ATTRACTIVE LADY'S UMBRELLA HANDLE IS DESIGNED IN A TYPICALLY DECO STYLE. THE STEM, GRIP AND HANDLE ARE ALL MADE IN THE THEN NEWLY FASHIONABLE MATERIAL – PLASTIC.
PRICE GUIDE 3

▶ THIS SIMPLE LADY'S UMBRELLA HANDLE HAS A BEATEN GOLD TOP. THE WOODEN STEM IS SEPARATED FROM THE SYNTHETIC HORN HANDLE BY A GOLD BAND.
PRICE GUIDE 3

▶ THE STEM OF THIS EDWARDIAN UMBRELLA IS MADE OF EBONIZED HOLLY AND THE NATURAL KNOTS HAVE BEEN LEFT STILL SHOWING. THE CRUTCH HANDLE IS MADE OF ENGRAVED SILVER.
PRICE GUIDE 3

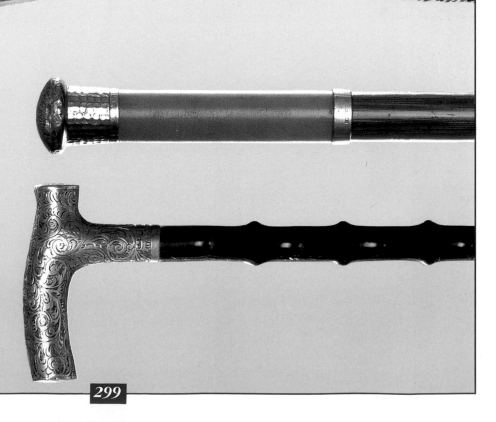

◀ THIS LATE VICTORIAN WALKING STICK HAS A SILVER HANDLE FASHIONED IN THE SHAPE OF A HORSE'S NECK AND HEAD. THE HORSE'S EYES ARE MADE OF GLASS AND THE SHAFT OF THE WALKING STICK IS MADE OF EBONIZED WOOD.
PRICE GUIDE 6

▼ THIS MALACCA CANE HAS AN IVORY HANDLE. SILVER BANDS ARE USED TO CAP THE ENDS OF THE HANDLE AND CONCEAL THE JOIN TO THE SHAFT. THE HANDLE HAS BECOME SLIGHTLY LOOSENED FROM THE WOODEN SHAFT.
PRICE GUIDE 5

▼ THIS SPY GLASS STICK WAS DEVISED FOR SURVEYING PEOPLE OR OBJECTS AT A SAFE DISTANCE. THIS PARTICULAR EXAMPLE, WHICH DATES FROM c.1880 HAS AN EBONIZED SHAFT, WITH AN IVORY AND GILT METAL HANDLE. THE GLASS IS EXTENDED BY PULLING OUTWARDS.
PRICE GUIDE 7

◀ THIS BAMBOO WALKING STICK DOUBLES AS A HORSE-MEASURE AND SPIRIT LEVEL. THE RULE CONCEALED INSIDE PULLS OUT AND HAS AN EXTENDING ARM FOR MEASURING ACROSS THE HORSE'S WITHERS AND IT ALSO DOUBLES AS A SPIRIT LEVEL.
PRICE GUIDE 6

POINTS TO WATCH

- THE HOLLOWED-OUT STICK OF A NOVELTY CANE IS PRONE TO SPLITTING.
- IMITATION IVORY WAS USED FOR HANDLESOF STICKS AND UMBRELLAS FROM THE LATE 19TH CENTURY.
- FERRULES (THE SMALL THIMBLE-LIKE ATTACHMENT THAT PROTECTS THE END OF A STICK) SHOULD SHOW SIGNS OF WEAR; NEW ONES ARE OFTEN ADDED TO SHORTENED OR DAMAGED STICKS.
- THE CURVED SILVER HANDLES OF DAMAGED UMBRELLAS ARE OFTEN CONVERTED INTO THE HANDLES OF WALKING STICKS.
- IF THERE IS A HALLMARK ON A SILVER BAND OR HANDLE, CHECK THAT THE DATE IS APPROPRIATE FOR THE STYLE OF THE STICK ITSELF.

▼ THE TOP OF THIS EARLY 18TH-CENTURY CANE IS MADE OF PORCELAIN. THE SIDES OF THIS BALL HAVE BEEN DECORATED WITH ELABORATE GILDED SCROLLS AND A SCENE IN PAINTED ENAMEL.
PRICE GUIDE 6

▼ THIS MID-VICTORIAN WOODEN WALKING CANE HAS A TOP IN THE SHAPE OF AN OWL. REALISTICALLY CARVED, GREAT ATTENTION HAS BEEN PAID TO TEXTURE AND DETAIL. THE FEATHERS HAVE BEEN CAREFULLY PICKED OUT AND THE EYES HAVE BEEN MADE OF GLASS.
PRICE GUIDE 5

▼ THIS JAPANESE CANE HAS BEEN TOPPED WITH AN IVORY FIGURE. THE SHAFT IS MADE FROM JAPANESE BAMBOO AND THE FIGURE HANDLE, DRESSED IN A KIMONO, IS TYPICALLY ORIENTAL. JAPANESE OBJECTS, ESPECIALLY THOSE IN BAMBOO AND IVORY, WERE FASHIONABLE AT THE END OF THE 19TH CENTURY.
PRICE GUIDE 7

DESIGN FEATURES

THE ETUI WAS, IN EFFECT, A POCKET SEWING KIT. SMALL ENOUGH TO SLIP INTO A HANDBAG OR COAT POCKET, OR EVEN TO HANG FROM A CHATELAINE, THE ETUI WOULD OFTEN HAVE BEEN CARRIED BY LADY'S MAIDS OR NANNIES WHEN TRAVELLING WITH THEIR CHARGES. THEY FIRST APPEARED IN THE 18TH CENTURY AND WERE MADE IN A VARIETY OF MATERIALS, SOME OF THEM BEING EXPENSIVE LUXURY ITEMS IN, FOR EXAMPLE, PRECIOUS METALS LIKE GOLD AND SILVER OR PAINTED ENAMELS.

THIS ETUI, DATING FROM AROUND 1850, IS BEAUTIFULLY MADE IN IVORY. THE INDIVIDUAL PIECES HARMONIZE WITH THE SHAPE OF THE CONTAINER AND ARE CLOSELY MATCHED IN STYLE. A PIECE SUCH AS THIS IS MORE COLLECTABLE IF ALL THE ORIGINAL PIECES ARE INTACT.

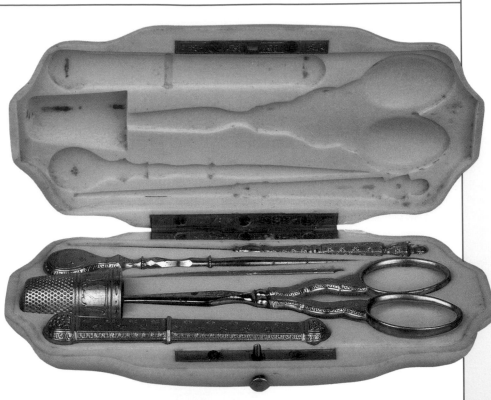

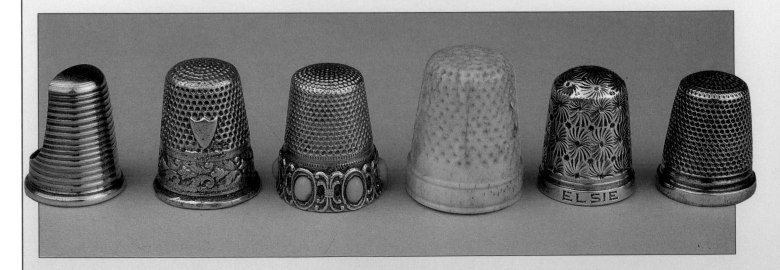

▲ THIMBLES HAVE LONG BEEN POPULAR WITH COLLECTORS. OVER THE CENTURIES, THEY HAVE APPEARED IN A VARIETY OF MATERIALS, INCLUDING WOOD, GLASS, PORCELAIN, IVORY, SILVER AND GOLD. ALTHOUGH IVORY THIMBLES TEND TO BE RARE, SILVER ONES ARE STILL COMMONLY FOUND AND OFTEN BEAR ORNATE DECORATION. SINCE THEY ARE QUITE SMALL, SILVER THIMBLES DID NOT TEND TO BE HALLMARKED BEFORE 1890.
PRICE GUIDE 3 — 4

▶ VICTORIAN AND EDWARDIAN BUTTONS CAN BE MINIATURE WORKS OF ART AND, BEING VERY REASONABLY PRICED, CAN BE THE BASIS FOR AN INTERESTING COLLECTION. THE MATERIALS OF THE BUTTONS SHOWN HERE INCLUDE CUT STEEL, BRASS, GLASS, PLASTIC AND MOTHER-OF-PEARL.
PRICE GUIDE 1 — 2

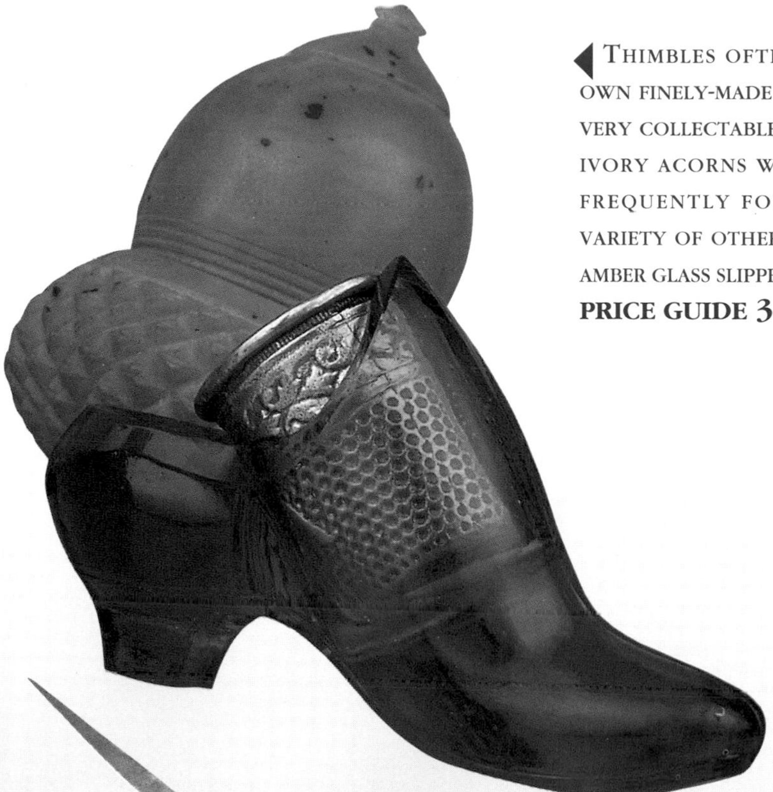

◀ THIMBLES OFTEN CAME WITH THEIR OWN FINELY-MADE CASES, AND THESE ARE VERY COLLECTABLE TODAY. WOODEN OR IVORY ACORNS WITH SCREW TOPS ARE FREQUENTLY FOUND ALONG WITH A VARIETY OF OTHER SHAPES SUCH AS THIS AMBER GLASS SLIPPER.
PRICE GUIDE 3

▼ DARNING MUSHROOMS WERE PRODUCED FROM MANY DIFFERENT WOODS. THE MUSHROOM SHAPE WAS THE MOST TRADITONAL AND WAS USED FOR SOCKS AND LARGER ITEMS. THE SMALLER DARNING MUSHROOM SHOWN HERE, THAT LOOKS LIKE A DUMB-BELL, WAS SPECIFICALLY INTENDED FOR REPAIRING THE FINGERS OF GLOVES.
PRICE GUIDE 1

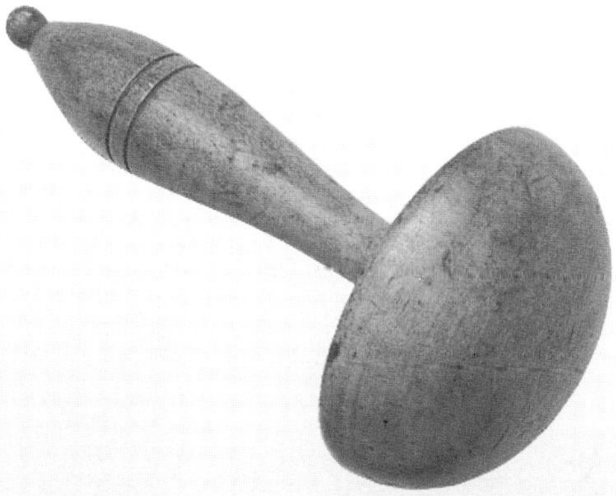

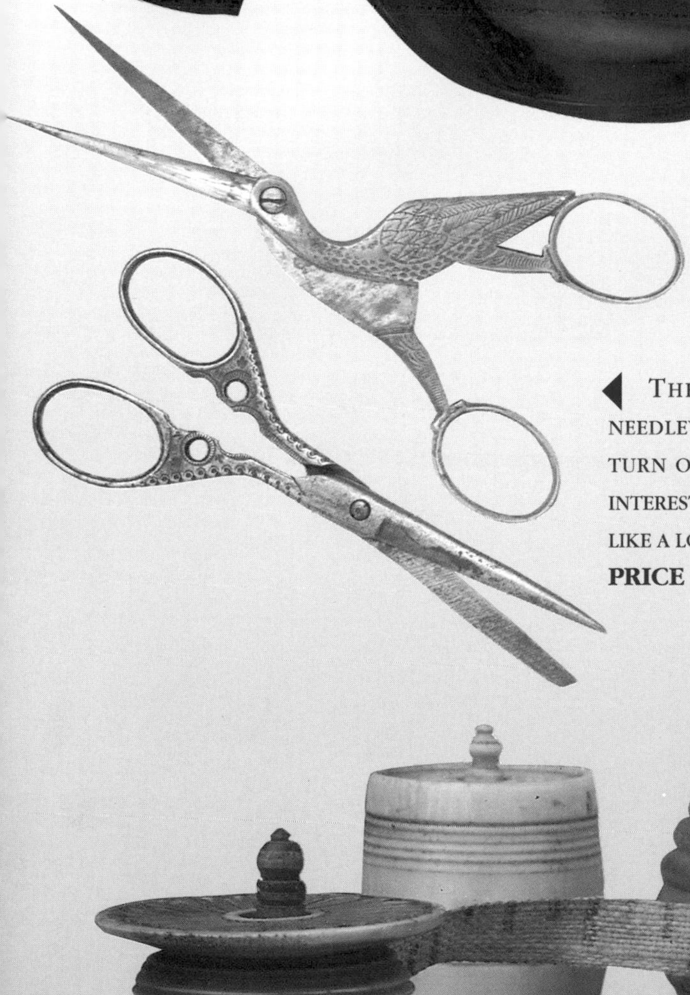

◀ THESE TWO PAIRS OF STEEL NEEDLEWORK SCISSORS DATE FROM THE TURN OF THE CENTURY. PARTICULARLY INTERESTING IS THE PAIR SHAPED TO LOOK LIKE A LONG-BEAKED BIRD.
PRICE GUIDE 2

▼ ONE INDISPENSABLE ELEMENT OF THE SEWING KIT WAS THE TAPE MEASURE. NEAT, WIND-UP TAPES IN CARVED WOOD OR IVORY CASES WERE WIDELY USED BY THE VICTORIANS AND EDWARDIANS AND THESE WERE FREQUENTLY MADE TO REPRESENT TINY BEEHIVES OR BARRELS.
PRICE GUIDE 1 – 3

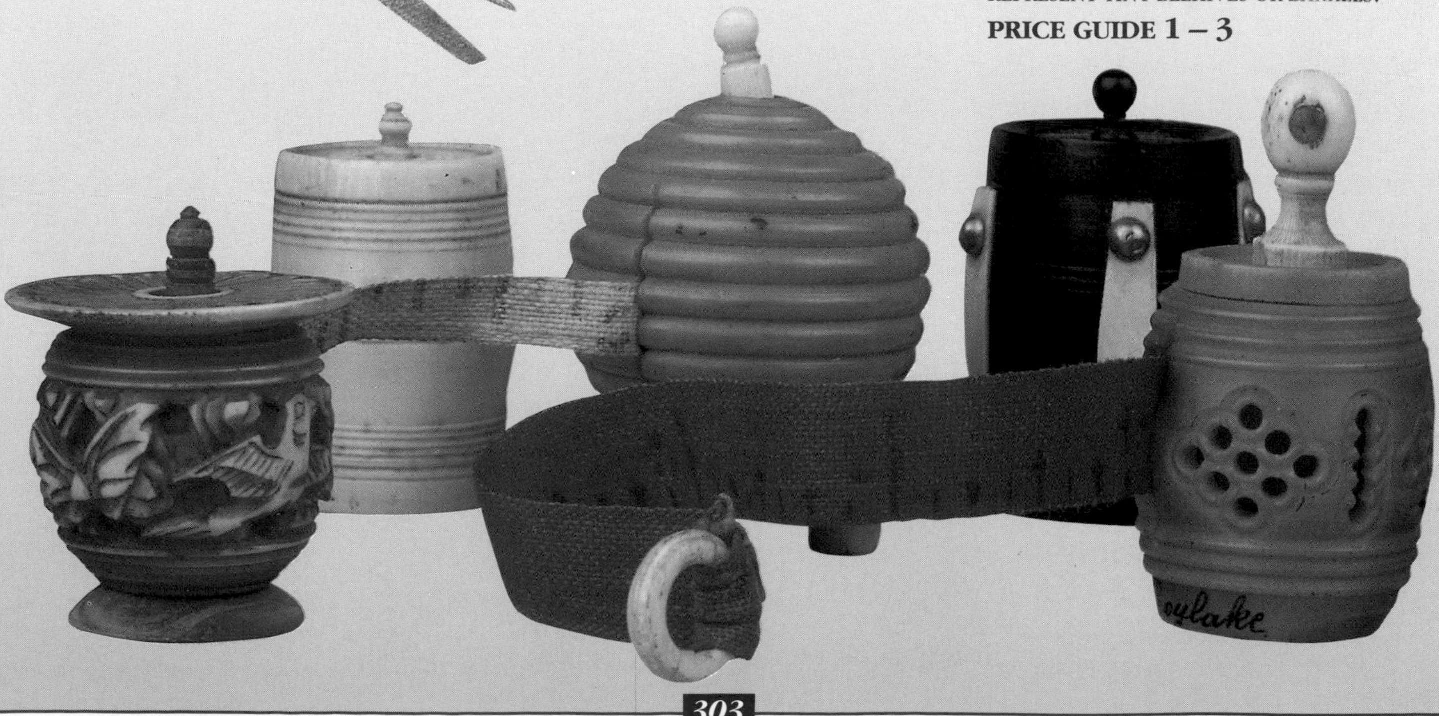

DESIGN FEATURES

▼ THIS WORKBOX IS MADE OF SEVERAL DIFFERENTLY COLOURED WOODS, WITH MARQUETRY BORDERS. INLAID IN THE TOP AND SIDES ARE NEO-CLASSICAL MEZZOTINT PRINTS. IT HAS A SHALLOW DRAWER AT THE FRONT, WITH AN IVORY KNOB, AND WAS MADE IN 1718.
PRICE GUIDE 7

▶ THIS FOB WATCH HOLDER DATES FROM 1850 AND IS MADE IN A SIMPLY DECORATED BRASS. A STAND SUCH AS THIS WOULD HAVE SAT ON A BEDSIDE TABLE AND THIS PARTICULAR EXAMPLE IS CREATED IN A DESIGN VERY SIMILAR TO THAT OF A BEDSIDE CANDLEHOLDER.
PRICE GUIDE 4

THIS OPEN-FACED POCKET WATCH, WITH EXQUISITE ENAMELLING, IS SET ON A BRASS WATCH STAND WITH INTRICATELY CARVED PILLARS. THE WATCH HAS STEM-WINDING, WHICH WAS FIRST INTRODUCED BY A SWISS WATCHMAKER, LOUIS AUDEMARS IN 1838. THIS MADE IT POSSIBLE TO SET THE HANDS AND WIND THE WATCH WITHOUT USING A KEY. THE BALANCE WHEEL IS VISIBLE BELOW THE NUMERAL SIX ON THE WATCH FACE. THIS CONTROLS THE RATE AT WHICH THE MAINSPRING IS ALLOWED TO UNWIND AND ALSO COMPENSATES FOR CHANGES IN THE ENVIRONMENT SUCH AS TEMPERATURE. THE METAL FACE HAS DELICATE ENAMELLING, A POPULAR DECORATION THAT HAS BEEN USED SINCE THE END OF THE 16TH CENTURY AND WHICH WAS OFTEN INSET WITH GILDING AND PRECIOUS GEMS. HERE, THE ENAMELLING IS INLAID WITH BLUE AND YELLOW FLOWERS AND THE HANDS OF THE WATCH ARE GOLD.

▼ THIS WORKBOX OF KINGWOOD, A PARTICULARLY BEAUTIFUL BRAZILLIAN HARD WOOD, IS DECORATED WITH A PAINTED FLORAL CENTRAL PANEL. THE PAW FEET AND LION'S HEAD HANDLES ARE MADE OF METAL.
PRICE GUIDE 7

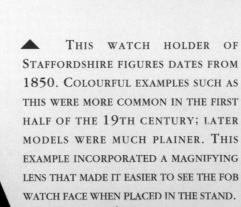

▲ THIS WATCH HOLDER OF STAFFORDSHIRE FIGURES DATES FROM 1850. COLOURFUL EXAMPLES SUCH AS THIS WERE MORE COMMON IN THE FIRST HALF OF THE 19TH CENTURY; LATER MODELS WERE MUCH PLAINER. THIS EXAMPLE INCORPORATED A MAGNIFYING LENS THAT MADE IT EASIER TO SEE THE FOB WATCH FACE WHEN PLACED IN THE STAND.
PRICE GUIDE 4

▲ STANDING ON SQUARE FEET, THIS WORKBOX IS OF ROSEWOOD WITH A SCROLLED BRASS INLAY. THE LID IS LINED WITH SILK AND THE COMPARTMENT LIDS ARE FABRIC-COVERED. MOST FITTINGS ARE IVORY, WITH SILVER-TOPPED SCENT BOTTLES, THIMBLE AND TAPE HOLDER.
PRICE GUIDE 8

▶ DATING FROM 1800, THIS WORKBOX IS OF BURR YEW WITH A WOODEN CARRYING HANDLE. THE INSIDE OF THE LID IS DECORATED WITH EMBROIDERY IN A FLORAL DESIGN. BOTH THE BOX PROPER AND THE DRAWER, WHICH HAS NEAT COMPARTMENTS, ARE LOCKABLE.
PRICE GUIDE 7

POINTS TO WATCH

- A WINDING HOLE IN THE BACK OF A WATCH THAT HAS BEEN FILLED IN INDICATES WHETHER THE DIAL OR MOVEMENT HAS BEEN REPLACED. THIS REDUCES THE VALUE OF THE WATCH.

- WITH A WATCH THAT IS OFFERED AS 'WHOLE', CHECK THAT THE DIAL, MOVEMENT AND CASE HAVE THE SAME NUMBER AND THAT THE OUTER AND INNER CASES HAVE THE SAME MAKER'S INITIALS AND THE SAME HALLMARK.

- WHEN BUYING A WATCH, CHECK THAT IT IS IN WORKING ORDER AS REPAIRS ARE EXPENSIVE, AND OBSOLETE PARTS MAY BE UNOBTAINABLE. IF THE WATCH IS WOUND WITH A KEY, CHECK THAT THE KEY IS WITH IT AND THAT IT IS THE ORIGINAL.

▲ A MAGNIFICENTLY DECORATED WATCH OF 1868 IN ENAMELLED GOLD. IT WAS, IN FACT, MADE FOR AN INDIAN MAHARAJAH AND IS EXTRAVAGANTLY SET WITH DIAMONDS AND RUBIES AND, OBVIOUSLY, COMMANDS A HIGH PRICE.
PRICE GUIDE 8

▲ DESIGNED IN A MUCH PLAINER STYLE, THIS FRENCH POCKET WATCH IS MADE IN GOLD WITH LITTLE DECORATION. IT IS A QUARTER REPEATER AND HAS THE UNUSUAL QUALITY OF A MUSICAL TONE.
PRICE GUIDE 8

▲ THIS QUARTER REPEATER DATES FROM 1810 AND IS DECORATED IN BOTH GOLD AND SILVER. POSITIONED AROUND THE WATCH FACE ARE TWO TINY AUTOMATED FIGURES WHICH STRIKE THE BELLS ABOVE THE CLOCK FACE ON THE QUARTER HOUR.
PRICE GUIDE 8

▲ THE FULLY SKELETONIZED MOVEMENTS OF THIS ENAMEL AND SILVER POCKET WATCH ARE VISIBLE AT BOTH FRONT AND BACK. THIS DATES FROM 1820 AND IS QUARTER REPEATING, AS WERE MANY WATCHES OF THE PERIOD.
PRICE GUIDE 8

▲ THIS FRENCH QUARTER REPEATING CALENDER WATCH IN GOLD AND SILVER DATES FROM ABOUT 1820. WITHIN THE FACE ARE THREE EXTRA DIALS, SHOWING THE SECONDS, THE DAY AND THE DATE.
PRICE GUIDE 8

▲ THIS SMALL 1930s BEDSIDE TABLE
CLOCK IS SET INTO AN ORANGE TINTED
SOLID GLASS CASE WITH BEVELLED FRONT
EDGES. CLOCKS LIKE THESE ARE QUITE
CHEAP TO BUY BUT CHECK THAT THEY ARE
IN WORKING ORDER.
PRICE GUIDE 3

▲ THIS PAINTED ENAMEL, TRAVELLING
ALARM CLOCK STILL HAS ITS ORIGINAL
CASE, GREATLY INCREASING ITS VALUE.
DATING FROM THE 1930s, IT BEARS MANY
TYPICAL DECO DESIGN FEATURES.
PRICE GUIDE 3

▲ THIS WRIST-WATCH FROM THE LATE
1930s IS MADE IN 9CT GOLD WITH A
RAISED DECORATION ON THE RIM OF THE
CASE. THE MOCK SNAKE-SKIN STRAP IS
NEW BUT QUITE IN KEEPING WITH THE
PERIOD OF THE WATCH.
PRICE GUIDE 5

◀ THIS FRENCH ART DECO CLOCK WAS
MADE IN THE 1930s. THE ATTACHMENT
AT THE TOP OF THE STEEL CASE IS AN
INCORPORATED LIGHTER. ITS SLIMLINE
SHAPE AND BOLD BLACK NUMERALS MAKE
THIS A VERY ATTRACTIVE PIECE.
PRICE GUIDE 5

▲ THIS 1930s WATCH WAS MADE BY
THE COMPANY BUREN. FAMOUS-NAME
WATCHES CAN FETCH VERY HIGH PRICES.
PRICE GUIDE 4

▼ THIS LATE 19TH-CENTURY CLOCK IS RATHER HEAVY AND VICTORIAN IN ITS PROPORTIONS. THE CLOCKFACE IS FRAMED BY TWO SLENDER, FREE-STANDING COLUMNS THAT ARE TOPPED BY A SWAN-NECKED BROKEN PEDIMENT. THE DIAL SURROUND IS PAINTED WITH DECORATIVE MOTIFS AND A SAILING SHIP.
PRICE GUIDE 7

▼ THIS CLOCK OF C.1745 IS VENEERED IN A BURR WALNUT OVER AN OAK CARCASE. THE SURROUND OF THE DIAL IS IN ENGRAVED BRASS AND IN THE ARCH IS A RARE FEATURE – A DIAL SHOWING THE PHASES OF THE MOON.
PRICE GUIDE 9

▼ THIS IS A CLOCK BAROMETER WHICH HOUSES BOTH A CLOCK AND AN ANEROID BAROMETER TOGETHER. DATING FROM AROUND 1900, THIS EXAMPLE TAKES THE FORM OF A FANCIFUL GOTHIC BUILDING.
PRICE GUIDE 6

▲ THIS VERY FINE EXAMPLE OF A LONGCASE CLOCK IS DUTCH IN ORIGIN AND DATES TO 1765. THE HOOD IS DECORATED WITH AN INTRICATE FRETTED PATTERN AND THERE IS A WINDOW IN THE SIDE OF THE BODY THAT SHOWS THE MOVEMENT OF THE CLOCK.
PRICE GUIDE 9

▲ THIS COMBINED THERMOMETER AND ANEROID BAROMETER, WITH A PORCELAIN FACE, IS ENCASED IN LIGHT OAK. AN ANEROID BAROMETER IS ONE THAT MEASURES ATMOSPHERIC PRESSURE BY THE EXPANSION AND CONTRACTION OF A SMALL METAL DRUM OR BOX PREVIOUSLY EXHAUSTED OF AIR.
PRICE GUIDE 5

▲ THIS ENGLISH BANJO BAROMETER IS ENCLOSED IN AN OAK CASE AND DATES FROM AROUND 1890. IT ALSO INCLUDES A THERMOMETER IN THE STEM. THE BODY OF THE CASE IS CARVED WITH ACANTHUS AND OTHER PLANT FORMS.
PRICE GUIDE 5

DESIGN FEATURES

THIS CASH REGISTER WAS MADE IN AROUND 1910. MADE BY NATIONAL CASH REGISTER, THIS EXAMPLE WAS PRODUCED FOR THE BRITISH MARKET AND IS A FULL-SIZED MODEL CASED IN NICKEL-PLATE WITH A PRINTER OF THE RIGHT.

THE REGISTER HAS METAL POP-UP NUMBERS RANGED RIGHT TO LEFT IN A GLASS CASE. JUST BELOW THE NUMBER CASE IS A SMALL SCREW-ON METAL PLATE DIE-STAMPED WITH THE TECHNICAL SPECIFICATIONS OF THE MACHINE. THE FRONT IS HINGED, SO THAT IS CAN BE LIFTED TO CHECK THE TOTALS.

THE KEYBOARD RUNS FROM A FARTHING ($^1/_4$ OF AN OLD PENNY) AT THE LOWEST PRICE TO £1/10 SHILLINGS AT THE HIGHEST. THOUGH ONLY £1.50 IN MODERN DECIMAL CURRENCY, THIS WAS QUITE A SUM WHEN THIS MACHINE WAS MADE. HERE, THE DRAWER TOP IS MADE OF MARBLE RATHER THAN WOOD, SUGGESTING THAT AT SOME TIME THE REGISTER WAS USED IN A BUTCHER'S, PHARMACY OR GREENGROCER'S.

▼ TYPEWRITERS ARE BECOMING A POPULAR COLLECTABLE AS MODERN COMPUTERS REPLACE THEM IN BOTH THE OFFICE AND IN THE HOME. THIS OLIVER TYPEWRITER WAS MADE AROUND 1915. IT FEATURES TWIN BANKS OF KEYS AND HAS A UNIVERSAL THREE BANK KEYBOARD.
PRICE GUIDE 2

▼ THIS MULTI-FUNCTION CASH REGISTER IS ENGLISH AND DATES FROM THE 1930s. THOUGH MADE OF METAL THE REGISTER HAS BEEN PAINTED TO SIMULATE WOOD. THE AMOUNT TENDERED WAS PUNCHED OUT ON THE KEYS AND THE DRAWER OPERATED BY A HANDLE ON THE SIDE. A PRINTED RECEIPT EMERGED FROM A SLOT ON THE LEFT. THERE ARE SEPARATE KEYS FOR CASH, CREDIT AND MONEY RECEIVED ON ACCOUNT.
PRICE GUIDE 5

▲ AS RECORDS ARE PHASED OUT TODAY, SO OLD GRAMAPHONE RECORDS ARE BECOMING INCREASINGLY COLLECTABLE. THE RECORDS HERE WERE ISSUED BY COLUMBIA, HIS MASTER'S VOICE (HMV), AND DECCA. THEY WERE PRESSED IN SHELLAC, A MATERIAL INTRODUCED IN 1896 TO REPLACE ZINC-COATED VERSIONS. ALSO SHOWN HERE ARE RECORD CATALOGUES THAT COMPANIES SOLD THROUGH WOOLWORTHS TO PUBLICIZE THEIR NEW RELEASES.

PRICE GUIDE 1

▶ THIS GRAMAPHONE'S MANUFACTURER REMAINS UNKNOWN BUT THE ELEGANT CABINET AND CONICAL SPEAKER ARE TYPICAL OF THIS KIND OF RECORD PLAYER. THIS PIECE IS DESIGNED TO BLEND IN WITH 1930S FURNITURE AND DECOR.

PRICE GUIDE 5

◀ EARLY GRAMAPHONE NEEDLES WORE DOWN QUICKLY AND WERE OFTEN REPLACED. MANY COMPANIES SOLD SMALL TINS OF REPLACEMENTS. THE BOX OF HMV NEEDLES SHOWN HERE OFFERS FOUR DIFFERENT KINDS; EXTRA LOUD TONE, LOUD TONE, HALF TONE AND SOFT TONE.

PRICE GUIDE 1

POINTS TO WATCH

- If buying an arcade machine to use, be sure to have a good supply of the appropriate coins.
- Few genuine early arcade machines survive. Many were destroyed or reconstituted to keep up with changing fashions and laws in pier amusements.
- Always insist in seeing and hearing a juke box in action before buying it.
- Rock-Ola and Wurlitzer have both reproduced old classics; though the cabinets are identical, the mechanisms are modern.

▶ This Wurlitzer 1250 dates from the 1950s. The perspex cylindrical top reveals the selection of records which the listener could chose by consulting the lists of songs in three panels at the front of the machine. The adapted Simplex mechanism has two pick-up arms to play either side of the 24 discs it contained.
PRICE GUIDE 9

▼ Working Model slot machines were a popular feature at the end of many British piers between the Wars. At the drop of a coin the scene inside came to life; in this 1930s version, a night watchman is beset with ghostly visitors.
PRICE GUIDE 7

▲ In the brief post-war boom in jukebox sales, many new companies formed, flourished and then folded. One such was Filben, whose Maestro featured a futuristic front of rippled glass with a dramatic visor grille over the speaker.
PRICE GUIDE 9

PLACE PENNY IN SLOT TO SEE MODEL WORK
THE NIGHT WATCHMAN

DANGER ROAD UP

Working Model

▶ Tests of skill or strength were a common role for slot machines in arcades. This punchbag features a dial on the front that offers to 'Test Your Strength'.
PRICE GUIDE 7

POINTS TO WATCH

● THE LENSES OF BOTH CAMERAS AND BINOCULARS SHOULD BE TREATED WITH CARE. ATTEMPTS TO CLEAN LENSES CAN LEAVE SMUDGES THAT WILL IMPAIR VISION AND LEAVE MARKS ON ANY PHOTOGRAPHS TAKEN.

● MANY OLD CAMERAS STILL WORK TODAY AND, IF NOT, THERE ARE MANY EXPERTS AROUND WHO CAN TACKLE REPAIRS AND RENOVATIONS.

● AS WITH MODERN FILMS, OLDER NEGATIVES AND TRANSPARENCIES WILL BENEFIT FROM BEING STORED IN COOL CONDITIONS. OLD PRINTS SHOULD, IDEALLY, BE KEPT IN ENVELOPES OR BAGS OF ACID-FREE PAPER.

▲ THE 'VICTORY' BELLOWS CAMERA HAS A DROP-DOWN, HINGED BASE FOR THE SLIDING FOCUS DEVISE. A BULB SHUTTER RELEASE ALLOWED THE PHOTOGRAPHER TO AVOID CAMERA SHAKE.
PRICE GUIDE 5

◀ THIS ROLLER BLIND SHUTTER FITTED OVER THE FRONT OF THE LENS. AS NEW, FASTER FILM WAS INTRODUCED, OLDER CAMERAS NEEDED ATTACHMENTS SUCH AS THIS TO ADAPT TO RESULTING CHANGES IN EXPOSURE TIME.
PRICE GUIDE 4

▲ BY THE EARLY 20TH CENTURY, TECHNICAL INNOVATIONS IN CAMERA DESIGN HAD MADE THE LARGE AND CUMBERSOME BELLOWS CAMERAS OBSOLETE. PHOTOGRAPHY WAS A POPULAR HOBBY AND SMALLER, LIGHTWEIGHT CAMERAS, THAT WERE EASIER TO USE FOR BOTH PROFESSIONAL AND AMATEUR ALIKE, WERE MUCH IN DEMAND. THE TWO EXAMPLES SHOWN HERE ARE BOTH STILL BELLOWS CAMERAS BUT DEVELOPMENTS IN LENS GRINDING AND FILM SIZE ALLOWED MANUFACTURERS TO MAKE MUCH SMALLER MODELS.
PRICE GUIDE 3

▲ THE BRASS RINGS SHOWN HERE ARE A SET OF LENSES MADE BY TAYLOR AND HOBSON, OF LEICESTER IN ENGLAND, C.1900. THE LIGHT METER SHOWN IS ALSO IN SOLID BRASS AND DATES FROM LATE IN THE 19TH CENTURY.
PRICE GUIDE 4

▲ THESE WOODEN SQUARES ARE PLATE HOLDERS, CAREFULLY MADE IN MAHOGANY WITH BRASS FITTINGS. THOSE SHOWN HERE ARE IN THREE SIZES; FULL, HALF AND QUARTER PLATE. THEY FITTED THE OLDER DRY-PLATE CAMERAS AND MAY SOMETIMES BE FOUND WITH PHOTOGRAPHIC PLATES.
PRICE GUIDE 1

◀ THIS ELEGANT PAIR OF BRASS BINOCULARS WERE MADE IN PARIS IN ABOUT 1910. PAIRS OF FIELD GLASSES SUCH AS THESE WERE VITAL TO THE EDWARDIAN GENTLEMAN OR LADY KEEN ON FIELD SPORTS SUCH AS HUNTING, SHOOTING OR RACING.
PRICE GUIDE 4

▼ THESE POWERFUL BINOCULARS WERE MADE IN AROUND 1905. LARGE AND SOLID THEY WERE DESIGNED TO HOLD STRONG LENSES. THE BRASS IS UNTARNISHED AND IN GOOD QUALITY.
PRICE GUIDE 3

▲ THIS PAIR OF BINOCULARS DATE FROM C.1910 AND ARE TRIMMED WITH LEATHER AND BRASS. STILL COMPLETE WITH THEIR ORIGINAL CASE, THIS CAN INCREASE VALUE IF BOTH ARE IN GOOD CONDITION.
PRICE GUIDE 3

▶ MADE IN 1910, THIS COMPACT PAIR OF BRASS BINOCULARS STILL HAS ITS LEATHER SHOULDER STRAP. LIGHTER IN WEIGHT AND SLIGHTLY SMALLER, THESE WERE PROBABLY PRODUCED AS A LADY'S MODEL.
PRICE GUIDE 3

▶ A BREECH-LOADING, MARTINI, ACTION SERVICE CARBINE – THE CARBINE HAD A SHORTER BARREL THAN THE MUSKET OR THE RIFLE. MADE IN EUROPE IN 1877, THIS PARTICULAR GUN WAS USED IN MUSCAT AND HAS ARABIC LETTERING ON THE ENGRAVED METALWORK.

PRICE GUIDE 4

▶ A RARE 40 BORE, PERCUSSION, TRANSITIONAL RIFLE, HAS A SPUR HAMMER FIRING MECHANISM AND REVOLVING CHAMBERS. MADE BY H. HOLLAND IN 1845, IT HAS AN OCTAGONAL BARREL AND A PISTOL GRIP INCORPORATED.

PRICE GUIDE 8

▲ THIS MILITARY, BREECH-LOADING, 450 BORE RIFLE WAS NICKNAMED 'THE MONKEY TAIL'. IT WAS MADE BY WESTLEY RICHARDS AND HAS A BRASS TRIGGER GUARD AND COLLAPSIBLE SIGHT.

PRICE GUIDE 6

▲ MADE IN 1912 BY F.W. KESSLER OF SUHL IN GERMANY, THIS IS AN 8MM, SINGLE-SHOT, DEER RIFLE. THE STOCK AND ACTION ARE ENGRAVED WITH HUNTING SCENES AND THE FLUTED, STEEL BARREL IS INLAID WITH SILVER. THIS PARTICULAR GUN HAS A SET TRIGGER.

PRICE GUIDE 8

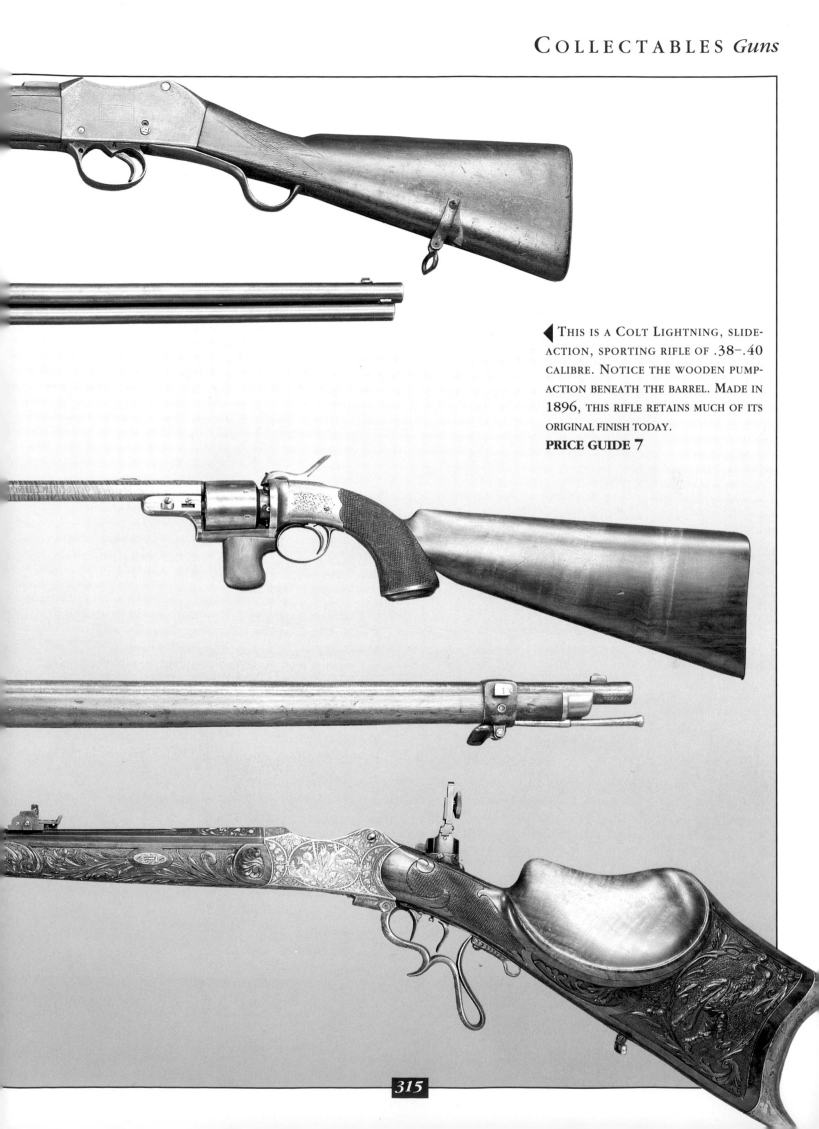

◀ THIS IS A COLT LIGHTNING, SLIDE-ACTION, SPORTING RIFLE OF .38–.40 CALIBRE. NOTICE THE WOODEN PUMP-ACTION BENEATH THE BARREL. MADE IN 1896, THIS RIFLE RETAINS MUCH OF ITS ORIGINAL FINISH TODAY.
PRICE GUIDE 7

DESIGN FEATURES

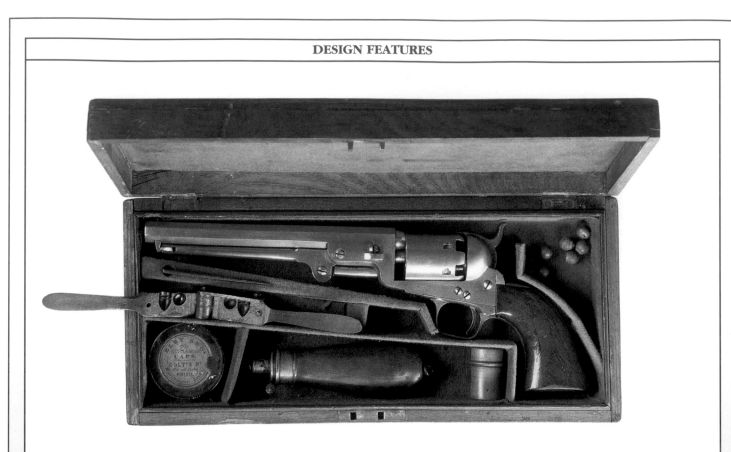

THIS IS A .36 CALIBRE, COLT NAVY PERCUSSION REVOLVER, MADE IN 1856, MAKING IT A RELATIVELY EARLY REVOLVER. MEASURING 12INS (30CM) OVERALL, IT HAS A 6 1/2IN (16CM) OCTAGONAL BARREL. THE CHAMBERS HOLD FIVE SHOTS AND FIRE EITHER LEAD BULLETS OR SPHERICAL LEAD SHOT. A SINGLE-ACTION WEAPON, THIS HAS TO BE COCKED EACH TIME IT IS FIRED. AN UNDERLEVER RAMMER, FOR CLEARING THE CHAMBERS, WAS AN INTEGRAL PART OF THE GUN'S BODY.

INCLUDED IN THE CASE IS A BULLET MOULD FOR MAKING ONE'S OWN BALLSHOT AND BULLETS; MOLTEN LEAD IS POURED INTO THE TOP OF THE CLOSED MOULD FOR TWO DIFFERENT SHAPES OF BULLET. A ROUND TIN CONTAINS PERCUSSION CAPS AND THE SMALL WOODEN BOX HAS SPARE STRIKING PINS IN IT. THE BAG-SHAPED WOODEN FLASK, WITH ITS GRADUATED BRASS NOZZLE, CONTAINED POWDER.

▲ THIS .41 CALIBRE, RIMFIRE PISTOL WITH OVER-AND-UNDER BARRELS WAS MADE BY REMMINGTON IN 1892. SMALL IN SIZE, IT FITTED INTO A WAISTCOAT POCKET AND WAS POPULAR WITH MISSISSIPPI GAMBLERS.
PRICE GUIDE 6

▶ THE PEPPERBOX REVOLVER WAS NOT EFFECTIVE FOR FIRING AT LONGER DISTANCES AND WAS DESIGNED FOR PERSONAL DEFENCE. MADE BY PERREZ OF BELGIUM IN 1870, THIS 6-SHOT, PINFIRE PEPPERBOX REVOLVER HAS A BLACK GRIP AND CHAMBERS. THE FOLDING TRIGGER ALLOWS IT TO FIT NEATLY INTO A CASE.
PRICE GUIDE 6

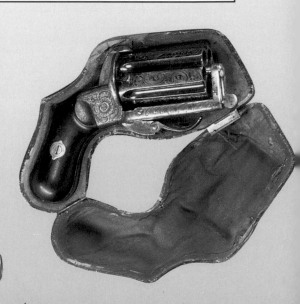

◀ MADE IN 1878, THIS IS A .41 CALIBRE, RIMFIRE COLT DERRINGER. IT HAS A BARREL THAT SWINGS OUT FOR LOADING.
PRICE GUIDE 5

▼ THIS PEPPERBOX, 6-SHOT GUN HAS RUSTED A LITTLE DUE TO LACK OF CARE. IT HAS AN IVORY GRIP AND DECORATIVELY ENGRAVED METALWORK. FITTING INTO A PURSE OR POCKET, PEPPERBOXES WERE ESPECIALLY POPULAR WITH THE LADIES.
PRICE GUIDE 6

▲ A .38 CALIBRE, BLACK POWDER, 5-SHOT CENTREFIRE REVOLVER. IT HAS SCROLL ENGRAVING AND A GILDED FINISH. MADE IN 1887, THE MAKER WAS J.M. MARLIN OF NEW HAVEN, CONNECTICUT.
PRICE GUIDE 5

▼ THIS IS A COLT .22 CALIBRE, RIMFIRE, OPEN FRAME REVOLVER. IT HAS A WOODEN GRIP AND WAS AN IDEAL LADY'S OR WAISTCOAT GUN. IT WAS MADE IN HARFORD, CONNECTICUT IN 1878.
PRICE GUIDE 5

▲ THIS IS A COLT .35 CALIBRE, SEMI-AUTOMATIC, POCKET PISTOL, SHOWN ALONGSIDE A SPARE MAGAZINE THAT CONTAINS 6 SHOTS. IT WAS SOLD IN A RED LEATHER AND PURPLE VELVET CASE. AUTOMATICS TOOK OVER FROM REVOLVERS AND COULD BE INCONSPICUOUSLY CARRIED IN TOWN.
PRICE GUIDE 5

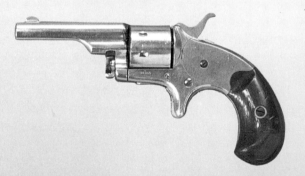

▶ NOW LEGENDRY, THE COLT 45 PEACEMAKER WAS THE GUN WITH WHICH THE WILD WEST WAS WON. IT IS A SINGLE-ACTION ARMY REVOLVER WITH AN IVORY HANDLE. PATENTED IN 1871, THIS PARTICULAR GUN WAS MADE IN 1880.
PRICE GUIDE 7

▼ THIS BRITISH NAVAL OFFICER'S
SWORD HAS A SHARK-SKIN HANDLE AND A
COPPERED-GILT GUARD. THE STANDARD
NAVAL MOTIF OF THE ROPE AND FOULED
ANCHOR IS JUST VISIBLE HERE, ON THE
FRONT CURVE OF THE GUARD.
PRICE GUIDE 5

▼ THE STYLE OF THIS LIGHT CAVALRY
SABRE, DATED 1830 – 40, IS KNOWN AS
THE 1796 PATTERN. IT HAS A
CHARACTERISTIC, P-SHAPED KNUCKLE-
BOW. THIS ONE ALSO HAS A PIPE-BACKED
BLADE AND STEEL SCABBARD.
PRICE GUIDE 5

THIS VICTORIAN ENGLISH ARMY SWORD HAS A GOTHIC-STYLE HILT; THAT IS, A LATTICE OF GILT BARS THAT MADE UP A HILT AND THAT WAS INTENDED FOR USE BY AN INFANTRY OFFICER. THE SINGLE-EDGED BLADE HAS A FINELY ETCHED DECORATION.
PRICE GUIDE 5

▼ THIS HEAVY CAVALRY SWORD HAS A BLACK FISH-SKIN HANDLE BOUND IN A GILT-WIRE WRAP. THE BRASS HILT IS OF THE TRIPLE-BAR DESIGN AND IS MATCHED BY A BRASS-MOUNTED SCABBARD.
PRICE GUIDE 6

▶ MADE IN THE EARLY 19TH CENTURY, THIS FINE PRESENTATION SWORD IS INSCRIBED ON THE REVERSE SIDE WITH THE NAME AND REGIMENT OF ITS OWNER. THE BLADE DECORATION IS WELL PRESERVED, AS IS THE SWORD'S SCABBARD.
PRICE GUIDE 8

POINTS TO WATCH

- CHECK THAT A SWORD'S BLADE IS CORRECT FOR THE STYLE OF THE HILT.
- THE HILT AND THE BLADE SHOULD FIT TOGETHER PERFECTLY – SOME SWORDS ON THE MARKET ARE MARRIAGES OF DIFFERENT PARTS OF OTHER SWORDS.
- CHECK THAT THE SCABBARD IS OF THE SAME AGE AS THE SWORD. AN ORIGINAL SCABBARD, HOWEVER BATTERED, INCREASES THE VALUE.
- LOOK FOR SIGNS OF WEAR AND TEAR; CRACKS, RUST, SCRATCHES AND MISSING BARS ON THE HILT.

▲ THIS STANDARD ISSUE BELT FROM
WORLD WAR I HAS BEEN TRANSFORMED
BY WOOL EMBROIDERY. THE FLAGS
SHOWN ARE THOSE OF BELGIUM, FRANCE
AND ITALY, WITH THE COLOURS REVERSED.
A PIECE LIKE THIS WOULD HAVE BEEN THE
WORK OF A SOLDIER, WHILING AWAY THE
TIME SPENT WAITING IN THE TRENCHES OR
BEHIND THE LINES.
PRICE GUIDE 3

▲ THIS PIECE OF WOOD IS SAWN FROM A
PLANE'S PROPELLER AND HAS BEEN
ADAPTED TO SERVE AS THE BASE FOR AN
INKPOT. THE INK WAS PLACED IN THE
METAL-LINED WELL AT THE TOP AND THE
GROOVES CUT INTO THE WOOD WERE
DESIGNED TO HOLD PENS.
PRICE GUIDE 3

◀ THIS CAR HAS BEEN MADE FROM PIECES
OF BRASS AND SHRAPNEL WELDED
TOGETHER. THE NUMBER PLATE BEARS THE
DATE 1914 AND THE LETTERS 'RE' –
PERHAPS THE INITIALS OF THE MAKER.
PRICE GUIDE 5

▶ ONE OF A PAIR, THIS VASE IS FASHIONED FROM SHELL CASE AND HAS INTRICATE ENGRAVED DECORATION SHOWING THE VICTORIOUS FRENCH COCKEREL TRAMPLING ON A VANQUISHED GERMAN EAGLE. TRANSFORMED SHELL CASES ARE THE ARCHETYPAL FORM OF TRENCH ART.
PRICE GUIDE 3

▲ INGENIOUS CRAFTSMANSHIP HAS CHANGED THIS SHELL CASE INTO A WINE BOTTLE HOLDER AND POURER, DECORATED WITH THE REGIMENTAL MOTIF.
PRICE GUIDE 2

▼ VARIOUS BITS OF SCRAP METAL THAT WERE FOUND AROUND THE BATTLE FIELD HAVE BEEN WELDED TOGETHER TO FORM THIS UNUSUAL SWORD-LIKE LETTER OPENER. THE BASE OF A BULLET CAN STILL BE CLEARLY DISTINGUISHED.
PRICE GUIDE 1

◀ THIS SELECTION OF MEDALS REPRESENTS JUST SOME OF THOSE AWARDED TO BRITISH SOLDIERS IN THE 19TH CENTURY. A REPRODUCTION OF THE VICTORIA CROSS (FIRST AWARDED IN 1856) IS SHOWN FAR LEFT; THE REST ARE FOR VARIOUS CAMPAIGNS IN OUTPOSTS OF THE BRITISH EMPIRE SUCH AS BURMA AND INDIA. THE AWARDING OF MEDALS FOR PARTICULAR CAMPAIGNS GREW IN THE 19TH CENTURY AND MANY WERE MINTED FOR NOW LONG-FORGOTTEN BATTLES.
PRICE GUIDE 1 – 3

▲ CIGAR SMOKERS USED ALL SORTS OF ACCESSORIES AND AMONGST THESE WERE CIGAR CUTTERS, USED FOR TRIMMING ONE END OF THE CIGAR BEFORE SMOKING. THIS SILVER CUTTER FROM 1896 BEARS AN ADVERTISEMENT FOR DEWAR'S WHISKY.

PRICE GUIDE 3

▼ CIGAR SMOKERS OFTEN USED HOLDERS THAT WERE DESIGNED TO PROTECT THE FINGERS FROM UNSIGHTLY TOBACCO STAINS. THESE AMBER EXAMPLES, DATING FROM 1906, ARE FINISHED WITH, ON THE RIGHT, A GILDED BRASS TRIM AND, LEFT, A SILVER BAND.

PRICE GUIDE 3

▲ BEFORE SAFETY MATCHES WERE INVENTED, MATCHES, ONCE PURCHASED, WERE OFTEN TRANSFERRED TO METAL CASES FOR SAFE KEEPING. DELICATELY ENGRAVED, THIS SILVER MATCH CASE BEARS A CREST IN THE CENTRAL RONDEL.

PRICE GUIDE 3

▲ AS WITH CIGARETTES, CIGARS WERE GENERALLY KEPT IN ATTRACTIVE CASES TO PREVENT THEM BEING CRUSHED IN THE POCKET. THIS SILVER CIGAR CASE HAS BEEN DECORATED WITH AN ATTRACTIVE ENGRAVED PATTERN.

PRICE GUIDE 5

◀ MEERSHAUM (A FINE, WHITISH CLAY) AND CLAY PIPES WERE WIDESPREAD IN THE 19TH CENTURY, WITH BRIAR EXAMPLES APPEARING AFTER 1860. THE LONG-STEMMED VERSIONS WITH BOWL TIPPING FORWARD AND SPUR AT BASE WERE DERIVED FROM AN 18TH-CENTURY STYLE. IN VICTORIAN TIMES, NOVELTY BOWLS CAME INTO THEIR OWN. SHOWN HERE, FOR EXAMPLE, ARE A CORN-COB MEERSCHAUM, AND A CLAY PIPE SHAPED IN THE FORM OF A MAN'S HEAD.

PRICE GUIDE 2 — 4

▼ THIS SMALL WOODEN CIGARETTE DISPENSER, IN THE FORM OF A 1930S RADIO, WAS MADE IN THE FAR EAST. WHEN THE LID WAS LIFTED, A SMALL BIRD POPPED UP WITH A CIGARETTE IN ITS BEAK.
PRICE GUIDE 3

▼ THIS CIGARETTE BOX IS MADE OF AN EARLY FORM OF PLASTIC. THE PLASTIC IS TRANSLUCENT, BUT IT HAS BEEN COLOURED TO RESEMBLE MARBLE. EVEN THE HINGES AT THE BACK HAVE BEEN MODELLED IN PLASTIC.
PRICE GUIDE 3

▲ MADE IN 1931, THIS CIGARETTE DISPENSER IS MADE IN ELECTRO-PLATED NICKEL SILVER. THE CIGARETTES WERE REVEALED BY PULLING THE SMALL KNOB AT THE TOP UPWARDS.
PRICE GUIDE 5

▼ THIS CHROME CIGARETTE BOX HAS BEEN ADORNED WITH BLACK ENAMEL DECO DESIGNS. CIGARETTE SMOKING IN THE 1930S WAS THEN A FASHIONABLE HABIT AND CIGARETTE BOXES WERE A COMMON FEATURE IN SMART LIVING ROOMS OF THE DAY.
PRICE GUIDE 3

▲ THIS LARGE ASHTRAY IS MADE UP OF DIFFERENT PIECES OF MIRROR-GLASS. TWO LONG STRIPS OF RIBBED GLASS EDGE THE ASHTRAY. ITS CLEAN AND MODERNISTIC LINES ARE TYPICAL OF ART DECO STYLING.
PRICE GUIDE 5

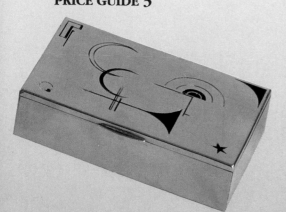

▶ BOTH OF THESE ASHTRAYS HAVE BEEN DECORATED WITH UPRIGHT FIGURES; ONE WITH A SILHOUETTE OF A NAKED LADY, THE OTHER WITH A SCOTTIE DOG. THE FIGURE OF THE WOMAN AND THE TRAY ARE BOTH MADE IN CHROME, AND THE SCOTTIE − A POPULAR 1930S MOTIF − IS MADE IN BAKELITE, A POPULAR MATERIAL THEN.
PRICE GUIDE 2

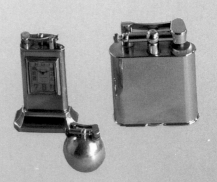

▲ THESE THREE TABLE LIGHTERS WERE ALL MADE BY DUNHILL. THE LARGE LIGHTER HERE IS A GIANT UNIQUE LIGHTER; ALSO SHOWN IS A GOLF BALL SHAPED LIGHTER IN SILVER AND AN 8-DAY CLOCK, IN SILVER, WITH LIGHTER INCORPORATED INTO THE DESIGN.
PRICE GUIDE 5 − 7

▼ THIS CHINESE SNUFF BOTTLE, C.1790, IS MADE OF CRYSTAL WITH A SCENE OF CHINESE WARRIORS PAINTED ON THE INSIDE. BOXES AND BOTTLES FOR SNUFF REMAIN ONE OF THE MOST SOUGHT AFTER OF COLLECTABLES.
PRICE GUIDE 7

▼ THIS ELEGANT, ENGLISH, SILVER SNUFF BOX IS SLIGHTLY LARGER IN SIZE THAN MOST AND WAS INTENDED TO BE KEPT OUT ON DISPLAY RATHER THAN IN THE POCKET. MADE BY JAMES PHIPPS, IT IS DATED 1777.
PRICE GUIDE 7

▼ MADE IN C.1740; THIS SILVER GILT SNUFF BOX IS FRENCH. THE CURVILINEAR SHAPES REFLECT THE ROCOCO STYLE THEN AT ITS PEAK IN FRENCH DECORATIVE ARTS.
PRICE GUIDE 6

◄ THIS TIBETAN SNUFF BOTTLE IS MADE OF CARVED IVORY PANELS, MOUNTED IN SILVER AND STUDDED WITH TURQUOISE AND AMETHYSTS. IT DATES FROM C.1800.
PRICE GUIDE 6

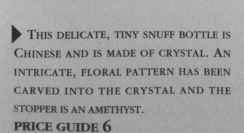

▶ THIS DELICATE, TINY SNUFF BOTTLE IS CHINESE AND IS MADE OF CRYSTAL. AN INTRICATE, FLORAL PATTERN HAS BEEN CARVED INTO THE CRYSTAL AND THE STOPPER IS AN AMETHYST.
PRICE GUIDE 6

▲ THIS TINY SILVER SNUFF BOX WAS PROBABLY MADE AROUND 1720. SIMPLE AND ELEGANT, IT WOULD HAVE SLIPPED UNOBTRUSIVELY INTO THE SMALLEST POCKET. A TINY SPOON, WITH WHICH TO TAKE THE SNUFF, IS ALSO INCLUDED.
PRICE GUIDE 8

POINTS TO WATCH

● The enamel of antique boxes is likely to have suffered some damage, even if it is only hairline cracks. The better the quality of enamel, the higher the price.

● Enamel cannot be repaired satisfactorily and imperfections are betterr than clumsy repairs.

● Smooth cylindrical hinges are generally preferable to protruding ones and the lid should close firmly and open comfortably.

▶ Inscribed 'Gift for a friend', this royal blue patch box is hand-painted with popular love birds and flowers. It dates from c.1790 and the manufacturer is unknown. Many patch boxes contained polished steel mirrors in the lid so fashionable ladies and gentlemen could check that their patches were still in place. **PRICE GUIDE 6**

◀ This Chinese, flask-shaped snuff bottle is made in blue and white porcelain and dates from the end of the 18th or early 19th centuries. Most Oriental snuff bottles feature an integral spoon, usually part of the bottle stopper. **PRICE GUIDE 6**

▶ Patch boxes were often decorated with sentimental inscriptions and pictures such as the doves and hearts on this enamelled box. This example was made in Bilston, in the Midlands, one of the major centres of enamel box manufacture. **PRICE GUIDE 6**

▶ In the 18th century, patches were used by both men and women alike as a fashionable accessory to cover facial blemishes. Patches were usually carried is small boxes such as this oval example dating from c.1790. The lid is illustrated with a hand-painted scene of birds sitting on a basket of flowers, with a delicate relief border. **PRICE GUIDE 7**

▲ THIS LARGE AND ORNATELY DECORATED CADDY IS CHINESE IN ORIGIN AND MADE IN LAQUER. THE IMPORTANCE OF TEA AND TEA-DRINKING IN BRITISH SOCIETY IS REFLECTED BY THE LAVISHNESS OF SOME OF THE CADDIES.
PRICE GUIDE 8

▶ THIS CADDY OF THE 1790s IS MADE OF ROLLED PAPER, FORMED INTO A FLORAL DESIGN. ALSO INCLUDED IS A PAINTED PANEL OF A YOUNG MAN. ROLLED PAPER WORK WAS MADE UP OF SMALL STRIPS OF PAPER, TIGHTLY ROLLED INTO DIFFERENT SIZED CIRCLES AND STUCK DOWN.
PRICE GUIDE 8

▶ THIS HEXAGONAL CADDY IS MADE OF IVORY. A SILVER SHIELD-SHAPE ADORNS THE FRONT, ETCHED WITH THE OWNERS INITIALS. TEA, IN EARLY CADDIES, WAS KEPT UNDER LOCK AND KEY, BUT BY 1850 TEA WAS CHEAP ENOUGH NOT TO WARRENT SUCH PROTECTION.
PRICE GUIDE 8

POINTS TO WATCH

● CHECK THAT INDIVIDUAL COMPARTMENTS WITHIN TEA CADDIES ARE STILL IN PLACE – THIS GREATLY EFFECTS THE VALUE.

● LATE VICTORIAN CADDIES WERE OFTEN FITTED WITH LOCKS TO MAKE THEM LOOK LIKE PRE-1850 CADDIES. THESE LATER CADDIES USUALLY HAVE STEEL LOCKS.

● LOOK AT THE HALLMARK ON A SILVER CADDY; ONE BY A WELL-KNOWN SILVERSMITH IS WORTH MORE THAN ONE BY AN UNKNOWN CRAFTSMAN.

◀ PAPIER MACHÉ WAS A VERY POPULAR MATERIAL IN THE 19TH CENTURY AND THIS CADDY WAS MADE IN 1837, THE YEAR OF VICTORIA'S ACCESSION, BY JENNENS AND BETTRIDGE, THE LARGEST MANUFACTURER IN THIS MEDIUM. THE LID OF THE BOX IS DECORATED WITH A PORTRAIT OF THE YOUNG QUEEN VICTORIA.
PRICE GUIDE 7

▼ THIS SMALL AND SIMPLE CADDY IS MADE UP OF EIGHT PANELS OF TORTOISESHELL. EACH PANEL IS SEPARATED BY A THIN STRINGING OF SILVER AND THE LOCK IS SURROUNDED BY SILVER.
PRICE GUIDE 7

▶ THIS BEAUTIFULLY CARVED WOODEN PEAR IS, IN FACT, A TEA CADDY. FRUIT-SHAPED CADDIES HAD BEEN INSPIRED BY CHINESE DESIGNS AND RANGED FROM APBLES TO AUBERGINES. ORIGINAL GEORGIAN CADDIES ARE MADE IN BEECH, BOX OR FRUITWOOD – VICTORIAN IMITATIONS OF FRUIT-SHAPED CADDIES ARE IN VARNISHED OR PAINTED WHITEWOOD.

PRICE GUIDE 6

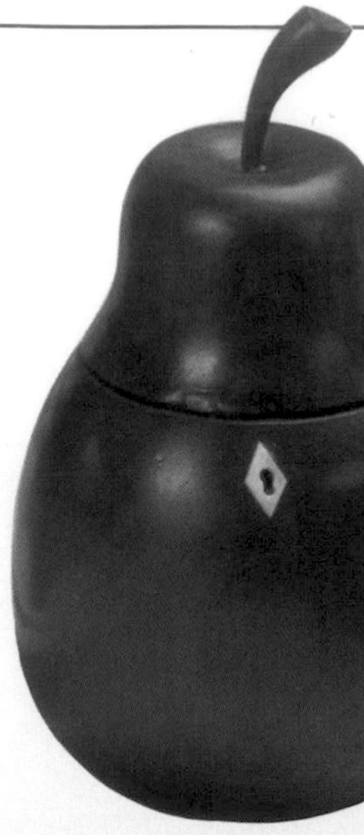

▶ THE INTRICATE AND DENSE DESIGN ON THIS CADDY IS A FORM OF DECORATION KNOWN AS PENWORK. THE TWO BOXES CONTAINED WITHIN THE CADDY WERE FOR STORING TWO DIFFERENT KINDS OF TEA, USUALLY GREEN AND BLACK.

PRICE GUIDE 7

▲ THIS WILLIAM IV ROSEWOOD CADDY, MADE IN 1835, HAS A MOTHER-OF-PEARL INLAY PATTERN IN A FOLIAGE DESIGN. THE CUT GLASS CONTAINER SHOWN HERE WOULD HAVE BEEN HOUSED INSIDE THE CADDY AND WAS FOR MIXING DIFFERENT KINDS OF TEA.

PRICE GUIDE 6

▶ THIS SIMPLE, SQUARE CADDY HAS BEEN DECORATED WITH A COMBINATION OF PENWORK AND TUNBRIDGE WARE STYLE. THIS PARTICULAR KIND OF DECORATION WAS A MOSAIC DESIGN MADE UP OF DIFFERENT COLOURED WOODS, POPULAR DURING THE 19TH CENTURY.

PRICE GUIDE 6

▲ THIS SMALL, OVAL, ROSEWOOD
CADDY DATES FROM AROUND 1780. OVAL
PANELS IN THE TOP AND SIDES HAVE BEEEN
INLAID WITH A PATTERN OF FLOWERS
POPULAR AT THE TIME.
PRICE GUIDE 7

POINTS TO WATCH

● LOOK OUT FOR BROWN OR BLACK STAINING THAT IS SOMETIMES USED TO MAKE JADE LOOK OLD.

● SOME JADE CAN SOFTEN AFTER YEARS IN A BURIAL CHAMBER, SO BEAR THAT IN MIND WHEN TESTING PIECES FOR AUTHENTIC JADE.

● IF STORING IVORY, AVOID WRAPPING THEM IN COLOURED PAPER AS THE IVORY MAY ABSORB THE COLOUR. ACID-FREE TISSUE PAPER IS BEST.

● DO NOT SOAK IVORY IN WATER AS IT GROWS IN LAYERS THAT CAN SEPARATE IF IMMERSED IN WATER.

▼ THIS CARVED JADE PENDANT WITH RUSSET MARKINGS WAS MADE IN THE 18TH CENTURY. IT TAKES THE FORM OF BLOSSOM – A COMMON THEME IN JADE CARVINGS IN CHINA, WHERE NATURAL IMAGES FEATURED STRONGLY IN ART AND DESIGN. SMALL PIECES SUCH AS THIS WERE OFTEN CARRIED AROUND IN THE POCKET WHERE THEY COULD BE HANDLED IN MUCH THE SAME WAY AS 'WORRY BEADS'.

PRICE GUIDE 6

▼ MADE DURING THE 18TH CENTURY, THIS DELICATELY CARVED FISH IS MADE IN A PALE CELADON JADE WITH RUSSET MARKINGS. ANIMALS WERE POPULAR SUBJECTS FOR JADE CARVING IN CHINA, WHERE THEY WERE TRADITIONALLY SEEN AS BEING IMBUED WITH ALMOST HUMAN CHARACTERISTICS.

PRICE GUIDE 8

▼ ONE OF THE MOST POPULAR FORMS OF *OKIMONO* ARE DETAILED FIGURE GROUPS SHOWING SCENES OF DAILY LIFE. THIS DELICATELY OBSERVED MOTHER AND CHILD HAVE BEEN ATTRIBUTED TO THE TOKYO SCHOOL. THIS, ALONG WITH THE OGAWA SCHOOL, WERE THE BEST KNOWN CENTRES FOR *OKIMONO*.

PRICE GUIDE 7

▼ PRODUCED PRIMARILY FOR THE EXPORT MARKET, JAPANESE IVORY CARVINGS ARE KNOWN AS *OKIMONO*. ANIMAL GROUPS ARE A VERY POPULAR FORM OF OF *OKIMONO* FROM A COUNTRY WHERE THE NATIONAL RELIGION, SHINTOISM, FOCUSES ON NATURE SPIRITS. THIS INTRICATE GROUP OF ENTWINED MONKEYS HAS BEEN STAINED WITH A SEPIA PIGMENT AND THE EYES ARE INLAID HORN.

PRICE GUIDE 8

▼ THE GIFT OF THE JAPANESE CARVERS OF *OKIMONO* FOR OBSERVING LIFE IS DEMONSTRATED IN THE CONVINCING INTERACTION BETWEEN THE MAN AND THE CHILD PLAYING WITH A SPIDER IN THIS LIVELY AND DELICATELY CARVED PIECE

PRICE GUIDE 8

▼ ORIGINALLY PART OF A FOUNTAIN, THE LION'S FACE HELD BY THE CHERUB FORMS A SPOUT. A TRADITIONAL DESIGN, THIS PIECE OF STATUARY WAS MADE IN ITALY, EARLY IN THIS CENTURY.
PRICE GUIDE 8

▲ THIS 17TH-CENTURY, MARBLE LION WAS MADE IN NORTHERN ITALY AND, AS PART OF A PAIR, IT HAS A RELATIVELY HIGH PRICE. BOTH LIONS WERE PROBABLY INTENDED TO FLANK AN ENTRY OR A FLIGHT OF STAIRS OUTDOORS.
PRICE GUIDE 9

▼ THIS GRIFFIN, A MYTHICAL BEAST COMBINING LION AND EAGLE, WAS MADE IN 1880 IN FRANCE. PAINTED TO LOOK LIKE STONE, THIS PIECE IS, IN FACT, MADE OF CAST IRON — EMINENTLY SUITABLE FOR GARDEN STATUARY.
PRICE GUIDE 8

▲ THIS 18TH-CENTURY PIECE OF GARDEN STATUARY, OF A LEAD FIGURE SURMOUNTED BY A SUNDIAL, WAS MADE BY JOHN CHEERE OF LONDON. IMBUED WITH AN ALLEGORICAL MEANING, THIS IS MEANT TO REPRESENT MAN ENSLAVED BY TIME.
PRICE GUIDE 9

▲ THIS MARBLE STATUE OF A FOX WITH A CAPTURED CHICKEN IS ENGLISH AND DATES FROM THE 1850S. FINELY DETAILED, EVEN THE TEXTURE OF THE FUR AND FEATHERS HAVE BEEN CAEFULLY PICKED OUT IN THE MARBLE.
PRICE GUIDE 9

◀ FOR A LONG TIME, SHELL BOXES HAVE BEEN THE IDEAL SOUVENIR TO BRING BACK FROM A TRIP TO THE SEASIDE. THIS WOODEN BOX, INTENDED TO HOLD JEWELLERY OR OTHER KNICK-KNACKS, HAS BEEN CREATIVELY COVERED WITH SHELLS.
PRICE GUIDE 4

▶ THIS SAILORS' VALENTINE PRESENTATION BOX HAS BEEN MADE UP OF A VARIETY OF EXOTIC SHELLS WHICH HAVE BEEN NEATLY ARRANGED IN COMPARTMENTS TO FORM A PLEASING PATTERN. ONE OF THE MOST ORIGINAL WAYS OF SENDING A MESSAGE OF LOVE FROM FAR AWAY PLACES, THESE VALENTINES WERE MOST COMMONLY MADE WITH SHELLS FROM THE WEST INDIES.
PRICE GUIDE 8

◀ THIS PAIR OF HORSESHOE-SHAPED SHELL PICTURES ARE FINE EXAMPLES OF ONE OF THE MOST POPULAR OF VICTORIAN SOUVENIR ORNAMENTS. A SEASHORE SCENE MADE UP OF SHELLS AND CORAL AND PAINTINGS OF MARINE SCENES ARE ENCLOSED IN GLASS, WHICH IS THEN SURROUNDED WITH A SHELL FRAME.
PRICE GUIDE 4

DESIGN FEATURES

IN TURKEY, A VARIETY OF KILIM BAGS WERE MADE FOR TRANSPORTING FAMILY BELONGINGS OR FOR HANGING UP AS STORAGE ITEMS ON THE WALLS OF A HOUSE OR TENT. SALT BAGS, SUCH AS THIS 19TH-CENTURY EXAMPLE, ARE SQUARE WITH DISTINCTIVELY NARROWED NECKS WHICH FOLD DOWN TO KEEP THE SALT DRY. THESE, ALONG WITH OTHER KILIM BAGS, ARE STILL MADE TODAY.

THE CENTRAL DESIGN IS A STYLIZED FORM OF THE TREE OF LIFE, SURROUNDED BY FLOWERS. A PARADE OF DRAGON'S HEADS ALONG THE BORDERS WERE INTENDED TO GIVE PROTECTION AGAINST EVIL.

► THIS BRIGHTLY COLOURED, LONG MARRIAGE CUSHION WAS WOVEN IN AROUND 1840. MOST TEXTILE PRODUCTION IN SWEDEN WAS CONCENTRATED IN SMALL RURAL COMMUNITIES. THIS PARTICULAR CUSHION COVER COMES FROM SKANE, AN AREA RENOWNED FOR FINE TEXTILES.
PRICE GUIDE 8

▲ THIS KILIM IS FROM CUMRA IN WESTERN TURKEY. IT WAS PROBABLY WOVEN BY A GIRL ANTICIPATING MARRIAGE, AS THE PATTERN IS FULL OF SYMBOLIC REFERENCES TO FERTILITY.
PRICE GUIDE 8

▶ THE DIAMOND-SHAPED MEDALLIONS THAT RUN IN BANDS ACROSS THIS KILIM ARE CHARACTERISTIC OF SHIRVAN RUGS WHICH, GENERALLY, HAVE NO BORDERS. KILIMS ARE FLAT-WOVEN RUGS AND FABRICS, WHICH REQUIRE LESS LABOUR AND MATERIAL TO PRODUCE, AND THAT WERE USED AS INEXPENSIVE FLOOR-COVERINGS, BAGS AND DRAPERIES.
PRICE GUIDE 8

▶ THIS IS A MID 19TH-CENTURY, OBRUK PRAYER KILIM. VARIOUS DECORATIVE MOTIFS MAKE UP A BORDER THAT SURROUNDS A CENTRAL PATTERN INTENDED TO REPRESENT A POINTED MIHRAB, OR PRAYER NICHE.
PRICE GUIDE 9

◀ THIS DARK BLUE SWEDISH MARRIAGE TAPESTRY CUSHION WAS MADE IN AROUND 1840. IN THE CENTRE IS A BIRD WITH NEST-BUILDING MATERIAL IN ITS BEAK. AROUND THIS MOTIF IS A WREATH OF LEAVES AND FLOWERS AND FOUR ANGELS. ALL THESE ELEMENTS SYMBOLIZE THE GOOD FORTUNE WISHED UPON THE MARRIED COUPLE.
PRICE GUIDE 8

THIS IS A TYPICAL MASS-PRODUCED FLAT IRON – MANY DIFFERENT SIZES WERE AVAILABLE RANGING FROM ONE TO 14. HEATED DIRECTLY ON THE RANGE, THE LAUNDRY MAID WOULD HAVE USED TWO IRONS AT A TIME, LEAVING ONE TO HEAT UP WHILE SHE IRONED WITH THE HOT ONE.
PRICE GUIDE 1

THE ELECTRIC IRON SOON CUT THE WORK OF MAIDS AND HOUSEWIVES WHEN THEY FIRST APPEARED. VALUE IS ADDED TO THIS DELUXE, DROP-HANDLE, GEC TRAVELLING IRON BY ITS BEING IN ITS ORIGINAL BOX, COMPLETE WITH SOCKETS.
PRICE GUIDE 4

THE BOX IRON WAS A HOLLOW METAL STRUCTURE THAT WAS THEN FILLED WITH HOT COALS OR CHARCOAL, PROVIDING A MORE CONSTANT SOURCE OF HEAT THAN WAS POSSIBLE WITH A FLAT IRON. THIS SCOTTISH EXAMPLE MADE IN IRON WITH AN ORNATE BRASS AND WOOD HANDLE.
PRICE GUIDE 6

THIS FINE BRASS AND IRON EDWARDIAN 'TALLY' IRON AND POKER WERE USED FOR IRONING RIBBONS AND FRILLS. THE CIGAR-SHAPED IRON CYLINDER HELD ON THE BRASS STAND IS HEATED BY INSERTING THE HOT POKER. THIS WAS THEN USED FOR IRONING BOWS, FRILLS, AND RIBBONS.
PRICE GUIDE 5

IN THE DAYS WHEN CRIMPED LINEN WAS A FASHIONABLE TRIM TO BOTH CLOTHES AND UNDERWEAR, THIS SMALL BOARD WAS A VITAL TOOL IN THE LAUNDRY. BOTH BOARD AND ROLLER ARE COVERED WITH SMALL RIDGES AND A PIECE OF LINEN COULD BE CRIMPED BY LAYING IT ON THE BOARD AND THEN PASSING THE ROLLER OVER IT.
PRICE GUIDE 5

▼ DESPITE ITS NAME, THIS TABLE-TOP MANGLE SAT ON THE DRAINING BOARD IN AN EDWARDIAN UTILITY ROOM OR KITCHEN. WHEN MOST WASHING WAS DONE BY HAND, THE MANGLE WOULD HAVE BEEN A VALUABLE AID TO WRINGING OUT THE LAUNDRY.
PRICE GUIDE 5

◄ THIS WHIRLWIND MODEL E CARPET SWEEPER PROUDLY CLAIMS TO BE 'ALL BRITISH' IN ORDER TO CONTEND WITH COMPETITION FROM FIRMS SUCH AS HOOVER AND ELECTROLUX WHO WERE IMPORTING VACUUM CLEANERS AND SWEEPERS INTO BRITAIN IN THE 1930s.
PRICE GUIDE 5

▼ THIS ELECTRIC VACUUM CLEANER WAS MADE BY VAC-TRIC OF CRICKLEWOOD, IN LONDON. THE RUNNERS UNDERNEATH THIS MODEL GAVE WAY TO CASTORS IN THE EARLY 1930s.
PRICE GUIDE 4

▼ THIS UNUSUALLY-SHAPED AND ATTRACTIVE, STEEL, KITCHEN CHOPPER DATES FROM AROUND 1800. USED FOR MEAT AND VEGETABLES, THIS CHOPPER COULD BE HELD BY THE T-SHAPED HANDLE.
PRICE GUIDE 5

▲ THIS ALL-BRASS VICTORIAN WARMING PAN HAS AN ENGRAVED LID. THE PAN PART OF THIS UTENSIL WAS FILLED WITH WARM COALS AND THEN PASSED OVER AND AMONG THE SHEETS TO TAKE THE CHILL OFF THE BED BEFORE RETIRING.
PRICE GUIDE 5

▼ THIS SMALL, MEAT CLEAVER DATES FROM THE LATE 18TH CENTURY. THE LARGE, STEEL BLADE IS FIXED INTO A BRASS AND WOOD HANDLE AND, THOUGH MOTTLED BY AGE, IS STILL GOOD AS A CUTTING BLADE.
PRICE GUIDE 4

▲ THIS SMALL, COPPER SAUCEPAN WITH LID DATES FROM 1790. AS WITH MOST COPPER POTS AND PANS, THIS ONE HAS BEEN LINED WITH TIN INSIDE TO PREVENT POISONS WITHIN THE COPPER CONTAMINATING THE FOOD.
PRICE GUIDE 5

▶ THIS LATE-GEORGIAN COFFEE POT IS MADE OF COPPER. THE WOODEN HANDLE IS ATTACHED TO THE POT WITH A HEART-SHAPED PLATE. FIXED TO THE SIDE OF THE POT, THE HANDLE MADE IT EASIER TO POUR THE COFFEE OUT.
PRICE GUIDE 5

▶ THE GLEAMING, BRASS BOWL OF THIS LADLE IS ATTACHED TO A STEEL HANDLE. DATING FROM AROUND 1800, UTENSILS LIKE THIS ONE WOULD HAVE BEEN USED IN THE KITCHEN FOR SERVING UP SOUPS AND STEWS INTO TUREENS BEFORE THEY WERE TAKEN TO THE TABLE.
PRICE GUIDE 5

▼ THIS HEAVY BRASS PESTLE AND MORTAR DATE FROM THE LATE 18TH CENTURY. HERBS AND SPICES FOR FLAVOURING FOOD AND SAUCES COULD BE CRUSHED BY THE PESTLE.
PRICE GUIDE 4

▲ THESE BRASS AND STEEL PINCERS WERE USED TO SUSPEND SLOWLY-COOKING MEAT OVER A FIRE. THE LENGTH OF DROP AND THE WIDTH OF THE PINCERS' GRIP COULD BE ADJUSTED WITH THE BRASS FITTINGS AT TOP AND CENTRE.
PRICE GUIDE 5

▶ THESE TWO TIN-PLATE RECEPTACLES ARE BOTH ALE MULLERS; ONE CONICAL AND THE OTHER SLIPPER-SHAPED. THEY COULD BE FILLED WITH BEER, AND A FEW SPICES, AND PUSHED INTO THE HOT COALS OF THE FIRE OR STOVE TO MULL.
PRICE GUIDE 3 & 5

▶ JELLIES — BOTH SWEET AND SAVOURY — AND BLANCMANGES WERE POPULAR DESSERTS DURING THE REGENCY PERIOD AND MOULDS CAME IN ALL SHAPES AND SIZES. COPPER MOULDS LINED WITH TIN, LIKE THESE EXAMPLES, WERE OFTEN USED EARLY IN THE 19TH CENTURY.
PRICE GUIDE 5

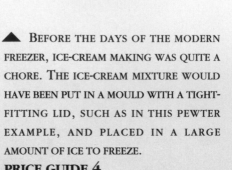

▲ BEFORE THE DAYS OF THE MODERN FREEZER, ICE-CREAM MAKING WAS QUITE A CHORE. THE ICE-CREAM MIXTURE WOULD HAVE BEEN PUT IN A MOULD WITH A TIGHT-FITTING LID, SUCH AS IN THIS PEWTER EXAMPLE, AND PLACED IN A LARGE AMOUNT OF ICE TO FREEZE.
PRICE GUIDE 4

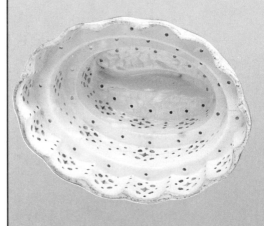

▲ THIS WELL-WORN, WOODEN, TWO-HANDLED BREAD BOARD DATES FROM AROUND 1790. IT WOULD FETCH A FAIRLY HIGH PRICE AT SALE DUE TO ITS AGE AND GOOD CONDITION.
PRICE GUIDE 5

▲ THIS CURD MOULD IN LEEDS CREAMWARE, DATING FROM AROUND 1820, IS DECORATED WITH A FISH THAT WOULD HAVE APPEARED ON THE TOP OF THE TIERS OF JELLY WHEN THE FINISHED DESSERT WAS TURNED OUT.
PRICE GUIDE 6

◀ THIS LARGE, OAK BOX WITH ITS SLOPING, HINGED LID WAS USED IN THE LATE 18TH CENTURY FOR STORING SALT. THIS WOULD HAVE HUNG BY THE FIRE OR STOVE TO HELP KEEP THE SALT DRY.
PRICE GUIDE 5

▲ AFTER BEING MADE, BUTTER WAS FORMED INTO SMALLER PIECES BY BEING PATTED INTO SHAPE. A WOODEN BUTTER STAMPER, LIKE THIS ONE FROM C.1800, WOULD HAVE BEEN USED TO STAMP AN ATTRACTIVE PATTERN INTO THE BUTTER.
PRICE GUIDE 5

◀ USED FOR CHOPPING CHEESE OR VEGETABLES, THIS EARLY, 19TH-CENTURY, WOOD AND STEEL SLICER OPERATED BY A GUILLOTINE ACTION.
PRICE GUIDE 3

◀ THESE TWO WOODEN CYLINDERS ARE SPICE TOWERS, DIVIDED INTO SECTIONS FOR THE DIFFERENT SPICES. THE SMALLER OF THE TWO CONTAINS A GRATER INSIDE THE LID FOR THE NUTMEG.
PRICE GUIDE 5

▲ THIS LATE-GEORGIAN RECTANGULAR EARTHENWARE DISH IS DECORATED WITH A SLIP DESIGN. SLIPWARE WAS TRADITIONALLY MADE BY COUNTRY POTTERS AND A DISH OF THIS FUNCTIONAL SIMPLICITY WOULD HAVE BEEN USED IN THE KITCHEN RATHER THAN AT THE TABLE.
PRICE GUIDE 4

DESIGN FEATURES

ALTHOUGH MOST PLASTIC TABLEWARE WAS SPECIFICALLY DESIGNED TO BE PRACTICAL AND DURABLE, ONE PARTICULAR RANGE WAS PRODUCED WITH A MORE DECORATIVE PURPOSE IN MIND. THIS WAS KNOWN AS JAXONITE, WHICH COMBINED A DARK MOTTLED BODY OF UREA FOMALDEHYDE, AS USED FOR BANDALASTA WARE, WITH BEAUTIFULLY CRAFTED SILVER-PLATED FITTINGS. THE MOTTLED PATTERNS ARE ACHIEVED BY THE BLENDING OF DIFFERENT COLOURED MOULDING POWDERS. AFTER SETTING, MOULDINGS LIKE THE KNOB ON THIS BISCUIT BARREL, WERE TRIMMED AND POLISHED, USING SPECIAL MACHINERY.

THE EFFECT THIS PRODUCED IS TYPICAL OF THE ART DECO FASHION FOR USING CONTRASTING COLOURS AND TEXTURES TO CREATE A DRAMATIC VISUAL EFFECT. LARGE JAXONITE BOWLS OR BISCUIT BARRELS WERE OFTEN BOUGHT AS WEDDING PRESENTS. THESE COULD BE MATCHED WITH A WHOLE RANGE OF TABLEWARE INCLUDING TABLE LAMPS, CANDLESTICKS AND COFFEE SETS.

▶ THE MAIN BODY OF THIS EARLY 'TEASMADE' IS MADE IN PLASTIC, THE KETTLE THAT HEATS THE WATER IS IN CHROME AND THE SQUARE-SHAPE TEAPOT IS CERAMIC. THE FIRST PATENTED AUTOMATIC TEA-MAKER WAS MADE IN 1904 OR 1905, BUT IT WAS NOT UNTIL THE 1930s THAT THE DESIGN WAS PERFECTED AND MANUFACTURED BY THE GOBLIN COMPANY.

PRICE GUIDE 5

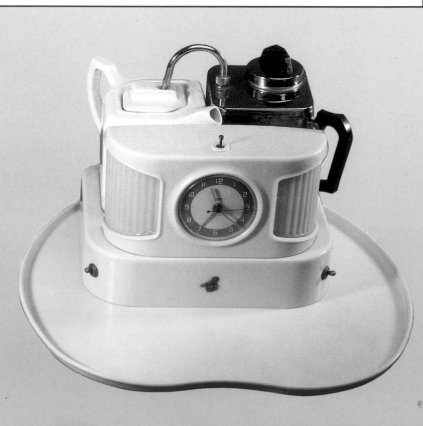

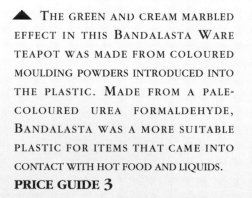

▲ THE GREEN AND CREAM MARBLED EFFECT IN THIS BANDALASTA WARE TEAPOT WAS MADE FROM COLOURED MOULDING POWDERS INTRODUCED INTO THE PLASTIC. MADE FROM A PALE-COLOURED UREA FORMALDEHYDE, BANDALASTA WAS A MORE SUITABLE PLASTIC FOR ITEMS THAT CAME INTO CONTACT WITH HOT FOOD AND LIQUIDS.
PRICE GUIDE 3

▲ THIS MOTTLED BLACK AND WHITE SALT POT WAS MADE IN THE 1930S FROM UREA FORMALDEHYDE. SMALL PIECES SUCH AS THIS ARE STILL AFFORDABLE AND CAN BE THE BASIS FOR AN INTERESTING COLLECTION OF EARLY PLASTICS.
PRICE GUIDE 1

▲ THESE TEACUPS AND SAUCERS AND EGG CUPS ARE ALL PART OF A MATCHING SET IN MOTTLED BROWN THIO UREA FORMALDEHYDE. BY THE 1930S, RATHER THAN IMITATE HISTORICAL STYLES OF SILVER OR CERAMIC TABLEWARE, PLASTIC DEVELOPED ITS OWN SIMPLE, CLEAN, AND MODERNISTIC LINES.
PRICE GUIDE 4

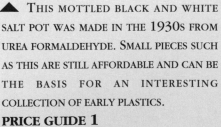

▲ THIS TOAST-RACK IS MADE IN A MARBLED UREA FORMALDEHYDE. THE MARBLED EFFECT WAS ACHIEVED BY PACKING DIFFERENT COLOURED POWDERS INTO STEEL MOULDS AND SHAPING UNDER PRESSURE AND HEAT, WHICH THEN MADE THE PLASTIC FLOW.
PRICE GUIDE 3

◀ THIS MARBLE, ORANGE JAMPOT WAS MADE IN UREA FORMALDEHYDE BY BEETLEWARE. MORE AFFORDABLE THAT BANDALASTA, WHICH WAS ONE OF THE EARLIEST AND MOST EXPENSIVE OF PLASTIC LINES, BEETLEWARE, MOSTLY SOLD AT WOOLWORTH'S, WAS A BEST-SELLER.
PRICE GUIDE 2

DESIGN FEATURES

THE PIANOS MADE BY JOHN BROADWOOD'S COMPANY WERE MUCH VALUED IN MUSIC HALLS AND OTHER PLACES OF ENTERTAINMENT FOR THEIR SOLID, METAL-FRAMED STRUCTURE AS WELL AS FOR THEIR MUSICAL QUALITY. AT THE SAME TIME, THE WOODEN CASINGS WERE DECORATIVE ENOUGH TO SIT IN THE PLUSHEST OF PARLOURS.

THIS UPRIGHT FROM THE 1880S IS CASED IN MAHOGANY, WITH A GOOD DEAL OF FINE INLAY WORK. THE TAPERED, SQUARE-SECTIONED LEGS AND THE FRONT PANELS ARE OUTLINED IN SATINWOOD STRINGING. LARGER PIECES OF SATINWOOD ARE USED IN THE FRIEZE RUNNING THE LENGTH OF THE TOP, AND FOR CROSSBANDING IN THE PANELS. EACH OF THESE CONTAINS A MARQUETRY PICTURE, OF MUSICAL INSTRUMENTS AT EITHER SIDE AND A BASKET OF FLOWERS IN THE CENTRE. THE CASTORS, PEDALS AND KEY ESCUTCHEON ARE ALL IN BRASS, WHILE THE KEYS THEMSELVES ARE MADE OF IVORY AND EBONY.

◄ THESE THREE VICTORIAN WRITING PENS WOULD HAVE BEEN KEPT ON AN INKWELL OR IN THE DRAWERS OF A WRITING DESK, ALONG WITH A BOX OF SPARE NIBS. THE TWO PENS AT THE TOP HAVE IVORY HANDLES, WHILE THE THIRD HAS A PRETTY PAINTED CERAMIC GRIP.
PRICE GUIDE 4

▶ THIS DELICATE SHEFFIELD PLATE INKSTAND DATES FROM AROUND 1830. THERE ARE TWO INKWELLS — ONE FOR BLACK INK AND THE OTHER FOR RED — AND A CONTAINER FOR THE WAFERS THAT WERE USED TO SEAL LETTERS.
PRICE GUIDE 6

◄ THIS COALPORT POUNCE POT IS DATED ABOUT 1810 AND IS PAINTED WITH A FLORAL DECORATION. THE PERFORATED TOP WAS FOR SPRINKLING THE POUNCE OVER THE WET INK OF A RECENTLY WRITTEN PAGE TO DRY IT.
PRICE GUIDE 4

▼ THE FOUNTAIN PEN WAS FIRST PATENTED BY J.J. PARKER IN 1832 BUT IT WAS NOT UNTIL 1884 THAT WATERMAN'S PRODUCED THEIR LEAK-PROOF FOUNTAIN PEN. THIS ELEGANT PEN, ON THE LEFT, WITH 14 CARAT GOLD DECORATION DATES FROM 1910 AND WAS MADE BY CONKLIN, AN AMERICAN COMPANY.
PRICE GUIDE 5

▼ THESE TWO SLENDER STICKS ARE CONDUCTOR'S BATONS, BOTH EBONY WITH SILVER MOUNTS. THE TIP OF THE SHORTER BATON IS DECORATED WITH A SILVER LYRE. BOTH DATE FROM THE EARLY 20TH CENTURY.
PRICE GUIDE 5

▼ MANY VICTORIAN MUSIC BOOKS ARE COLLECTED FOR THEIR ATTRACTIVE BINDINGS. SHOWN HERE ARE A PRACTICAL INSTRUCTION BOOK FOR THE BOEHM FLUTE IN G FLAT, THE COMPLETE BOOK OF CHOPIN'S NOCTURNES AND THE CURSCHMANN ALBUM.
PRICE GUIDE 4

▲ THIS BECHSTEIN GRAND PIANO OF ABOUT 1890 IS MADE IN ROSEWOOD WITH AN ELABORATE FRETTED MUSIC STAND AND HEAVY OCTAGONAL, TURNED LEGS. THE FINEST OF PIANOS CAN FETCH A HIGH PRICE AND WILL BE OF MOST INTEREST TO THE MORE DEDICATED PIANO PLAYER.
PRICE GUIDE 9

▲ THIS WATERMAN'S FOUNTAIN PEN, ON THE RIGHT, FROM 1920 HAS A DECORATIVE BROWN AND BLACK PLASTIC BODY. THE FOUNTAIN PEN ALLOWED AT LEAST A WEEK'S WRITING WITHOUT HAVING TO BE REFILLED WITH INK.
PRICE GUIDE 3

▲ THIS IVORY PAPER KNIFE HAS AN INTRICATELY CARVED HANDLE IN THE FORM OF A HAND AND SLEEVE. THE HAND IS CLUTCHING THE WIDE, FLAT BLADE. A PAPER KNIFE WAS USED FOR CUTTING THE PAGES OF NEW BOOKS AS WELL AS FOR OPENING LETTERS.
PRICE GUIDE 5

IN 1935, THE PUBLISHER ALLEN LANE HIT UPON THE IDEA OF PRODUCING POCKET-SIZED, PAPERBACK BOOKS FOR SIXPENCE – THEN THE COST OF A PACKET OF TEN CIGARETTES. THE SERIES HE HAD DEVELOPED WAS PUBLISHED UNDER THE IMPRINT OF PENGUIN. PAPER COVERS HAD BEEN USED BEFORE, BUT BY THE 1930s SALES GREW CONSIDERABLY.
PRICE GUIDE 1

EARLY MAGAZINES WERE ILLUSTRATED WITH BLACK AND WHITE WOODCUTS OR ENGRAVINGS, WITH SOME OCCASIONAL COLOUR PRINTING. PHOTOGRAPHY WAS NOT REALLY USED UNTIL THE 1930s.
PRICE GUIDE 1

THE COVER OF THIS COPY OF THE *AMERICAN SUNDAY MAGAZINE* OF 9TH MARCH 1913 SHOWS A FASHIONABLE YOUNG WOMAN PULLING ON A LONG AND ELEGANT GLOVE. THE MAGAZINE WAS A MONTHLY SECTION OF THE SAN FRANCISCO EXAMINER, AIMED AT WOMEN.
PRICE GUIDE 3

THESE FOUR BRITISH WOMEN'S MAGAZINES DATE FROM BETWEEN 1898 AND 1915. THEY INCLUDE THE FIRST EDITION OF A MAGAZINE CALLED *MARY BULL*, ISSUED AS A SISTER PUBLICATION TO *JOHN BULL*, AND THE SPECIAL CORONATION NUMBER OF *OUR HOME*.
PRICE GUIDE 3

▶ COLOUR COMICS FOR CHILDREN WERE AN EDWARDIAN INTRODUCTION, AND SOON FOUND A LOYAL READERSHIP. PUBLISHED WEEKLY, CHILDREN COULD FOLLOW THEIR FAVOURITE CHARACTERS AND STRIPS THROUGH THEIR ADVENTURES. **PRICE GUIDE 1**

▼ THIS SUPPLEMENT, *LA MODE*, WAS PUBLISHED WITH *PETIT JOURNAL*, A FRENCH MAGAZINE. CONCERNED WITH CLOTHES AND ACCESSORIES, THE COVER OF THIS ISSUE SHOWS FOUR OF THE LATEST FASHIONS FOR YOUNG WOMEN AND GIRLS. **PRICE GUIDE 3**

▲ THIS COPY OF *THE LADY* IS OPEN AT ITS FIRST EDITORIAL PAGE. A YOUNG, SOCIETY BEAUTY IS PHOTOGRAPHED IN A POSE CAPTIONED 'MEDITATION' AND OPPOSITE, MAISON NICOL OF THE HAYMARKET, LONDON, ADVERTISE THEIR SPECIALIST HAIR PREPARATIONS. **PRICE GUIDE 4**

▲ THIS ISSUE OF *THE QUEEN*, 'THE LADY'S NEWSPAPER', WAS PUBLISHED IN 1915, DURING WORLD WAR I. IN KEEPING WITH OTHER MAGAZINES OF THE PERIOD, THE FRONT PAGE IS GIVEN OVER TO ADVERTS. LATER ON, THIS MAGAZINE MERGED WITH *HARPERS BAZAAR* TO BECOME *HARPERS AND QUEEN*. **PRICE GUIDE 4**

▲ UNDER THE FASHION-CONSCIOUS EYE OF MME ALINE RAYMOND, *LA MODE ILLUSTRÉE* WAS PUBLISHED WEEKLY AND SAW ITSELF AS 'A FAMILY MAGAZINE', THE 'JOURNAL DE LA FAMILLE'. THIS ISSUE APPEARED IN 1912. **PRICE GUIDE 3**

POINTS TO WATCH

● DO NOT BUY A CARD JUST BECAUSE YOU NOTICE AN ERROR ON IT AND HOPE THAT THIS MAY MAKE IT VALUABLE. WRONG CAPTIONS OR SPELLING MISTAKES ARE REGARDED MERELY AS INTERESTING ODDITIES AND, UNLIKE ERRORS ON POSTAGE STAMPS, DO NOT NECCESSARILY COMMAND A PREMIUM.

● STORE CARDS CAREFULLY IN FRAMES OR ALBUMS THAT CAN GUARD AGAINST ACCIDENTAL DAMAGE.

● DAMAGED CARDS HAVE LITTLE VALUE, ALTHOUGH THE SUBJECT MATTER MAY STILL APPEAL. IF YOU BUY SUCH CARDS TO CUT COST, YOU MAY FIND IT DIFFICULT TO FIND A BUYER, SHOULD YOU EVER WISH TO SELL.

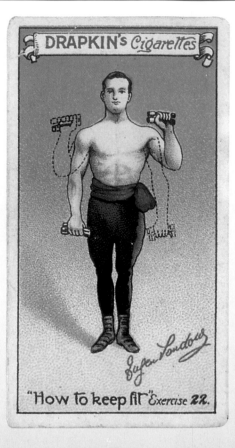

"How to keep fit" Exercise 22.

▲ DRAPKIN'S CIGARETTES GAVE AWAY CARDS THAT FEATURED, RATHER IRONICALLY SEEN FROM TODAY'S POINT OF VIEW, 'HOW TO KEEP FIT' EXERCISES. SHOWN HERE, EXCERCISE 22 INSTRUCTED THE EDWARDIAN MAN ON HOW TO DEVELOP THE MUSCLES IN HIS UPPER AND LOWER ARMS.
PRICE GUIDE 1

▼ KNOWN AS THE DIXIE KID, THIS BOXER'S REAL NAME WAS AARON L.BROWN. AN AMERICAN BOXER, HIS CAREER DETAILS WERE LISTED ON THE BACK OF THIS CARD GIVEN AWAY WITH COPE'S CIGARETTES.
PRICE GUIDE 1

DIXIE KID

▼ OGDEN CIGARETTES ALSO PRODUCED A 'RACEHORSES' SERIES OF 50 GREAT HORSES. SHOWN HERE IS PRINCE BATHYANY'S CHESTNUT BROWN, GALOPIN, THE DERBY WINNER OF 1875.
PRICE GUIDE 1

MR. P. F. WARNER (MIDDLESEX).

▲ SPORTING STARS WERE ONE OF THE MOST POPULAR OF SUBJECTS FOR CIGARETTE CARDS. THIS WILL'S CIGARETTE CARD SHOWS 'PLUM' WARNER, THE CAPTAIN OF THE 1903 ENGLAND TEAM, VICTORIOUS AGAINST AUSTRALIA.
PRICE GUIDE 1

GALOPIN.

PROMINENT FOOTBALLERS.

J. LUMLEY,

BRIGHTON & HOVE ALBION.

OGDEN'S CIGARETTES.

OTTO MADDEN

◀ J. LUMLEY OF BRIGHTON AND HOVE ALBION IS ONE OF THE SPORTSMEN INCLUDED IN TADDY'S & CO'S 'PROMINENT FOOTBALLERS' RUN. THE BACK OF THE CARD PROMOTES TADDY'S 'RIPE, FULL FLAVOURED PIPE TOBACCO'.
PRICE GUIDE 1

▶ JOCKEY OTTO MADDEN, DRESSED IN THE RED AND YELLOW COLOURS OF HORSE OWNER G.A. PRENTICE, IS PART OF A SET OF 50 RACING CARDS. THEY SHOWED 'OWNERS' RACING COLOURS AND JOCKEYS' AND WERE GIVEN AWAY WITH OGDEN'S CIGARETTES.
PRICE GUIDE 1

◀ TADDY & CO PRODUCED A SERIES OF CARDS FEATURING FAMOUS JOCKEYS. THIS PARTICULAR CARD SHOWS A PORTRAIT OF L.H. HEWITT IN A NEAT PICTURE FRAME.
PRICE GUIDE 2

▼ JOB CIGARETTES RAN A SERIES OF HORSE RACING CARDS THAT FEATURED PHOTOGRAPHS OF FAMOUS RUNNERS AND RIDERS. HERE, A JOCKEY IS SEATED ON MINORU, ONE OF THE KING'S HORSES.
PRICE GUIDE 1

FAMOUS JOCKEYS.

L. H. HEWITT

MINORU. JOB CIGARETTES

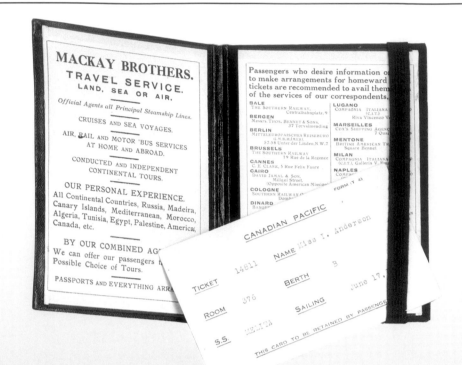

THIS SMART, LEATHER TICKET WALLET WAS GIVEN TO CUSTOMERS WHO BOOKED THEIR HOLIDAYS THROUGH MACKAY BROTHERS, A SCOTTISH TRAVEL FIRM. AS WELL AS GIVING A LIST OF THEIR OVERSEAS CORRESPONDENTS, THE TRAVELLER'S TICKET DETAILS WERE ENCLOSED.
PRICE GUIDE 2

THIS EYE-CATCHING, 1930s, LUGGAGE LABEL WAS FOR PASSENGERS STOPPING OFF FOR A FEW DAYS, OR STAYING, AT THE MIKADO HOTEL ON THE ISLAND OF KOBE, JAPAN.
PRICE GUIDE 1

THIS P & O BROCHURE ADVERTISES THEIR TOURIST CLASS CRUISES OF 1933. SELLING THEIR SERVICE WITH GLAMOUR, EVEN TOURIST-CLASS PASSENGERS ARE SHOWN BEING SALUTED BY THE CAPTAIN.
PRICE GUIDE 2

THIS CHARMING BON VOYAGE CARD FROM THE 1920s HAS A SHORT VERSE WHICH WISHES THE TRAVELLER A SAFE JOURNEY. SENT TO ANYONE ABOUT TO EMBARK ON A LONG SEA TRIP, THE MESSAGE WOULD HAVE BEEN WRITTEN ON THE BACK OF THIS CARD.
PRICE GUIDE 1

THIS BLOTTER, ADVERTISING THE SERVICES OF A TRAVEL AGENT, WAS FOR THE BRITISH & NORTHERN SHIPPING AGENCY OF LONDON. HERE, THE TRAVELLER IS OFFERED A CHOICE BETWEEN PLANE OR BOAT, THOUGH AIR TRAVEL EVENTUALLY SUPERSEDED SEA VOYAGES.
PRICE GUIDE 1

▶ THIS COLOUR ADVERTISEMENT FOR ROLLS ROYCE APPEARED IN AUGUST 1919. A PICTURE OF TRANQUILLITY IS PAINTED AS A CHAUFFEUR-DRIVEN ROLLS, 'THE BEST CAR IN THE WORLD', IS DRIVEN THROUGH A FOREST.
PRICE GUIDE 2

▼ THE PICTURE USED IN THIS ADVERTISEMENT FOR VAUXHALL CARS IS ENTITLED 'SUNSHINE AFTER STORM'. THE PASSENGERS OF THIS CONVERTABLE CAR ARE ABLE TO PUSH BACK THE HOOD AND VIEW THE LANDSCAPE AFTER THE RAIN.
PRICE GUIDE 2

▶ THIS ADVERTISEMENT FROM A 1919 MAGAZINE EXTOLS THE VIRTUES OF THE HUMBER CAR. ADVERTISED AS THE CAR FOR THE OWNER-DRIVER, THIS IS THE KIND OF CAR THAT WAS BEING BOUGHT BY A WIDER SECTION OF THE PUBLIC.
PRICE GUIDE 2

▼ THIS CARDBOARD POSTER ADVERTISES 'COLLEGE SWEETS'. MADE AROUND 1920, ITS EYE-CATCHING ILLUSTRATION SHOWS TWO CHEERFUL BOYS IN ETON SCHOOL UNIFORM, EACH CARRYING A LARGE AND SHINY TIN OF SWEETS.
PRICE GUIDE 3

▼ THIS CLASSIC BISTO GRAVY POSTER WAS DESIGNED IN 1929. THE PUNNING HUMOUR AND ARTISTIC TALENT OF ITS DESIGNER, WILL OWEN, AND THE ENDURING APPEAL OF HIS 'BISTO KIDS' ARE REFLECTED IN THE HIGH PRICE.
PRICE GUIDE 6

◀ THIS FREEDOM SOAP CARDBOARD POSTER WAS MADE AROUND 1920. IT CARRIES AN UNUSUALLY PROGRESSIVE AND FEMINIST MESSAGE FOR ADVERTISEMENTS OF THE TIME AND, APART FROM THE SLOGAN AT THE BOTTOM, THERE IS NO OTHER REFERENCE TO THE PRODUCT.
PRICE GUIDE 3

◀ THIS RYVITA SHOWCARD WAS INTENDED TO ADVERTISE THE PRODUCT AT THE POINT OF SALE. THE MAIN POINT OF THIS ADVERT IS THAT THE CRISPBREAD WAS BEING MADE IN BRITAIN; ITS 'SLIMMING' QUALITES ARE STILL PROMOTED TODAY.
PRICE GUIDE 4

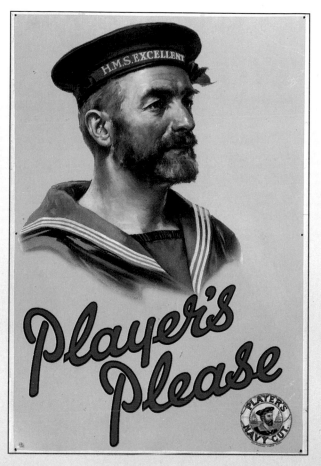

▶ THIS PLAYER'S CIGARETTES ENAMELLED TIN SIGN WAS MADE AROUND 1920. ITS REGISTERED TRADE MARK FEATURING A STALWART SAILOR IS USED TO THIS DAY.
PRICE GUIDE 3

◀ THIS FAMOUS BOVRIL BEEF EXTRACT POSTER WAS ILLUSTRATED BY THE ARTIST H.H. HARRIS IN 1923. ITS CHEERFUL, INFECTIOUS MESSAGE WAS — AND STILL IS — VERY APPEALING.
PRICE GUIDE 6

POINTS TO WATCH

- THE POSITION OF THE WATERMARK AFFECTS THE VALUE OF A NOTE: ON THE WORLD WAR I, 'BRADBURY' TREASURY NOTES IT WAS NORMALLY SIDWAYS, AND EXCEPTIONS ARE EXTREMELY RARE.
- OVERPRINTING CAN DRAMATICALLY INCREASE VALUE: FOR EXAMPLE, BRITISH BANKNOTES ISSUED FOR THE DARDANELLES CAMPAIGN OF 1915 HAVE ARABIC OVERPRINTING.
- FORGERIES CAN OFTEN BE WORTH MORE TO COLLECTORS THAN THE ORIGINALS THEMSELVES.

▲ THIS BANK OF ENGLAND £5 NOTE IS THEIR FAMOUS 1915 'WHITE FIVER' ON WHICH THE DESIGN FOR THE £1 NOTE HAD BEEN BASED. WRITTEN OUT IN AN ELEGANT COPPERPLATE SCRIPT, THE SERIAL NUMBER OF THIS NOTE IS PRINTED OVER THE TOP OF THE WORDS.
PRICE GUIDE 5

▲ THIS GRECIAN 100 DRACHMA NOTE DATES FROM 1912. TO REDUCE THE RISK OF FORGERY, THE DATE IS OVERPRINTED IN PURPLE ABOVE THE THREE SIGNATURES, THE GREEN BACKGROUND GRADUALLY FADES TO A YELLOW CENTRAL STRIPE, AND THE COLOURED AREAS ARE TINTED WITH A COMPLEX LINEAR DESIGN.
PRICE GUIDE 5

▶ THIS BULGARIAN 100 LEVA NOTE FROM 1916 IS COVERED IN COMPLEX PATTERNS INTENDED TO REDUCE THE RISK OF FORGERY. NEW TECHNIQUES ALLOWED MORE INTRICATE DESIGNS TO BE PRINTED.
PRICE GUIDE 1

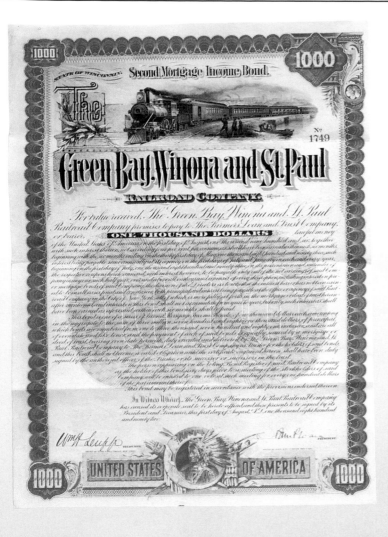

◀ THIS GREEN BAY, WINONA AND
ST. PAUL RAILROAD COMPANY BOND,
C.1890, FEATURES AN ENGRAVING OF A
SPEEDING STEAM TRAIN AS ITS LOGO. THIS
BOND PROMISES TO PAY THE FARMERS
LOAN AND TRUST COMPANY $1000.
PRICE GUIDE 3

▲ THIS CERTIFICATE OF A SHARE OF £25
IN THE GREAT WESTERN RAILWAY
COMPANY IS DATED 13TH OCTOBER
1845. RAILWAY SHARES WILL INTEREST
RAILWAY EPHEMERIS COLLECTORS.
PRICE GUIDE 4

◀ THIS RUSSIAN SHARE CERTIFICATE,
LOOKING VERY MUCH LIKE A BANKNOTE, IS
WORTH 500 ROUBLES. DATING FROM
1912, THIS ENTITLED THE PURCHASER TO
SHARES IN A RUSSIAN MINE.
PRICE GUIDE 2

▶ THIS FRENCH BANK NOTE FOR THE SUM
OF 20 FRANCS FEATURES THE PORTRAIT OF
A FAMOUS FRENCH PERSONALITY – JUST AS
MODERN NOTES DO. DEPICTED IN THE
LEFT-HAND VIGNETTE IS BAYARD, A 15TH-
CENTURY SOLDIER RENOWNED FOR HIS
COURAGE. THE RIGHT-HAND VIGNETTE
CONTAINS THE WATERMARK.
PRICE GUIDE 3

DESIGN FEATURES

VICTORIAN AND EDWARDIAN STAMP ALBUMS ARE ALWAYS INTRIGUING. THE BOOKS THEMSELVES COME IN A VARIETY OF DESIGNS, FROM SMALL PAPERBACKS TO DE-LUXE TOOLED LEATHER VOLUMES FASTENED WITH METAL CLASPS, SUCH AS THIS ONE. SOME ALBUMS ARE FOR STAMPS FROM A SINGLE COUNTRY, OR FOR A LARGER AREA, SUCH AS THE BRITISH EMPIRE. MOST INCLUDE PRINTED ILLUSTRATIONS AND INFORMATION ABOUT STAMPS. AND MANY, AS HERE,

HAVE NUMBERED RECTANGLES IN WHICH THE STAMPS ARE TO BE STUCK. THIS, AND THE PRINTED INFORMATON OF THE OPPOSITE PAGE, ENSURE THAT THE COLLECTOR IS AWARE OF ALL THE DENOMINATIONS.

HOWEVER ATTRACTIVE AN ALBUM MAY BE, ITS REAL INTEREST AND VALUE TO THE PHILATELIST LIES IN THE COLLECTION OF STAMPS IT HOLDS. THE COLLECTION MAY BE RUN-OF-THE-MILL, OR IT MAY HOLD SOME EXCITING RARITIES.

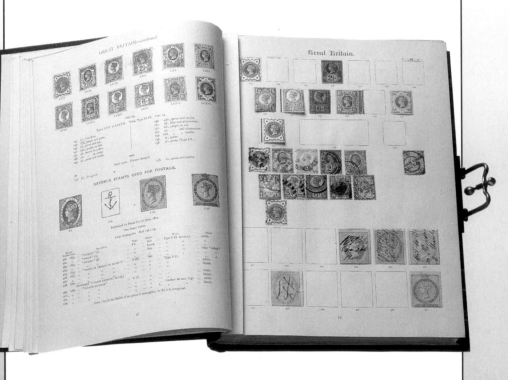

◀ THE PENNY BLACK WAS THE FIRST AND MOST FAMOUS POSTAGE STAMP. IT WAS FIRST ISSUED IN 1840. USED EXAMPLES ARE QUITE COMMON, AND WILL NOT NECESSARILY FETCH A HIGH PRICE, BUT MINT ONES ARE RARER.
PRICE GUIDE 6

◀ THESE TWO ENVELOPES WERE BOTH SENT TO A MISS WILLIS AT DIFFERENT ADDRESSES. DRAWINGS HAVE BEEN ADDED TO EACH THAT INCORPORATE THE STAMPS – VICTORIAN PENNY REDS – INTO THE ILLUSTRATIONS. THIS HUMOUROUS AND PERSONAL TOUCH WILL GREATLY INCREASE THE INTEREST TO A COLLECTOR OF COVERS AND OTHER EPHEMERIS.
PRICE GUIDE 1

▼ NEW ZEALAND, LIKE CANADA AND AUSTRALIA, ISSUED ILLUSTRATED STAMPS LONG BEFORE BRITAIN. THEY OFTEN DEPICTED THE LANDSCAPES AND FLORA AND FAUNA OF THE COUNTRY.
PRICE GUIDE 4

◀ THE BLACK TRIM OF THIS ENVELOPE WOULD HAVE INDICATES THAT IT CARRIED BAD NEWS. MOURNING STATIONARY WAS COMMONLY USED IN THE VICTORIAN AND EDWARDIAN PERIOD TO SEND NEWS OF DEATHS. THIS LETTER WAS SENT IN 1904 TO LADY HIGGINSON IN MARLOW ONLY TO BE FORWARDED TO HER AT THE PRINCES HOTEL, BRIGHTON.
PRICE GUIDE 1

▼ THESE TWO STAMPS, FROM A SET OF EIGHT, WERE ISSUED IN THE FALKLAND ISLANDS FROM 1904 TO 1912. LIKE MOST COLONIAL AND BRITISH STAMPS THEY HAVE THE MONARCH'S HEAD, IN THIS CASE EDWARD VII, IN A CLASSICAL DESIGN.
PRICE GUIDE 1

◀ THIS REGISTERED LETTER BEARS A 3 PENNY EDWARDIAN STAMP. THE ENVELOPE IS PRINTED NOT ONLY WITH THE SENDER'S ADDRESS, BUT ALSO WITH THAT OF THE ADDRESSEE IN FRANCE.
PRICE GUIDE 1

▼ THESE FOUR STAMPS ARE THE HIGHEST VALUE OF A SET OF 13 ISSUED IN 1904. THEY ARE ALSO WORTH THE MOST TODAY. THESE ARE IN MINT CONDITION, BUT WOULD, SUPRISINGLY ENOUGH, BE MORE VALUABLE IF THEY HAD BEEN USED.
PRICE GUIDE 5

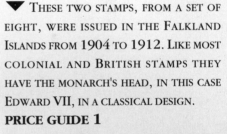

DESIGN FEATURES

WILLIAM HOGARTH (1697 – 1764) WAS THE OUTSTANDING BRITISH PAINTER AND ENGRAVER OF HIS PERIOD. HE PRODUCED SEVERAL SERIES OF PICTURES DEPICTING THE SOCIAL ABUSES OF THE TIME, OF WHICH *A RAKE'S PROGRESS* AND *MARRIAGE À LA MODE* ARE PERHAPS THE MOST FAMOUS. HOGARTH PAINTED WITH A VIEW TO HIS WORK BEING ENGRAVED SINCE HE WANTED HIS IMAGES TO REACH AS MANY PEOPLE AS POSSIBLE. SATIRE NEEDED A WIDE AUDIENCE, AND MANY HOGARTH PRINTS WERE SOLD BY PENNY BROADSHEET SELLERS.

HIS ENGRAVINGS WERE HUGELY POPULAR AND WERE SOON PIRATED, PROMPTING HIM TO AGITATE FOR A COPYRIGHT LAW, WHICH WAS PASSED IN 1735, PROTECTING ARTISTS' DESIGNS FOR 14 YEARS. HOGARTH SATIRIZED A WIDE AND VARIED CROSS SECTION OF SOCIETY – HERE, BORED AND INATTENTIVE STUDENTS ARE BEING LECTURED BY A POMPOUS-LOOKING READER. THE HIGHLY INDIVIDUAL QUALITY OF THE STUDENTS' FACES DOES SUGGEST THEY MIGHT BE CARICATURES OF PEOPLE KNOWN TO HOGARTH.

▲ ENGRAVINGS WERE OFTEN DONE OF FAMOUS PAINTINGS AND IN THE 18TH CENTURY THIS WAS USUALLY OF THE LEADING PORTRAITS OF THE DAY. THIS MEZZOTINT OF LADY ELIZABETH CROMWELL, PUBLISHED IN 1742, IS AFTER A PAINTING BY SIR GODFREY KNELLER.
PRICE GUIDE 4

▶ ONE OF THE MOST FAMOUS SERIES OF GEORGIAN PRINTS IS THE 'CRIES OF LONDON'. PAINTED BY FRANCIS WHEATLEY R.A. (1747 – 1801), A FAMOUS ARTIST OF THE DAY, MANY NOTABLE ENGRAVERS REPRODUCED THE PAINTINGS. THIS PARTICULAR PRINT SHOWS A FLOWER SELLER WITH HER BASKET AND BUNCHES OF PRIMROSES.
PRICE GUIDE 4

◀ ENTITLED 'BANDITTI AT MARKET', THIS COPPERPLATE ENGRAVING, PUBLISHED IN 1780, BY JOHN HALL WAS DONE AFTER A PAINTING BY JOHN HAMILTON MORTIMER. THE WORD 'SCULP.' AFTER A NAME INDICATES THAT THIS IS THE ENGRAVER; THE ORIGINAL ARTIST'S NAME IS FOLLOWED BY THE WORD 'PINXT.' BEFORE THE DAYS OF PHOTOGRAPHIC REPRODUCTIONS, ENGRAVINGS LIKE THIS ALLOWED IMAGES OF GREAT PAINTINGS TO BE MORE GENERALLY SEEN.
PRICE GUIDE 3

▶ SATIRICAL PRINTS WERE IMMENSELY POPULAR DURING THE LATE 18TH CENTURY AND REGENCY PERIOD AND ROWLANDSON AND GILLRAY WERE AMONG THE MOST FAMOUS OF ARTISTS WORKING IN THIS GENRE. THIS GILLRAY PRINT, 'VERY SLIPPY WEATHER', SHOWS, IN THE BACKGROUND, INTERESTED CUSTOMERS IN FRONT OF A PRINT SHOP. GILLRAY WAS MAKING A PERSONAL JOKE AS THE SHOP HE SHOWS IS THAT OF MRS. HUMPHREY'S, WHO WAS HIS PUBLISHER.
PRICE GUIDE 4

◀ THIS RECTANGULAR-SHAPED MINIATURE HAS BEEN PAINTED ON IVORY AND WAS EXECUTED IN AROUND 1830. SET IN A RATHER ORNATE GILT FRAME WITH PLAIN BLACK SURROUND, THIS PICTURE WOULD HAVE BEEN HUNG ON THE WALL, PROBABLY ALONGSIDE OTHER FAMILY PORTRAITS.

PRICE GUIDE 6

▼ THIS TYPICAL PAGE FROM A LARGE FAMILY PHOTO ALBUM SHOWS A VARIETY OF SHOTS. A TRADITIONAL WEDDING GROUP AND A POSED PORTRAIT OF A CHILD IN COSTUME ARE PLACED ON THE SAME PAGES AS VIEWS OF THE HOUSE AND GARDENS, AND OF LOCAL EVENTS.

PRICE GUIDE 3

▼ THIS OVAL-SHAPED MINIATURE OF AN UNKNOWN GENTLEMAN IS PAINTED IN THE STYLE OF THE AMERICAN SCHOOL. THE IMAGE HAS BEEN DELICATELY PAINTED ON IVORY AND HAS BEEN SET IN A GILT FRAME THAT COULD BE WORN ON A CHAIN.

PRICE GUIDE 6

▲ LEATHER-BOUND PHOTOGRAPH ALBUMS WERE IMMENSELY POPULAR ONCE PHOTOGRAPHY CAME WITHIN THE REACH OF MOST PEOPLE. SPECIAL ALBUMS WERE DESIGNED TO KEEP FAVOURITE SHOTS IN, WHETHER TAKEN BY PROFESSIONALS OR BY THE FAMILY THEMSELVES.

PRICE GUIDE 2

▲ THIS STUDIO PORTRAIT OF A BRIDE WAS TAKEN IN INDIA, NO DOUBT TO SEND TO RELATIVES AT HOME IN BRITAIN. PRINTED ON STIFF, GOLD-EDGED CARD, THIS KIND OF MOUNTED PHOTOGRAPH WAS KNOWN AS A CARTE-DE-VISITE, A POPULAR FORM OF PHOTOGRAPHIC PRINT.

PRICE GUIDE 1

▲ THIS STYLISH ART POSTCARD BY THE VIENNESE ARTIST RAPHAEL KIRCHNER BEARS A LIVELY IMAGE OF A YOUNG WOMAN SKIING.

PRICE GUIDE 3

▲ BEAUTIFUL YOUNG WOMEN WERE A POPULAR SUBJECT FOR ART NOUVEAU POSTCARDS. IN THIS PORTRAIT BY RAPHAEL KIRCHNER, A TYPICAL SECESSION DESIGN FRAMES THE PICTURE. SECESSION ARTISTS DESIGNED SPECIFICALLY FOR THE POSTCARD FORMAT RATHER THAN HAVING THEIR PAINTINGS REPRODUCED IN THIS FORM.

PRICE GUIDE 3

▲ THIS POSTCARD OF A YOUNG GIRL EMBRACING HER PHONOGRAPH IN APPARENT ADORATION OF THE SINGER CARUSO, IS, IN FACT, A GERMAN ADVERTISEMENT FOR TOOTHPASTE.

PRICE GUIDE 3

▼ A FRENCH ARTIST, JACK ABEILLE, DESIGNED THIS CARD WHICH WAS PUBLISHED IN 1899 BY HEGG OF BONN. LIKE MANY CARDS OF THE PERIOD, THERE IS ROOM FOR ONLY A BRIEF SALUTATION AT THE SIDE OF THE PICTURE.

PRICE GUIDE 3

▶ STYLIZED, UNDULATING SUNBEAMS, A DISTINCT ART NOUVEAU MOTIF, PROVIDE A DYNAMIC BACKGROUND FOR THIS 1900s IMAGE OF A YOUNG WOMAN LEANING FORWARD TO SMELL LILIES.

PRICE GUIDE 3

DESIGN FEATURES

ALTHOUGH TINPLATE CONTAINERS HAD BEEN AROUND FOR SOME TIME, THE IMPROVED METHODS OF PRODUCTION IN THE EARLY DECADES OF THIS CENTURY ALLOWED A WIDER USE OF TINS, MAKING THEM ESPECIALLY SUITABLE FOR COSMETIC APPLICATIONS.

DESIGNS AND COLOUR SCHEMES WERE USUALLY DICTATED BY THE FASHION OF THE DAY, BUT, ONCE ESTABLISHED, COMPANIES FOLLOWED THE DESIGN FOR THE LENGTH OF THEIR ADVERTISING CAMPAIGN, AND IF THE STYLE BECAME IDENTIFIED WITH THE PRODUCT.

THE ART DECO INFLUENCE ON PACKAGING MATERIAL IS SHOWN ON THIS TALCUM TIN BY THE STREAMLINED CONTOURS AND STRAIGHT VERTICAL LINES WHICH STAND OUT AGAINST A LIGHT BACKGROUND.

▼ THE GLASS JAR ITSELF COULD ALSO BE ATTRACTIVELY MOULDED SO AS BEST TO DISPLAY THE CONTENTS, AS IN THIS JAR OF PERFUMED BATH CRYSTALS FROM POTTER AND MOORE'S.
PRICE GUIDE 1

▲ THIS FRENCH CYLINDRICAL BOTTLE WITH ITS GLASS STOPPER RETAINS A PHARMACEUTICAL FEEL. IT CONTAINED AN ASTRINGENT MADE, ACCORDING TO THE LABEL, TO THE FORMULA OF THE MONKS OF THE ABBEY OF FÉCAMP.
PRICE GUIDE 1

▼ GEOMETRIC LINES AND THE USE OF MINIMAL COLOUR WERE TYPICAL OF ART DECO PACKAGING. THIS OVAL TIN CONTAINED BRILLIANTINE, A HAIR PREPARATION FOR MEN.
PRICE GUIDE 1

▼ GRAPHIC DESIGN CAME INTO ITS OWN DURING THE ART DECO PERIOD AND NEW, CLEAN-CUT TYPEFACES BEGAN TO APPEAR. THE MANUFACTURER'S NAME IS MADE THE FEATURE OF THE DESIGN OF THIS PHILLIPS' TOOTHPASTE PACKAGE.
PRICE GUIDE 1

▼ THE NAME OF THE PRODUCT AND ITS INGREDIENTS ARE THE MAIN DESIGN ELEMENTS ON THE LID OF THIS SHAVING SOAP TIN. THIS IS SET AGAINST THE SIMPLE STRIPES OF THE TIN ITSELF.
PRICE GUIDE 1

▲ THESE 1930S TINS CONTAINED THREE DIFFERENT MAKES OF THE SPECIAL SHAVING SOAP VITAL TO THE GROOMING OF ANY FASHIONABLE, CLEAN-SHAVEN MAN.
PRICE GUIDE 1

▲ THIS GLASS COLOGNE BOTTLE WAS ON SALE IN THE 1930S. THE DESIGN OF BOTH LABEL AND BOTTLE IS MORE REMINISCENT OF VICTORIAN STYLING.
PRICE GUIDE 1

POINTS TO WATCH

● DECORATIVE AND MULTI-BLADED KNIVES ARE MORE VALUABLE THAN PLAINER EXAMPLES.

● BLADES SHOULD FIT PROPERLY INTO THE HANDLE AND THE SPRING MECHANISM SHOULD PRODUCE A CLEAN AND CRISP MOVEMENT.

● SILVER BLADES WILL BEAR HALLMARKS AND MAKER'S MARKS INDICATING THE DATE AND PLACE OF MANUFACTURE.

▼ MORE DECORATIVE THAN FUNCTIONAL, THIS FOLDING KNIFE FROM THE FRENCH TOWN OF AIX LES BAINS WAS PRODUCED FOR THE SOUVENIR MARKET. MADE OF HORN, THIS KNIFE HAS BEEN INLAID WITH SILVER AND PIECES OF SHELL.
PRICE GUIDE 3

▼ THE RIVET HEADS OF THIS TWIN-BLADED FRUIT KNIFE HAVE BEEN CONCEALED BY SILVER PICQUÉ WORK, SET INTO THE BANDED MOTHER-OF-PEARL HAFT. HALLMARKS ARE CLEARLY VISIBLE ON THE BLADE.
PRICE GUIDE 4

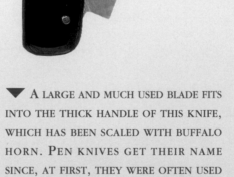

▲ THE DOUBLE BLADES OF THIS QUILL KNIFE ARE HOUSED IN AN IVORY HANDLE. THIS HAS BEEN CRAFTED INTO THE FORM OF A CLOAKED WOMAN HOLDING A SMALL BIRD, PROBABLY A PARTRIDGE.
PRICE GUIDE 4

▼ A LARGE AND MUCH USED BLADE FITS INTO THE THICK HANDLE OF THIS KNIFE, WHICH HAS BEEN SCALED WITH BUFFALO HORN. PEN KNIVES GET THEIR NAME SINCE, AT FIRST, THEY WERE OFTEN USED TO TRIM QUILLS INTO PENS FOR WRITING.
PRICE GUIDE 3

▲ THIS TWIN-BLADED SILVER FRUIT KNIFE HAS A CAST FLORAL MOTIF HAFT AND A SEED-PICKER AND DATES FROM ABOUT 1870. SILVER WAS MOST COMMONLY USED FOR THE BLADES OF FRUIT KNIVES SINCE IT WAS NOT STAINED BY FRUIT ACID.
PRICE GUIDE 3

▲ THE SMALLER, NARROW BLADE OF THIS SILVER AND MOTHER-OF-PEARL FOLDING KNIFE IS A 'PIPPING' BLADE, USED TO PICK THE PIPS OUT OF CUT FRUIT. THIS KNIFE STILL COMES IN ITS SUEDE CASE.
PRICE GUIDE 3

▼ THIS TORTOISESHELL FRUIT KNIFE HAS A SILVER BLADE AND IS INLAID WITH SILVER FLOWERS AND A SMALL PLAQUE THAT IS ENGRAVED WITH THE OWNER'S INITIALS.
PRICE GUIDE 4

▲ THE BLADE AND TINES OF THIS FOLDING KNIFE AND FORK SET ARE MADE OF SILVER AND A FINE PATTERN HAS BEEN DELICATELY ENGRAVED AROUND THE EDGES. HARVEST MOTIFS HAVE BEEN CARVED INTO THE IVORY HANDLES.
PRICE GUIDE 6

▶ THIS SOL-PERAM 'VICTORIA' PRAM WAS MADE IN THE 1920S. IT HAS PAINTED COACHWORK, AND A MATCHING HOOD AND COVER. THE DESIGN OF THE BODY MEANT THAT THE CHILD WAS MORE PROPPED UP, AND WITH THE PRAM BEING PUSHED FROM BEHIND THE BABY, IT IS MORE LIKE THE MODERN PUSHCHAIR.
PRICE GUIDE 6

◀ THIS BLACK PRAM WAS MADE BY HITCHINS IN C.1930, AND IT HAS A WOODEN BODY. THE FLAP AT THE HANDLE-END OF THIS PRAM IS A FOOT EXTENSION SO THAT AN OLDER CHILD COULD SIT AT THIS END OF THE PRAM IN GREATER COMFORT.
PRICE GUIDE 6

▶ THIS 1920S HARRIS PRAM HAS A LOW-SLUNG BODY AND SMALL WHEELS. IT HAS DELICATE ART DECO DESIGNS ALONG EACH PANEL, AND A CONVENIENT WICKER BASKET, PROBABLY FOR SHOPPING, HANGING FROM THE HANDLES.
PRICE GUIDE 6

◀ THIS DEEP-BODIED PRAM WAS MADE IN THE EARLY 1920S. IT HAS DRESS GUARDS ON THE WHEELS; LOOKING RATHER LIKE MUD GUARDS ON A BIKE, THEY WOULD HAVE KEPT LONGER SKIRTS OUT OF THE SPOKES. ONE INTERESTING DETAIL HERE IS THE WICKER UMBRELLA HOLDER ATTACHED TO THE BASE OF ONE HANDLE.
PRICE GUIDE 6

DESIGN FEATURES

THIS LADY'S ROVER, MADE IN 1891, IS ONE OF THE EARLIEST EXAMPLES OF A DROP-FRAME SAFETY BICYCLE, ON WHICH THE CROSS-BAR HAS BEEN REMOVED IN ORDER TO ACCOMODATE A WOMAN'S SKIRTS. AS A FURTHER SAFEGUARD, STRANDS OF THREAD HAVE BEEN STRETCHED FROM THE REAR WHEEL HUB OVER THE MUDGUARD TO PREVENT A

DRESS BEING CAUGHT IN THE SPOKES.

THE WHEELS HAVE TANGENTIAL SPOKES AND SOLID TYRES. THE ARAB-SPRUNG SADDLE IS DESIGNED TO ABSORB SOME OF THE SHOCK TRANSMITTED BY THE RUBBER TYRES. THERE IS A SPOON BRAKE ON THE FRONT WHEEL, OPERATED BY A LARGE LEVER SITUATED BELOW THE HANDLEBARS. THE FRAME IS OF TUBULAR STEEL, WITH A

RAKISH CURVE TO THE FRONT FORKS AND A BOTTOM TUBE WHICH CLOSELY FOLLOWS THE CONTOURS OF THE FRONT WHEEL. AS A FURTHER SAFETY FEATURE, THE CHAIN IS GUARDED BY A METAL FRAME COVERED IN LEATHER AND BOUND BY A CORD MATCHING THE PAINTWORK. THE MAKER'S NAME IS ON A METAL EXCUTCHEON ON THE STEERING COLUMN.

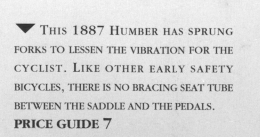

▼ THIS 1887 HUMBER HAS SPRUNG FORKS TO LESSEN THE VIBRATION FOR THE CYCLIST. LIKE OTHER EARLY SAFETY BICYCLES, THERE IS NO BRACING SEAT TUBE BETWEEN THE SADDLE AND THE PEDALS.
PRICE GUIDE 7

▼ THE RUDGE WHITWORTH COMPANY ENJOYED THE PATRONAGE OF ROYALTY AND OF SOME OF THE TOP RACERS IN THE EARLY 20TH CENTURY. THIS IS THEIR STANDARD MODEL FROM 1910.
PRICE GUIDE 4

▶ IN BRITAIN, IN THE EARLY DAYS OF MOTORING, DRIVERS WERE GRANTED ONE YEAR'S LICENCE AT A TIME. THIS LICENCE WAS ISSUED BY THE COUNTY OF LONDON AND WAS VALID FOR THE YEAR FALLING BETWEEN 1917 AND 1918.
PRICE GUIDE 3

▲ THIS RUBBER AND METAL BULB HORN WAS THE BASIC HORN FOR EARLY CARS, AND WAS FOUND IN ALL MOTORING ACCESSORY CATALOGUES. THE MOTORIST COULD MAKE A NOISE TO ALERT OTHER TRAVELLERS BY SQUEEZING THE RUBBER BULB AT THE END OF THE HORN.
PRICE GUIDE 3

▼ CAR MAKERS' BADGES THAT WERE ATTACHED TO THE RADIATOR GRILLE OF EARLY CARS ARE NOW VERY COLLECTABLE. SEEN HERE ARE THE BADGES FOR TRIUMPH, RILEY AND MORRIS.
PRICE GUIDE 3

▶ THIS EGYPTIAN MOSQUE LAMP IS MADE FROM COPPER WITH A SILVER INLAY. THE GREEN GLASS TUBE THAT HANGS BENEATH THE LAMP HAS BEEN DECORATED USING THE ACID ETCHING TECHNIQUE.
PRICE GUIDE 6

▲ THIS PATINATED, EGYPTIAN, BRONZE MOSQUE LAMP HAS A HINGED DOOR IN THE SIDE FOR TENDING THE OIL AND THE WICK. NINETEENTH-CENTURY LAMPS FETCH A HIGH PRICE TODAY AND COPIES ARE OFTEN MADE, THOUGH THE WORKMANSHIP IS GENERALLY POORER.
PRICE GUIDE 8

▲ A RICH PATTERN IS CREATED ON THIS ORNATE 19TH-CENTURY EGYPTIAN BRASS MOSQUE LAMP BY DELICATELY STAMPED SMALL HOLES. THIS LAMP WOULD HAVE BEEN SUSPENDED FROM THE CEILING BY THE FOUR DELICATE CHAINS.
PRICE GUIDE 7

▲ THIS SYRIAN BRASS MOSQUE LAMP DATES FROM THE 19TH CENTURY. ITS ROUNDED BODY, WHICH TAPERS TO A POINT, IS PIERCED WITH INTRICATE GEOMETRIC FLORAL PATTERNS.
PRICE GUIDE 8

- I T IS ALWAYS A GOOD IDEA TO ASCERTAIN WHETHER OR NOT A LAMP IS IN WORKING ORDER BEFORE DECIDING TO BUY A LAMP TO USE.
- T HERE ARE VERY GOOD MODERN REPRODUCTIONS AVAILABLE, SO PROSPECTIVE PURCHASES SHOULD BE EXAMINED CAREFULLY TO ENSURE THEY ARE GENUINE ANTIQUES.
- O IL AND GAS LAMPS AND CANDLE HOLDERS, THAT HAVE BEEN CONVERTED TO ELECTRICITY WILL NOT BE AS VALUABLE AS THOSE LEFT ALONE.

▲ THIS BRASS STUDENT'S LAMP FROM THE EARLY 19TH CENTURY HAS A FINGER RING AT THE TOP OF THE STAND TO ENABLE THE USER TO CARRY IT FROM ROOM TO ROOM. THE BURNER CAN BE MOVED UP AND DOWN THE STAND BY AN ADJUSTABLE SUPPORT.
PRICE GUIDE 4

◀ THIS ROUND, GREEN, GLASS HANGING LAMP HAS A BRONZE COLLAR, FINIAL AND CHAIN. THE GLASS BOWL WOULD HAVE BEEN FILLED WITH OIL AND THEN THE WICK WOULD HAVE FLOATED IN THAT.
PRICE GUIDE 5

◀ THIS OIL LAMP FROM 1820 IS MADE ENTIRELY OF GLASS. THE OIL WOULD HAVE BEEN HELD IN THE BULBOUS RESERVOIR IN THE CENTRE, AND THE WICK WOULD HAVE BEEN FED THROUGH INTO THE CHIMNEY BY TURNING THE BRONZE DIAL ON THE SIDE.

PRICE GUIDE 6

▲ THISI IS AN EARLY, 19TH-CENTURY, GILDED TABLE LAMP. THE TOP OF THE URN LIFTS OFF SO THAT OIL CAN BE FED INTO THE RESERVOIR, BUT THIS LAMP HAS BEEN CONVERTED TO ELECTRICITY AND THE BURNERS FITTED WITH SOCKETS.

PRICE GUIDE 5

▶ THE 'PIERROT' MUSICIAN RESTING ON A CRESCENT MOON WAS A POPULAR ART DECO THEME. HERE, A LIGHT IS PLACED IN THE CRESCENT SHAPE SUPPORTED IN A SWIRL OF BRONZE CLOUDS.
PRICE GUIDE 7

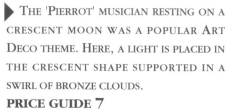

◀ THE FIGURINE OF THIS TABLE LAMP IS MADE OF SPELTER, A CHEAP METAL THAT WAS THE BY-PRODUCT OF ZINC ORE REFINEMENT. FIXED TO A SMALL MARBLE PLINTH, THIS NAKED WOMAN SUPPORTS A BEACHBALL ON ONE HAND, A CHARACTERISTIC DECO LAMP DESIGN.
PRICE GUIDE 6

▲ THIS EXOTIC-LOOKING DANCING GIRL HAS BEEN POSED BETWEEN TWO PILLARS OF ALABASTER FROM WHICH THE LIGHT EMANATES. IT HAS BEEN SIGNED BY THE CRAFTSMAN WHO MADE IT, LE FAGUAYS.
PRICE GUIDE 8

INDEX

Acknowledgements

The pictures in this book were taken by the following photographers:

Chris Barker
Steven Bartholomew
Steve Bisgrove
Aubrey Dewer
Ray Duns
Melvin Grey
John Hollingshead
Syd Hughes
Ranald MacKechnie
Michael Michaels
Ian O'Leary
Lyndon Parker
Peter Reilly
Pam Rigby
Duncan Smith
Rosemary Weller